BEHAVIORAL PSYCHOTHERAPY

Basic Principles and

Case Studies in an

Integrative Clinical Model

Edited by

Herbert Fensterheim, Ph.D.
and
Howard I. Glazer, Ph.D.

BRUNNER/MAZEL, *Publishers* • New York

Library of Congress Cataloging in Publication Data
Main entry under title:

Behavioral psychotherapy, basic principles and case
studies in an integrative clinical model.

   Includes bibliographies and index.
   1. Behavior therapy. I. Fensterheim, Herbert.
II. Glazer, Howard I. [DNLM: 1. Behavior therapy.
2. Models, Psychological. WM 425 B424]
RC489.B4B4377   1983   616.89'142   82-20622
ISBN 0-87630-325-4

Published by
BRUNNER/MAZEL, INC.
19 Union Square West
New York, N.Y. 10003

MANUFACTURED IN THE UNITED STATES OF AMERICA

Preface

This is a book written by working therapists for working therapists of all persuasions. All of the contributors have been trained in the traditional psychodynamically oriented methods of treatment. All of us have switched to the behavioral orientation, not in revolt against the psychodynamic concepts but rather because we chafed at the limitations of that model and were seeking new perspectives. The behavioral model, however, soon proved to have its own limitations. Patients are human beings, too complicated for their problems to be approached in terms of isolated behaviors; the therapeutic interactions are too intensely personal to be formulated in terms of stimulus and response. Yet the strengths of the behavioral model, the selection and systematic attempts to change target behaviors, are too great to abandon. The problem facing us in our daily work was one of how to perceive the full richness and complexity of our individual patients in such a manner that we could bring to bear the power of the behavioral methods to help them.

In an attempt to solve this problem we have developed a therapeutic approach which we call *behavioral psychotherapy*. For ten years now we have been working to sharpen and refine this approach through our own clinical experiences at the Payne Whitney Clinic of The New York Hospital-Cornell University Medical College, as well as in our own individual practices. During this period we constantly applied our approach to the treatment of specific patients and there were ongoing discussions of its strengths and weaknesses in our case conferences. Behavioral therapy stems from just such hard clinical experience, although it does of course utilize theoretical models and experimental findings when they are found to be helpful.

Evaluation and formulation are the core of behavioral psychotherapy. Specific behaviors are considered in terms of their underlying processes as well as of their phenotypic characteristics. Behaviors are in functional relation to each other and combine to form a behavioral organization, an organization that is more than the mere sum of its parts and that possesses its own emergent characteristics. The major task of the therapist is to formulate this behavioral organization in problem areas and to use this formulation as the basis for his therapeutic decisions. The concepts used in making the formulation can be biological, psychodynamic, behavioral or social. However, specific behaviors and their interactions are always included, for the aim of the formulation is planned action, i.e., the determination of key target behaviors for change and the determination of the order in which such changes are to be attempted. These methods are described and elaborated upon in practical, clinical terms in Section I of the book.

The second section of the book presents a series of case reports to demonstrate the application of the behavioral psychotherapy model to actual patients. Complicated and difficult cases have been deliberately selected. The emphasis is on the therapist's thinking and decision-making and such complicated cases provide the best context for illustrating these. A generally narrative style of presentation has been used in order to highlight the therapist's perspective. However, each presentation loosely follows a general outline: presenting problem, life history, psychiatric diagnosis, behavioral paradigms, behavioral formulation and treatment plan, ongoing treatment with problems and reformulations, treatment results and follow-up. The patients treated range from an adolescent boy with asthma to a woman with a 40-year history of agoraphobia and very difficult life problems. The therapists, with the single exception of Wilder (Chapter 9), had been trained in our behavioral psychotherapy unit.

The case presentations provide neither magical solutions nor astounding results. Rather, they provide a model of a systematic approach to difficult problems. This approach, coupled with hard work and sensitive concern, achieves the limited but important changes with which working therapists are so familiar.

The clinical orientation of behavioral psychotherapy should make it quite clear that it is neither dogmatic nor righteous. The application of its principles will be modified according to the characteristics of the therapist and the characteristics of the specific patient. There will be times when these principles must be deliberately violated. Also, just as behavioral organizations need to be reformulated as new information about the patient becomes available, so will these principles be reformulated with increased clinical experience. It is a model that allows for systematic treatment planning and decision-making and it is intended to be used with clinical flexibility.

Herbert Fensterheim, Ph.D.
Howard I. Glazer, Ph.D.

Contents

Contributors

JOHN BORONOW, M.D.
Staff Psychiatrist, Neuro-Science branch, National Institute of Mental Health

DAPHNE BURDMAN, M.D.
Major, United States Army, P & N 5th General Hospital, West Germany

HERBERT FENSTERHEIM, Ph.D.
Clinical Associate Professor of Psychology in Psychiatry, Cornell University Medical College/New York Hospital, Private Practice, New York, New York

MARY M. FITZPATRICK, Ph.D.
Clinical Instructor of Psychology in Psychiatry, Cornell University Medical College/New York Hospital, Chief Psychologist, The League Center, Brooklyn, New York

HOWARD I. GLAZER, Ph.D.
Clinical Assistant Professor of Psychology in Psychiatry, Cornell University Medical College/New York Hospital, President, Corporate Stress Control Services, Inc., Private Practice, New York, New York

GEORGE GREENBERG, Ph.D.
Clinical Instructor of Psychology in Psychiatry, Cornell University Medical College/New York Hospital, Private Practice, New York, New York

MARIE EDWARDS JACOBSON, C.S.W.
Clinical Instructor of Social Work in Psychiatry, Cornell University Medical College/New York Hospital, Supervisor of Psychiatric Social Work, Jewish Board of Family & Children's Services, Private Practice, New York, New York

HELENE SANDS, C.S.W.
Clinical Instructor of Social Work in Psychiatry, Cornell University Medical College/New York Hospital, Private Practice, New York, New York

JOHNATHAN H. WEISS, PH.D.
Clinical Assistant Professor of Psychology in Psychiatry, Cornell University Medical College/New York Hospital, Private Practice, New York, New York

STEPHEN WILDER, PH.D.
Private Practice, New York and Westchester County, New York

BEHAVIORAL PSYCHOTHERAPY

Basic Principles and

Case Studies in an

Integrative Clinical Model

PART I

The Model

1

Introduction to Behavioral Psychotherapy

Herbert Fensterheim

There is a constant and ongoing search for new methods to help people who suffer psychological distress. This search for more effective and more efficient ways of doing psychotherapy has resulted in the proliferation of varied therapeutic techniques. Each of these methods, however, is based on one of the two major theoretical paradigms that dominate the field: the psychoanalytic and the behavioral.

On the surface these two models appear to be antithetical. The psychoanalytic model emphasizes the dynamic forces operating within the individual and assumes that symptoms emerge from the balance of these forces and that only through a corrective emotional experience where these dynamic forces are realigned can meaningful change be brought about. The diverse methods stemming from this model are simply different methods for providing such a corrective emotional experience. The behavioral model, on the other hand, holds that symptoms are freestanding behaviors in the sense that even though they may be maintained by rather complex contingencies, they are discrete psychological entities. As discrete behaviors, whatever their origins, they can be directly modified (usually) through learning and conditioning methods or indirectly modified by changing the contingencies that maintain them. Only through such systematic attempts to modify specific behaviors can

effective and efficient change be brought about. The concept of psychodynamics is rejected, ignored, or considered to be irrelevant. The diverse
treatment methods that emerge from this model are all different ways
of providing a meaningful corrective learning experience.

There has been surprisingly little cross-fertilization between the two
models and, indeed, little productive communication. The adherents of
each model strongly reject the core theory of the other and reject almost
all aspects of the work they produce, from the data to which they attend
to the therapeutic goals towards which they strive. When phenomena
cannot be ignored, adherents from the opposing camp translate them
into their own terms. Thus, a behavior therapist may see the transference
as a product of the therapist's acting as a reinforcing agent, and the
psychoanalytic therapist may see conditioning as a part of the transference relationship. Several attempts have been made to integrate these
two models, the most noteworthy, thoughtful and thoroughgoing such
attempt being that of Wachtel (1977), but the tendency toward separa-
tism has largely persisted. There is no clear-cut evidence of the therapeutic superiority of one model over the other, although the adherents
of each are certain of the eventual justification of their own model.

Behavioral psychotherapy combines the two approaches in the actual
practice of psychotherapy. It eschews theoretical arguments, holding
that both perspectives are necessary for complete and adequate treatment of patients. As people are capable of being conditioned and as
they are capable of acting in a purposive, teleological manner, concepts
from both the behavioral and the psychoanalytic areas may need to be
called upon for effective treatment. However, behavioral psychotherapy
is also aware that these different models call for very different styles of
therapeutic actions: differences in thinking, in therapeutic attitudes, in
the processes to which therapists attend, and in the therapeutic goals
they set. These differing styles are held to be of crucial importance.

Once it is granted that neither motivational nor learning variables hold
exclusive sway in the patient, it becomes possible to apply selectively
the different styles in such a manner as to maximize their strengths and
to minimize their weaknesses. For the past eight years the behavioral
psychotherapy group at the Payne Whitney Clinic of The New York
Hospital and the Cornell University Medical College has been attempting
just such an integration within the framework of the clinical treatment
of adult neurotic and character disorder patients.

Behavioral psychotherapy attempts to take the strongest aspect of
each style. From the psychoanalytic model it takes the emphasis on the
processes, psychodynamic and behavioral, that underlie a given behav-

ior, rather than stressing the outward characteristic of that behavior. It also states that many behaviors, rather than being discrete entities under the direct control of specific contingencies, may emerge from the context of dynamic interactions within biological, intrapsychic-behavioral, and social organizations. From the behavior therapy model it takes the concept of specific target behaviors and of direct, deliberate, and systematic attempts to modify these behaviors. The goal is not merely to modify those behaviors involved in the problem or symptom, but also to modify behaviors crucial to changing the organizational context from which these behaviors arose. Under the best of conditions it begins to approximate that "direct approach to the reconstruction of personality" that is the subtitle of Salter's (1949) influential book.

Thus, behavioral psychotherapy uses the psychoanalytic style to formulate hypotheses concerning the underlying organization and to select target behaviors. It uses the behavior therapy style to change these behaviors in a deliberate and systematic manner. The approach is empirical. It involves as a first step the careful derivation of a *behavioral formulation* to serve as a basis for selecting targets. It then tests this formulation through the changes brought about by the therapeutic procedures used. These procedures also provide new information about the patient that is needed for the reformulations so often necessary.

It once again is stressed that the emphasis is on the form, the style, and the attitude of the therapist, rather than on the specific facts he uses. Such an emphasis is not new to the clinical area. Although a number of examples may be cited, perhaps the most direct illustration is provided by Hanfmann's (1952) consideration of projective techniques.

Hanfmann (1952) raises the question of what is a projective technique. She notes that a child can be given a blank piece of paper and be instructed to draw a picture of a person. The resultant drawing can be used in two different ways. It can be scored to yield an IQ following the method of Goodenough. This is called an objective test. Or it can be interpreted to throw light on the emotional functioning and conflicts of the child. This is called a projective technique. In the two situations the instructions to the child and the child's behavior are identical. The difference, Hanfmann argues, is in the attitudes of the examiners. The attitude, of course, is shaped by whether the examiner at the moment is functioning within the psychometric model or the psychodynamic one. Further, the examiner can deliberately shift his attitude, first scoring the test objectively and then interpreting it projectively.

So in behavioral psychotherapy we focus on the attitude or style of the therapist and on the deliberate shifts in these attitudes as required by the aspect of the therapeutic problem being considered. To explicate this point, the styles stemming from each model, their strengths and weaknesses, must be presented in some detail. These styles influence everything the therapist does from the initial interview to the final decision to terminate treatment.

PSYCHOANALYTIC PSYCHOTHERAPY

In his style of functioning, the psychoanalytically oriented psychotherapist has as his major and almost exclusive concern the formulation of the psychodynamic processes taking place within the patient's unconscious. This information cannot be gained directly, and the therapist must work under the heuristic assumption that everything the patient does or says is a reflection of these forces. The presenting problem, the patient's symptoms, whether the patient is early, on time, or late for the session—all are not only behaviors in their own right but gain added importance as they throw light on the psychodynamic processes. The therapist not only uses the content of the patient's associations and the feelings the patient communicates as data but also attends to his own feelings and associations. Then, using essentially deductive thinking, he formulates to himself the interplay of the psychodynamic forces. It is only as the dynamic imbalances that came about in the course of development are realigned that true and meaningful change can take place.

The therapist must also attend to the things the patient cannot express, experience, or understand, for many subtle defense mechanisms are actively at work to protect the patient from a knowledge of these forces. These self-protective needs also make it unwise for the therapist simply to pass along his own understanding to the patient. The timing of interpretations is crucial, for presenting them too soon strengthens the defenses and presenting them too late may lead to a missed opportunity for gaining knowledge. Knowledge in this instance does not mean a simple knowing but refers to that syncretic cognitive-emotional experience known as insight. When this does occur, when id is replaced by ego, there is a realignment of the psychodynamic forces, the protective role of the symptoms is no longer needed, and so the presenting problem, along with others, disappears.

The task of the therapist is to provide the interpersonal setting that allows the patient to move towards this corrective emotional experience, to allow him to recognize and to work through his resistances, and to guide him towards a deep understanding of himself. The specific concepts the therapist uses in his formulations vary according to the psychoanalytic model he follows. He may use such concepts as oral fixations, grandiose self-image, or parataxical distortions in interpersonal relations. The exact therapeutic procedures may vary from the active approaches of bioenergetics, Gestalt, and Primal Scream to the permissive encouragement of free association that follows the model of classical psychoanalysis. Despite the varieties of theories, concepts, and procedures, all these therapists have similar tasks, styles of thinking, and attitudes: the uncovering of crucial psychodynamic processes.

In actual practice this model and the style of thinking to which it leads has certain limitations and difficulties:

1) It is a single-minded approach. The heuristic assumption that everything is motivated, the almost exclusive attention to the psychodynamic processes, excludes other processes from consideration. Thus, despite the theorizing of the ego psychologists, there is no place for the conception of certain behaviors as the product of learning or of external reinforcement contingencies, each of which may be unconnected with conflict energy. Yet we do know that people are capable of being conditioned, of learning, and of being under control of external contingencies. Hence a wide area of the human psychological organization is excluded.

Of course it would be incorrect to state that the therapist pays no attention to the patient's life situation or to his interpersonal relations. However, he does so only fleetingly and for the main purpose of uncovering dynamic motivations. Wachtel (1977, p. 50) discusses one such example. The psychoanalytic therapist reflects "You'd like me to feel sorry for you" or "You're trying to get me to help you." These reflections invite associations to the feelings involved, aimed at gaining further understanding of the unconscious psychodynamics. An alternate interpretation might be "You get people to feel sorry and help you out, and so you never get the chance to learn and try things out yourself." Wachtel elaborates on the implications of this alternate reflection.

> Following through on the latter way of understanding, the therapist might note that since the patient is deprived of chances to learn, he's left with the feeling that *all he can do* is get people sorry for him and hope they help. This further perpetuates the cycle. As long as he succeeds in eliciting help, he continues to *need* help. . . . When the problem is viewed this way, the therapist is less likely to rely solely on interpretation. Helping the patient to

> undergo experiences that will help to break up the cycle, perhaps through actively learning certain modes in a protected situation, begins to look like a useful course (italics in original).

The style and attitude of the psychoanalytic therapist preclude the consideration of such alternate approaches.

2) It leads to a therapeutic inflexibility. This goes beyond the exclusion of alternate formulations discussed above. All patients are treated in basically the same way. It is true that the therapist relates differently to different patients. It is true that even with the same patient he acts differently at different times. He may be supportive, reflective, probing, challenging, or confronting, depending on his perception of therapeutic requirements at that point. However, at all times his main task is to guide the patient towards an insightful uncovering of psychodynamic forces.

Lack of therapeutic progress is often seen as a sign of resistance or a lack of readiness that in due time will be worked through. There is no basis for challenging the applicability of the basic method for that patient with that problem. Therapists do at times declare that a person is "not an analytic patient," based usually on either lack of verbal skills or a lack of desire to explore internal events. However, just as often other (good) therapists would take on these very same patients with the sincere belief that with patience and with the provision of a permissive, encouraging atmosphere, the patient will eventually open up and treatment will then proceed on its designated course. If a patient is not taken on in analytically oriented psychotherapy, the therapist feels that it is too bad that the patient must settle for something second-rate and that he is not accessible to the one truly meaningful form of treatment.

The core of the treatment approach is the same at all times for all patients. The patient must be able to adapt to the demands of the treatment situation. If he cannot do so, this points to some deficit in himself which he must try to work out within the analytic framework. There are no criteria for showing when the therapist himself is using a wrong approach.

3) There is a lack of attention to overt behavior. As noted, the necessary concentration on the psychodynamics and on the ongoing processes of treatment leads the therapist away from the examination of overt behavior. Working hypotheses are formulated in psychodynamic terms. Even when these hypotheses are formulated in terms of a specific prob-

lem area, they tend to be overgeneral and diffuse. At best, as illustrated by Normand, Fensterheim, and Schrenzel (1967), it leads to extremely limited forms of intervention aimed at reestablishing a previous equilibrium rather than bringing about real change. Most usually it leads to treatment of uncertain length and course. Hence, whatever its efficacy, it is often inefficient and overly costly in terms of time, money, and energy.

The clinical strength of the psychoanalytic psychotherapy approach thus is in the attention it pays to underlying psychodynamic processes and their organization. The therapist develops a style and attitude that sensitizes him to possible cues that may throw light on these and develops a powerful mode of deductive thinking that helps to organize his observations. The weaknesses of this style are that it becomes too exclusive, is oblivious to alternate approaches, becomes an inflexible set of therapeutic procedures, and may lead to inappropriate or inefficient treatment. It was in part a reaction to shortcomings such as these that behavior therapy gained professional attention.

BEHAVIOR THERAPY

The clinical style of the behavior therapist differs vastly from that of his psychoanalytically oriented colleague. His basic assumption is that he can identify specific patterns of unadaptive behavior in the present and that these behaviors, overt or covert, follow the laws of general psychology. The emphasis is not so much on the genesis and the development of these behaviors as it is on the variables that maintain them in the present. He is constantly searching for such patterns in such areas as motor behavior, affect, cognition, imagery, and interpersonal relations. Once identified, a thorough behavioral analysis is crucial. Among the variables investigated in such an analysis are the stimulus contingencies that surround these behaviors, the incorrect cognitions that may be involved, and the alternate behaviors (or lack of them) that are available in the patient's repertoire. With this as a basis, treatment centers around systematic and rigorous attempts to change the target behaviors. A varied and constantly growing change technology, based mainly but not exclusively on the psychology of learning and conditioning, is available for this purpose. The laboratory researcher is presented as a model for the therapist, who systematically varies the conditions surrounding the target behaviors until change in the desired direction occurs. Constant evaluation and measurement of change are an integral part of the treatment process, and, if the desired change does not take place, it is the responsibility of the therapist to modify his own behaviors and procedures until such change does come about. Contrary to the unfortunate belief held in some professional circles, in the hands of a good therapist this style becomes neither mechanistic nor mechanical, as Wolpe (1976) demonstrates with a series of case reports.

There are many great clinical strengths not present in the traditional psychotherapeutic approach that are to be found with this therapeutic style. The selection of target behaviors serves as a focus for making therapy more efficient, as well as supplying a goal that in turn becomes a motivator for the patient. The ongoing measurement and evaluation of change keep both therapist and patient from deceiving themselves that progress is being made when it really is not so. Of equal and perhaps even greater importance is that continual evaluation alerts the therapist to when the patient may be getting worse. Again, the focus on specific behaviors leads to the need for methods that are effective with just those behaviors. Hence, the experimental development and evaluation of a treatment technology gain a high order of importance, and the work of the clinical researcher becomes the bedrock for clinical practice.

Despite these strengths and despite the demonstrated efficacy of this approach with a series of difficult clinical problems, there are a number of weaknesses for the clinical practitioner. These weaknesses must be examined in some detail.

1) *Target behavior.* As noted, the identification and the systematic treatment of very specific target behaviors are the core of behavior therapy and the aspects that most differentiate it from the traditional psychotherapeutic approaches. Yet the field as a whole gives no rules, no guidelines, no models for the selection of these targets nor for determining the order in which these behaviors should be modified. While it is true that there are rules for behavior analysis, there are no rules for determining which behaviors to analyze. While it is true that there are a number of methods for the fine measurement of behaviors—indeed there is now an entire journal devoted to this subject—there are no rules for determining which behaviors to measure.

It is most interesting to note that in listing the major characteristics of behavior therapy, Kazdin and Hersen (1980) do not even mention this key element. The selection of target behaviors poses no problem for the clinical researcher; it is his research goal that determines his target. If he wants to investigate different treatment procedures with depressed patients, he chooses depression as the target behavior. If he wants to determine the relative effectiveness of different parts of the desensitization procedures, he selects phobias as his target. Hence, the researcher pays little attention, feels little need, to approach this problem of target selection. To the practitioner, however, it is a major, if not *the* major, problem.

Take the injunction "to do no harm," an injunction basic to clinical practice for millenia. How can the working therapist be certain that changing a specific set of behaviors will not bring harm to his patient? There are two types of harm that may be brought about. One type, to which the behavior therapists do pay some concern, is the subsequent emergence of new or greater disturbances. The other type, which is generally ignored by behavior therapists, is where, by virtue of changing a set of behaviors, the patient is deprived of an opportunity for growth and greater change. Fensterheim (1972) does report one such instance in the "successful" behavioral treatment of a man with sexual impotence. He had been in traditional psychotherapy, appeared to be at the point of major insight and change, but to avoid the anxiety this was eliciting he withdrew from that treatment in favor of the behavioral approach. Thus, the successful removal of the symptom that most disturbed him may well have done him harm.

The first type of harm where the patient becomes worse may be illustrated by the "successful" treatment of a voyeur (Fensterheim, 1974). In the published report it had been stated that no follow-up data were available. Since that time (and not hitherto reported) it was found out that immediately following treatment the patient became severely depressed and required years of hospitalization; eventually he got into a fight where he became permanently physically disabled. A retrospective evaluation of the case indicated that his rage reactions should have been treated before attempts were made to modify his voyeurism. This same reevaluation, however, indicates that at the time of treatment there was no way of knowing this using the behavior therapy model.

While the possibility of doing harm to a person may (or may not) be a low probability event, when we deal with individuals rather than with "populations," each patient must be considered as a potential low probability event. However, this possibility is presented primarily to illustrate the great importance of the selection of target behaviors and the failure of the behavior therapy approach to provide solutions in this area.

2) *Phenotypic behaviors.* Behavior therapists emphasize the phenotypic characteristics of the behavior. It is true that such therapists do attend to a series of psychological processes that support or maintain those

behaviors. They attend to the reinforcing relationships between different behaviors, to the stimulus contexts in which the behavior occurs, to the cognitive variables influencing those behaviors, and to other such processes. Almost completely ignored are the conative, the purposive, behaviors, be they conscious or unconscious. Also ignored are those behaviors which emerge from the balance and interplay of these conative forces within the person. This leads to a number of potential limitations in the formulation of treatment strategies for certain patients.

Behaviors possessing similar superficial characteristics may be treated in the same manner even though the processes underlying them may be quite different. Sexual impotence, for example, may have different underlying processes (Fensterheim and Kantor, 1980). It may be a simple conditioned anxiety response to the sexual situation, most often in the form of the "fear of inadequacy," which is a major basis for the Masters and Johnson (1970) treatment approach. However, the consequence of the impotence may be the frustration of the partner or feelings of self-humiliation on the part of the patient. As human beings are quite capable of teleologic behavior, the sexual impotence may be motivated to bring about just these consequences of partner frustration or self-humiliation. Thus, a completely different treatment strategy would be called for than were it a simple conditioned response. It may be noted that calling these consequences "reinforcers" and removing them in some manner from the situation leads to an inadequate treatment outcome. Should the sexual impotence be relieved, the motive is still present and undoubtedly influences other aspects of the person's life. Beyond that, with the underlying need still present, there may be a chance for the return of the symptom or the development of a substitute symptom.

It may be noted that this approach generally follows the principles of sex therapy formulated by Kaplan (1974). It may also be noted ahat LoPiccolo (1975), a behavior therapist, severely criticizes her for adopting just such an approach. Thus LoPiccolo advises us to ignore an entire area of human function and so limits our range of potential treatment strategies.

The current models of neurotic depression can further illustrate this point. Depression has its own unique phenotypic behaviors. Hence, because of the emphasis on phenotypy, depression requires a unique treatment strategy. A number of models thus have been proposed including learned helplessness (Seligman, 1975), cognitive (Beck , Rush, Shaw, and Emery, 1979), activity (Rehm, 1977), and self-control (Goldfried, 1971). The need for distinctive models has recently been challenged by Wolpe (1979), who argues that neurotic depression may be a manifestation of conditioned anxiety, and by Fensterheim (1981), who discusses a number of other possible variables, such as temperamental characteristics, loss of mastery, blind habits, and even hyperventilation, that may lead to the depressed behaviors. A specific phobic reaction, kept from the patient's awareness by defense mechanisms, may also fuel the depression (see Chapter 2). The phenotypic characteristics of the depression, such as learned helplessness or diminished activities, may be emergent behaviors, and their direct treatment, under these conditions, will at best yield transitory improvement.

The obverse is also true. Behaviors may be phenotypically quite different and yet have similar underlying processes. Hence they will require similar treatment. For example, the fear of heights, a mother constantly yelling at her children, and compulsive sexual exhibitionism all appear quite different on the phenotypic level. Yet all may have the similar underlying process of a direct conditioned response of the autonomic nervous system and, therefore, all may require a similar treatment strategy. It must be noted in this example that the process involved directly supports the target behavior. Hence, it would be expected that a careful behavioral analysis would indeed lead to a similar treatment for these phenotypically different behaviors. However, even here there may be some doubt. The Cautela and Upper (1973) behavioral diagnostic system emphasizes the phenotypic characteristics and carries with it the implication, as any diagnostic system must do, that it furnishes a blueprint for action.

However, it must also be noted that these phenotypically different behaviors may also emerge from processes that do not directly support them. To illustrate this, and to illustrate that indirect underlying processes need not always be psychodynamic ones, the model proposed by Salter will be presented.

Salter (1949) is one of the very few behavior therapists who does give certain processes a central role and does consider disturbed or symptomatic behaviors as emerging, directly or indirectly, from these processes. The processes central to his model are the Pavlovian cortical processes of excitation and inhibition. It is the balance of these forces that is critical, and to Salter a neurosis is always due to an excess of inhibition. Such an excess, according to this model, may well lead to a fear of heights, the mother constantly yelling at her children, or a compulsive sexual exhibitionism. The aim of therapy is to bring about a new balance where the excitatory processes play a more dominant role. To achieve this, target behaviors having no direct connection with the problem behaviors may be selected. Such target behaviors may include increased emotional expression or more appropriate eye contact. Training the patient in such behaviors strengthens the dominance of excitatory processes which, in turn, leads not only to a resolution of the presenting problem but also to a general psychological reorganization and to a "reconstruction of the personality." It is interesting to note that, despite its initial major impact on behavior therapy, Salter's model is now generally ignored within that field. It does, however, furnish at least a partial foundation for the behavioral psychotherapy approach presented herein.

3) *Rejection of the "medical model."* The so-called medical model has long been a *bête noir* for the behavior therapist (Ullmann and Krasner, 1966). According to Kazdin and Hersen (1980), to this day the rejection of this model is one of the characteristics behavior therapists hold in common. This position is much more than a spurious dismissal of an admittedly inadequate system of classifying behavior pathology. Basically it is a rejection of a certain concept of psychological organization and of the concept of behaviors emerging from that organization.

The medical model, using the analogy of physical illness, holds that when the normal workings of the organism are interfered with, symptoms arise. Psychological symptoms are signs of disorder or malfunctions within the person and are not themselves the disorders to be labeled and treated. To treat these symptoms directly without confronting those dysfunctions from which they stem is essentially futile. In actual practice, the psychoanalytically oriented therapist follows this model and assumes that symptoms always stem from a disturbance in the underlying organization and that it is that underlying disturbance that must be treated. Behavior therapists reject this perspective and hold the opposing point of view that disturbed behavior in itself is the pathology and is always accessible to direct intervention.

Behavior therapists do indeed have a concept of the organization of behavior. However, they hold a different one from that of the medical model. The major concept is one of chains of behaviors, some chains being quite complex indeed. The behaviors composing such a chain are all freestanding behaviors differing only in the number of contingencies that maintain them and in the number of contingencies they themselves provide. There is no concept of a hierarchical order where some behaviors are central to the problem area and some peripheral to it; where some behaviors are important and some are trivial; where some behaviors are directly maintained and others emerge from the context of the organization. This last point leads to a difficulty in distinguishing between those behaviors that maintain the problem and those that are a by-product of the problem, as negative thought may be a by-product of depression rather than a primary problem in its own right. All these points lead to selection of inappropriate target behaviors.

The total rejection of the concept of a psychological organization implied by the medical model leads to a further difficulty: How can the therapist determine when treatment is complete? Many times the mere removal of a symptom may not be a sufficient goal, and by stopping treatment there, there is a good probability for return of that symptom or the development of other symptoms stemming from the same inadequate organization and core problem. The commonly accepted behavior therapy goals of establishing "adaptive and prosocial behaviors" (Kazdin and Hersen, 1980) cannot take these organizational characteristics into account.

4) *Emphasis on the experimental model*. Although the model of the laboratory scientist has been replaced by that of the research clinician as the paradigm for the treatment situation, the emphasis remains on the operations the therapist performs rather than on his style of thinking. This is understandable when research goals predominate, for in research the evaluation and replicability of treatment methods are primary. However, when patient change is primary it leads to a mechanization and inflexibility of the treatment itself. It assumes that a given procedure works on the same principle for all patients; that it works the same way for a given patient at all times; that the patient learns what the therapist thinks he is learning. The therapist-patient relationship is important only as it facilitates or interferes with the conduct of the procedures. Few of these assumptions are often true.

When one is concerned with individual people rather than with populations, with the person rather than with the behavior, the uniqueness of each treatment situation comes to the fore. Behavior therapy practitioners are well aware of this. David C. Tinling (personal communication, 1980) writes that he does "1001 different things" in the course of conducting a systematic desensitization procedure and, therefore, cannot conduct a clinical desensitization within a research framework. Stephen Wilder (personal communication, 1980) states that behavior therapy training prepares the student to function within situations he rarely meets in reality. The Wolpes, the Salters, the Lazaruses of behavior therapy are superb clinicians by any standard and do conduct treatment with great sensitivity and flexibility. However, the dominance of the experimental model places the emphasis on the operations they perform rather than on their personal characteristics and the relationships they form with specific patients. There is no room to account for the observation that no matter how mechanical a reinforcing procedure is, some people consistently are better reinforcing agents than are others (Breger and McGaugh, 1965).

In emphasizing the procedures we run the risk of not listening to the patient, of not attending to the feeling/meaning communications that may uncover targets that are important for the complete treatment of the person. Emphasis on procedure may also lead to the demand that the patient conform to our style of doing things, distracting us from the need to tailor the treatment situation so that the patient can best function—or even so that he will remain in treatment. Emphasis on the procedures themselves rather than on the systematic, scientific, and empathic style of thinking by the therapist leads to the stereotyped application of these procedures, consequent failure of treatment, and, eventually, to the disillusionment of the therapist with behavior therapy in general. This, incidentally, is not a straw man being set up. Mozer (1979) reports just such an experience in a letter to *The Behavior Therapist*, and Barlow (1980), in commenting on this letter, states that he had received many other such letters of disillusionment.

Thus, in considering behavior therapy as a method of clinical treatment, despite its many obvious strengths, many weaknesses are noted. These lead to practical difficulties in such matters as the selection of target behaviors, determining the order in which behaviors are to be treated, and setting criteria for determining the goals of treatment. A strict behavior therapy approach may lead to a stereotyped and inflexible mode of treatment. These shortcomings, it is held, stem from an overemphasis on the phenotypic characteristics of behavior and on the operations performed by the therapist to change these behaviors. They also stem from a limited concept of psychological organization which is nonhierarchical and does not allow for the concept of emergent behaviors. It is just these shortcomings that behavioral psychotherapy attempts to resolve.

BASIC PRINCIPLES OF BEHAVIORAL PSYCHOTHERAPY

In the clinical integration of the strengths of both of these approaches to psychotherapy, behavioral psychotherapy places its major emphasis on the identification of appropriate target behaviors and on the selection of the strategy for changing these behaviors. It places great weight on the processes that underlie any given behavior, processes which may range from simple conditioned responses to the conative forces emerging from psychodynamic conflict. Further, it always attempts to place behaviors within the context of a psychological organization. Even behaviors that are identical in phenotypic appearance and underlying processes may have very different meanings and roles as their organizational contexts differ, a point of great importance in the selection of target behaviors and in the determination of their order of treatment.

Behavioral Paradigms

The processes underlying a given behavior are usually identified through a thorough behavioral analysis, and a number of such behavioral processes have been identified. These may range from behaviors maintained by external reinforcers to deficits in the behavioral response repertoire. We have found that many of these processes do possess common elements and can be grouped together into behavioral paradigms. The processes grouped within the same paradigm generally call for similar treatment tactics and for similar therapeutic procedures. Although processes falling into different paradigms may underlie a specific behavior, usually one predominates at a given moment and so determines the treatment during that phase of therapy.

The paradigms we most commonly use are: general tension, automatic emotional responses (phobias), obsessions, assertive difficulties, behavioral deficits, and unwanted behaviors. A detailed discussion of the automatic emotional response paradigm will be found in Chapter 2. The characteristics, diagnostic considerations, and main treatment approaches of the other paradigms will be found in Chapter 3. These paradigms determine therapeutic actions once the target behaviors have been selected.

The Organization

Behaviors occur not in a vacuum but rather in a functional relation to other behaviors and psychological characteristics within the person, to biological variables, and to the social context. These form an organization in which the different aspects may facilitate, inhibit, or distort each other and where the organization itself possesses unique characteristics that are greater than the sum of the different components. Specific behaviors may emerge from and be maintained by these organizational characteristics. Emphasis is placed on the present organization; psychodynamic characteristics are considered in terms of their current status rather than of their developmental history. Traumatic childhood memories are important only if they elicit disturbances (or defenses against disturbances) in the present and influence behaviors in the problem area being treated.

Any and all information concerning the patient may provide clues about the organization. The important point is for the therapist, using deductive thinking, to derive a *behavioral formulation*. This behavioral formulation is actually a working hypothesis of the organization of behavior patterns (including psychodynamic features) relevant to the treatment problem. It allows the therapist to identify key behaviors and so to select target behaviors for treatment. The methods for deriving such behavioral formulations are described in Chapter 3.

The Therapeutic Process

The behavioral formulation thus determines where to intervene, which behaviors to select as targets, and in what order the targets should be approached. The behavioral paradigms into which the target behaviors fall indicate the form the intervention should take and the therapeutic procedures to be attempted. The success or failure of these interventions serves as a therapeutic test of the adequacy of the behavioral formulation. This requires a constant monitoring of change in the target areas; therefore, evaluation becomes an essential part of the therapeutic process. The methods might fail to bring about the anticipated changes, interferences with treatment such as resistances or lack of cooperation may appear, or new information concerning the patient may become available, all of which may require a reformulation of the organizational structures. Hence reformulation, too, becomes an essential part of the therapeutic process.

This model enables the therapist to maintain the clinical strengths of both the psychodynamic and the behavioral approaches. It sensitizes him to underlying processes, be they behavioral or psychodynamic. It facilitates his deductive formulations of behavioral interactions and organizations. At the same time, it focuses on the treatment of selected target behaviors and on the empirical evaluation of treatment effectiveness as do the behavior therapists. As will be illustrated through case reports, this combination of strengths can lead to flexible and systematic treatment with severe and complicated problems.

REFERENCES

Barlow, D. Behavior therapy: The next decade. *Behavior Therapy*, 1980, *11*: 315-328.
Beck, A.E., Rush, A. J., Shaw, B. F., and Emery, G. *Cognitive Therapy of Depression*, New York: Guilford Press, 1979.
Breger, L., and McGaugh, J. L. Critique and reformulation of "learning theory" approaches to psychotherapy and neurosis. *Psychological Bulletin*, 1965, *63*: 338-358.
Cautela, J. R., and Upper, D. A. A behavioral coding system. Presidential Address to the Seventh Annual Meeting of the Association for the Advancement of Behavior Therapy, 1973.
Fensterheim, H. The initial interview. In A. A. Lazarus (Ed.) *Clinical Behavior Therapy*, New York: Brunner/Mazel, 1972.
Fensterheim, H., Behavior therapy of the sexual variations. *Journal of Sex and Marital Therapy*, 1974, *1*: 16-28.
Fensterheim, H., and Kantor, J. S. The behavioral approach to sexual disorders. In B. B. Wolman and J. Money (Eds.) *Handbook of Human Sexuality*, Englewood Cliffs, NJ: Prentice-Hall, 1980.
Fensterheim, H. Clinical behavior therapy of depression. In J. Clarkin and H. Glazer (Eds.) *Depression: Behavioral and Directive Intervention Strategies*, New York: Garland Press, 1981.
Goldfried, M. R. Systematic desensitization as training in self-control. *Journal of Consulting and Clinical Psychology*, 1971, *37*: 228-234.
Hanfmann, E. Wilhelm Stern on "Projective Techniques." *Journal of Personality*, 1952, *21*: 1-21.
Kaplan, H. S. *The New Sex Therapy*, New York: Brunner/Mazel, 1974.
Kazdin, A. E., and Hersen, M. The current status of behavior therapy. *Behavior Modification*, 1980, *4*: 283-302.
LoPiccolo, J. Book Review of H. S. Kaplan, *The New Sex Therapy*. *Behavior Therapy*, 1975, *6*: 136-138.
Masters, W. H., and Johnson, V.E. *Human Sexual Inadequacy*, Boston: Little, Brown, 1970.
Mozer, M. H. Confessions of an ex-behaviorist. *The Behavior Therapist*, 1979, *2*(3): 3.
Normand, W. C., Fensterheim, H., and Schrenzel, S. A systematic approach to brief therapy for patients from a low socioeconomic community. *Community Ment. Health J.*, *1967*, *3*: 349-354.
Rehm, L. P. A self-control model of depression. *Behavior Therapy*, 1977, *8*: 787-804.
Salter, A. *Conditioned Reflex Therapy*, New York: Farrar, Straus and Giroux, 1949.
Seligman, M. E. P. *Helplessness: On Depression, Development and Death*, San Francisco: W. H. Freeman, 1975.
Ullmann, L. P., and Krasner, L. (Eds.) *Case Studies in Behavior Modification*, New York: Holt, Rinehart and Winston, 1966.
Wachtel, P. I. *Psychoanalysis and Behavior Therapy*, New York: Basic Books, 1977.
Wolpe, J. *Theme and Variations: A Behavior Therapy Casebook*, New York: Pergamon, 1976.
Wolpe, J. The experimental model and treatment of neurotic depression. *Behavior Research and Therapy*, 1979, *17*: 555-565.

2

The Behavioral Psychotherapy Model of Phobias

Herbert Fensterheim

The behavioral psychotherapy model and its contrast to other approaches is presented here through a consideration of the area of phobias. Both the psychoanalytic and the behavior therapy modalities accept the same definition of phobias as " . . . excessive fear of some particular type of object or situation; fear that is persistent and without sound grounds . . . " (English and English, 1958), "an abnormally intense fear of an object or situation" (Eysenck and Rachman, 1965) " . . . leading to avoidance . . . " (O'Leary and Wilson, 1975). Note that these definitions all involve the phenotypical characteristics of the phobic condition.

The psychodynamic approach to phobias uses Freud's (1909) analysis of "little Hans" as a model. Anxiety stemming from oedipal conflicts involving castration fears threatens to become conscious. The repressive defenses are not completely adequate for controlling this anxiety. Hence another defense mechanism is brought into play and the fear and anxiety are displaced to an external object. The choice of object has some symbolic relation to the underlying conflict. In the treatment of phobias Freud himself notes that the patient must attempt to face the phobia in order to bring in relevant associations for analysis.

The behavior therapy approach uses the Watson and Rayner (1920) never-replicated demonstration with "little Albert" as the model. While it may be true that the nervous system is "prepared" to learn some phobias more readily than others, some form of learning is sufficient to account for their acquisition. Behavior therapy has become more concerned with the maintenance rather than the acquisition of phobias. Several theories, such as Mowrer's two-factor theory stressing escape and avoidance (1939) or Eysenck's more recent work considering the intensity of the stimulus (1968), have been advanced in this area. The major treatment approach is to have the patient face the phobia under controlled conditions so that unlearning and/or new learning can take effect.

The behavioral psychotherapy approach differs fundamentally from these paradigms. It emphasizes the process involved rather than the phenotypic characteristics of the behavior, and it takes into account the organizations from which they stem. A closer consideration of each of these points is necessary.

THE PROCESS

The phobic response may be defined as a conditioned direct response of the autonomic nervous system to a given stimulus or class of stimuli. Whenever the stimulus appears, the autonomic nervous system (ANS) kicks off. The response is automatic, persistent, and not under voluntary control. At times the chain of behaviors may be slightly more complex: stimulus—> word or thought—> ANS reaction. Nevertheless, all steps are automatic, and true thinking is not involved in the reaction itself. Any thinking that comes about is either beside the fact (epiphenomenal) or after the fact.

Because the phobia is a direct response of the ANS and because it does not involve the cognitive centers, people cannot "be reasoned" out of their phobias. Ellis and Harper's (1962) cognitive approach must be reevaluated in this light. By examining the belief system that supposedly intervenes between the stimulus and the response, what Ellis may actually be doing is changing the meaning of the stimulus to the person. As its meaning changes, it no longer is the same stimulus and, hence, no longer elicits the same response.

The ANS response may lead to different subjective experiences. The most usual experiences appear to be fear, anxiety, or tension. However, differences in temperament and differences in the meaning of the situation to the person may lead to feelings of anger, depression, desire to withdraw, or any other disturbance. Indeed, it has been argued that the elicited feelings need not be only disturbed ones. The sudden and pleasurable flashes of sexual excitement that provoke such sexual variant behavior as exhibitionism or transvestism may fall into this paradigm. Hence, they may be classified and successfully treated as phobias (Fensterheim and Kantor, 1980).

Following this process-oriented approach, many phenotypically different behaviors may fall into the same grouping. A fear of dogs, a mother's constant yelling at her children, a recurring depressive reaction, or a compulsive sexual exhibitionism may all be products of an automatic, persistent, and out-of-voluntary-control reaction of the ANS. Thus, these very different-appearing behaviors may call for essentially similar treatment tactics.

THE ORGANIZATION

The identification of the phobic process, while necessary, is not in itself sufficient for the evaluation of the disturbed behavior. The phobic reaction does not occur in a vacuum but within a biological, intrapsychic, and social organization. These, too, need be considered.

Biological Organization

Many biological variables need be considered with every patient. Among these variables are temperamental characteristics, body appearance and coordination, bodily rhythms, physiological dysfunctions, and endogenous psychological conditions. In the consideration of phobias, two biological variables will be presented for special consideration: the weak nervous system and habitual chronic hyperventilation.

These biological conditions appear to facilitate the acquisition of phobic reactions and to make their removal more difficult. Even when successful removal of the phobia is accomplished under these conditions, the return of the phobia or the acquisition of a different phobia is most probable unless some change in the biological condition is brought about.

The weak nervous system is one where small stimuli will produce strong reactions. It may be indicated by a high score on the Neuroticism Scale of the Maudsley Personality Inventory (Eysenck and Eysenck, 1975). Part of the variance for this may be through inherited temperamental characteristics, part due to continued stress. In any event, the strong disturbed reactions may become associated with specific stimuli, thereby facilitating the acquisition of phobias. This high level of reactivity makes the direct removal of phobias most difficult and, usually, the high level of general tension must be the first target for treatment. This may be accomplished through the initial use of appropriate medication, intensive relaxation training, or a combination of both. Coping desensitization, which trains the patient to control his anxiety reactions in the presence of disturbing stimuli, is often helpful with these conditions. Once the heightened reactions are somewhat controlled, approaches to specific phobias may be carried out. Even after the removal of such phobias, treatment cannot be considered complete until some combination of reduced nervous system reactivity and skills in coping with excessive reactions are brought about.

Habitual chronic hyperventilation (Lum, 1976) is a second biological variable associated with phobias. Unlike the well-known acute hyperventilation which is the product of anxiety, this type of breathing is often the cause of anxiety. During childhood the patient had learned to breathe with the upper thorax rather than with the diaphragm and, hence, continually throws off too much carbon dioxide. This results in a number of profound and pervasive changes in the physiological functions (Lum, 1978/1979), which, in turn, bring on psychological disturbances and symptoms including phobic reactions. Initial treatment must be aimed at training the patient in correct diaphragmatic breathing habits; this many times proves to be a sufficient treatment for the phobias. Direct treatment of phobias without treating the habitual chronic hyperventilation when it is present is usually unsuccessful or, at best, transitory.

Intrapsychic-Behavioral Organization

Phobias, like all symptoms, occur within the framework of a psychological organization. There is a growing body of evidence that personality variables do influence a successful course of treatment. Some examples: Morgenstern, Pearce, and Rees (1965) found that transvestites who scored low on the Neuroticism Scale of the Maudsley Personality Inventory (MPI) responded better to their treatment procedures than did those who scored high on that scale. Rahman and Eysenck (1978) found that patients who scored high on the Psychoticism Scale of the MPI (showing hostility and lack of cooperativeness) in general did not make satisfactory treatment progress. In so simple a treatment as the use of autogenic training procedures for the treatment of Raynaud's disease, the feeling of control over one's life (as measured by the Alienation Scale of the

Psychological Screening Inventory) was highly associated with success (Sunwit, Bradner, Fenton, and Pilon, 1979). Variables such as these must routinely be taken into consideration.

The individual psychological organization of the person may play an even more important role. We will discuss three characteristics of the individual organization that relate directly to phobias: autonomy, coping, and fueling.

The autonomous phobia

Each phobia tends to form a psychological organization of its own. Behaviors in anticipation of the occurrence of the phobic stimulus form one part of this organization. These often include ruminative thoughts and increasing anxiety. The consequences of the phobic reaction itself may be avoidance or escape behaviors which may have a profound influence on the entire life-style of the person. Finally, there are the direct reactions to the phobic response. These typically include secondary anxieties such as fear of losing control, of having a heart attack or of going crazy, as well as the loss of self-respect, self-esteem, and feelings of control over life.

Any aspect of the phobic organization may intrude into other parts of the general psychological and social organization of the person. The anticipatory ruminative thoughts may interfere with concentration at work or disrupt interpersonal relations. The avoidance patterns may lead to an unsatisfactory life-style in general, and the loss of self-esteem may have a profound effect on all areas. For instance, most women we have seen with cat phobias presented not because of that phobia itself but because of its disruptive effect on their marriage.

Nevertheless, the phobic reaction may be essentially autonomous; that is, it is not reinforced or maintained by other parts of the psychological organization. However it originated, in the present it is being maintained solely by its own characteristics. The avoidance-escape patterns may protect the phobic reaction from extinction. The secondary anxiety reactions may lead to the reinforcement of the phobic reaction through the attention paid to it. The anticipatory thoughts may lead to a self-fulfilling prophecy. It is primarily these characteristics, rather than other aspects of the organization, that perpetuate the phobia. Psychoanalytic theory would say that it is involved with ego rather than conflict energy. Many phobias do attain such autonomy.

Such autonomous phobias can usually be treated in a direct, straightforward manner using desensitization or flooding methods. With relief of the phobia, it is expected that the entire organization surrounding it will collapse and so bring about widespread changes and a "complete cure." However, that is not always the case. Sometimes aspects of the phobic organization may themselves become autonomous and require separate treatment. The persistence of avoidance patterns long after the phobia has been removed and the person knows that it has been removed has been a matter of some concern to the theorists. It is difficult to predict when the avoidance will persist and when it will just dissipate with the removal of the phobia. Hence, in therapeutic practice, we tend to use vacations as a test. When the technical indications are that the phobic response has been removed, the patient takes a two-month vacation from treatment. This usually is sufficient time to determine whether the phobic organization will break up or whether further treatment is indicated.

Coping devices

Part of the phobic organization concerns attempts to cope with the phobia. Two such coping devices are extremely important because they have widespread effects, are often misleading, and must be recognized for what they are in order even to know that a phobic reaction is present. One of these concerns the need to anticipate the appearance of the phobic stimuli so that they may be avoided. This leads to a state of *hypervigilance*. The second concerns the need to retain some feeling of mastery in the phobic area. This leads to *counterphobic repetition*. Both coping patterns may be quite subtle and quite complex.

Most people with phobias become highly sensitive to the potential appearance of the phobic stimulus. They are constantly prepared, alert, vigilant, so that at the first sign of its appearance they can take the necessary defensive actions. Hypervigilance is an exaggerated state of this. The person is so supersensitive to the potential appearance of danger that there are disruptive misperceptions and judgments. It is particularly disabling when it occurs in the area of social phobias (i.e., those automatic, persistent reactions that are elicited by such social cues as anger, criticism, or emotional closeness).

The paradigm of this condition (and the example usually used to explain it to patients) concerns a young adult man who presented with a depression of moderately severe intensity. His depression was an appropriate reaction to a depressing life-style; his social life was minimal because he never left his apartment after dark. The reason for this was his terror of cats. During the daylight hours he was able to see the cats and take necessary evasive action. At night he couldn't see them. Hence every shadow was a potential cat poised to leap. Every rustle of leaf or paper against the sidewalk was a cat stalking him. These tensions were too great to bear, so he stayed home, a consequence of his hypervigilance.

Transfer this situation to the area of social phobias. Instead of cats, a person has an intense fear of criticism. He, too, may become hypervigilant, oversensitive to the possible appearance of criticism. The two people across the room talking to each other may be criticizing him. The person he has just left may say something critical to a mutual friend. He begins to feel angry with those people or to avoid them. Superficially it looks very much like paranoid ideas of reference, but the underlying process is phobic and the treatment is for a phobia. Patients with this condition, incidentally, are often worried that they are paranoid. Explaining it to them in these terms usually brings great relief, somewhat lowers general tension, and facilitates the progress of treatment.

Counterphobic repetition, clinically most important in the social area, is an attempt to cope with a different aspect of the phobic organization. As previously noted, one of the main characteristics of the phobic reaction is that it is out of control. The person is aware of this and takes steps to attain some measure of mastery. He cannot do this through controlling the response itself. Nor can he have complete control over the appearance of the phobic stimulus, particularly if it is a social phobia. He can have no guarantees that the other person will not get angry, reject, show tenderness, or whatever it is the patient fears. Yet some feeling of control is needed.

One way to control the situation is to make inevitable the appearance of the phobic stimulus. He can act in a way that practically guarantees that the other person will get angry, will reject, will show tenderness. Then, when this does happen, the phobic reaction sets in and he escapes at its height. So, although he does achieve mastery of a kind, he also strengthens and perpetuates the entire phobic constellation.

Clinically this pattern often appears as a form of testing. A man is terrified of rejection and has a counterphobic repetition. He acts in ways that upset, irritate, and anger his girlfriend. In the midst of these bad feelings he demands sexual relations. Should the girlfriend understandably reject these sexual advances, he becomes extremely angry and abruptly leaves, feels hurt and furious at the same time. Should by chance she acquiesce to his sexual advances under those conditions, the pattern will soon be repeated under escalating pressure until she has no choice whatever but to refuse him.

Fueling phobias

All phobias are not autonomous; rather, they may be related to and maintained by other aspects of the psychological organization. These may be fears directly feeding into each other, derived fears, or fears that attain some reinforcer (gain) for some other aspect of the organization.

Paired phobias: These are fears that feed into each other. Usually they are obvious to the clinician during the initial interview, although the importance of the pairing may not be fully appreciated until phobic reduction procedures are attempted.

The most common examples of these are usually found in patients who present with agoraphobia with panic. An illustrative example concerns a woman with this condition who also had a fear of "sick people." She was afraid that some person near her (usually in a public place or on public transportation) would get sick and would vomit over her. The fear could be set off by pregnant women, by someone who might be slightly drunk, by an adolescent who might just have taken some drug, by someone who coughs or looks a bit pale. In other words, she was hypervigilant. She had had this fear in a milder form long before the onset of the agoraphobia. Now, however, when a potential phobic stimulus presented itself, an agoraphobic panic would be set off. Beyond that, the anticipation of a panic attack would heighten her general level of tension so that she became even more hypervigilant than formerly. Thus, the two phobias fueled each other.

The two phobias also fueled each other during treatment. *In vivo* desensitization could be carried out only in situations where there was little chance that someone who might get sick would appear. At all other times, nothing could be done to prevent escape. The treatment of these fears through behavioral procedures in the office also proved impossible. Attempts to reduce the fear of sick people were complicated by her fear of having a panic attack during the procedure. Attempts to reduce her anticipation of panics were complicated by the fear that, should she overcome the agoraphobia, she might then be forced to expose herself to sick people. Over an eight-month course of treatment, only slight progress was made. Treatment was then discontinued by mutual agreement.

Derived phobias: Not all phobias can be taken at face appearance. Some phobias are the end product of a series of associations to a core fear, often going back to childhood experience. The phobic reaction in the present is some disturbed re-action to either a specific memory or, more usual, a series of childhood memories. This phobia is not directly experienced because of the action of two mechanisms. The first is avoidance; the person rarely allows himself to recall these incidents. The second is the defense mechanism of isolation. The person does not make the connection between these memories and the current problem. Further, when he does recall these incidents, although there may be some feelings of disturbance, the affect originally attached to it is not experienced.

Such a chain of fears is usually connected to a social phobia, but not necessarily so. A woman presented with a fear of sailboats. This was an important fear, because her husband was addicted to sailing and insisted she share this interest with him. Yet every time she even approached a sailboat she experienced intense anxiety. Forcing herself to sail over a period of time only exacerbated this fear.

The fear was vague and she could not identify the main cues. Anything connected with sailboats elicited severe anxiety. A hierarchy was finally made up which first included pictures of sailboats and then looking at sailboats in a store. As the anxiety in these areas decreased, she was able to identify the core fear that the boat would turn over. The critical variable involved the degree the boat heeled before the wind. This served as the basis for a new hierarchy.

The boat hierarchy did not work. Desensitization to the specific lowest scenes did bring about an anxiety reduction during that session, but this did not hold to the next session. Various attempts to modify the hierarchy brought no better results.

However, something did happen during these attempts at desensitization, for in the discussion of the cause of this failure she was now able to identify her fear of drowning. She had always been aware of this fear but had been able to avoid situations where this might be a factor. She would comfortably spend long days at the beach with the knowledge that she would not go near the water. She had not connected the fear of drowning with the fear that the boat might turn over. Beyond that, in discussing the fear of drowning she recalled a specific incident from mid-childhood where she was present at the time a close friend did drown. Desensitization to this memory yielded a series of different feelings. The first disturbance was experienced as a fear that this might happen to her. Next, strong feelings of guilt emerged. Finally, she recalled looking at her friend's body lying on the beach and experienced profound feelings of helplessness. As the helplessness was reduced, her fear of sailboats dissipated to the extent that when she was actually caught in a severe squall she was so busy handling the ropes that she did not notice whether she was frightened or not. It must be noted that this memory had been mentioned in passing and without affect during the initial interview, but at the time neither patient nor therapist recognized its possible connection to the sailboat fear. It must also be noted that the logic of behavioral psychotherapy would have required further exploration of the helplessness. However, for practical clinical reasons, this could not be undertaken with this particular patient.

The core fear need not always come down to a childhood memory, nor need the emotional response be a disturbed one. Feather and Rhoads (1972) report on a young man who had a fear of driving because he might hit a pedestrian. After a failing attempt at the direct desensitization of this fear, they had the patient fantasy deliberately running over people and enjoying it. This procedure did result in a definite marked decrease of the driving phobia. Note that in this instance the emotional reaction was enjoyment, a pleasant feeling. The writers interpret the phobia as emerging in an attempt to keep from acting out to gratify aggressive fantasies. These writers (Feather and Rhoads, 1972; Rhoads and Feather, 1974) cite several similar illustrations of what has been called here fueling phobias.

The fueling phobias are most common in the social area, where the patterns of association often become rather complicated. In our experience most of them do reduce to childhood fears or memories.

A woman presented with a long history of mild to moderate depression, difficulties in close relationships, a current problem of an inability to work, and years of only slightly helpful psychotherapy. The current work problem was formulated as a phobic reaction to criticism, and deconditioning procedures were instituted. Following Pavlov's suggestion to question people about their conditioning, the therapist encouraged her to tell of the feelings and associations she experienced during the desensitization. As the fear of criticism decreased, two other phobic lines emerged (see Figure 1). In one phobic line the criticism was turned into self-criticism, to which she had a phobic reaction experienced as self-hate. Underlying this was the belief that she was truly "evil" in the moral sense of the word, but this remained vague and she could give no specifics. In the second line the fear was that criticism would lead to rejection, and this set off fear reactions. Underlying this fear of rejection was the fear of abandonment, of being helpless and alone in a hostile world. These led to a series of childhood memories of threatened abandonment which, when they were recalled in the present, elicited strong fear responses. These memories were chosen as the new target for desensitization.

These target memories had been often discussed during her psy-

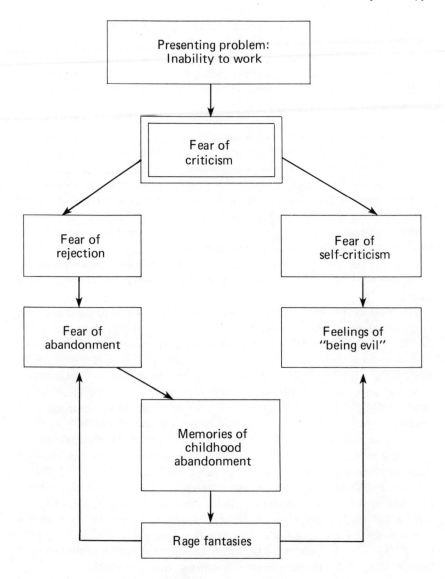

Figure 1. Fueled phobia of criticism.

chotherapies, but she had not been able to get beyond the fear. With desensitization, other feelings rather quickly emerged. The fear was replaced by helplessness, depression (fleetingly), guilt, anger, and finally rage. At that point she recalled a series of vindictive fantasies she had had as a child where she "got even" with her parents, mainly by abandoning them. As the rage reactions were reduced through desensitization, no other feelings replaced them. She experienced an insight that it was the vindictive fantasies that caused her to believe she was evil; the phobic reaction to criticism disappeared; for the first time she could remember she was free of the chronic depression. It appears very much as though the defense mechanism of isolation was involved. As disturbance was reduced through desensitization, there was less need for this defense, and the core phobic reactions themselves became accessible for desensitization.

Many other similar examples may be given. The pattern, though not common, is not rare. Unfortunately, it usually cannot be formulated during the early stages of treatment but becomes clear only as work with the phobia progresses and then only if the therapist looks for it. We seem to be affirming Freud's statement about the necessity of having the patient face the phobia in order to bring in the relevant material. However, when it comes to the need for free association, we tend to follow Pavlov. Pavlov's statement was: "Children, not being dogs, should be questioned about their conditioning." In this instance, the patient only need be questioned about his changing feelings during the phobic reduction procedure. Indeed, most patients are eager to talk about these and about the associations they have during the process. All the therapist usually needs do is to listen and to reflect the feelings in a Rogerian manner. Eventually, a core area for further desensitization will be recognized by both patient and therapist. The final target core in a given area is easily recognized: Successful phobic reduction is attained without being replaced by other disturbances. Although this is not an infallible criterion, it usually means that this is as far as the phobia can be followed at that time.

Reinforced phobias: At times the phobias are reinforced by other aspects of the psychological organization. Among these are secondary gains which help to maintain the phobia and make it difficult for the person to give it up. Often these gains allow the person to avoid other areas of which he is even more fearful. The woman discussed above, who had both agoraphobia and a separate phobia of people being sick near her, is one example. She found it difficult to give up the agoraphobia, for then she would be placed into situations where people might become sick. Often, when another phobia is involved, the connection is more subtle. Fear of novelty, fear of loss of control, fear of being in anxiety-provoking situations are often behind such subtle connections.

The different phobic organizations may also interact. There have been patients in whom an autonomous phobia masked a fueled phobia. One woman had a fear of cats which severely restricted her social life. She could not accept invitations from people she didn't know well lest they or their neighbors had cats. Nor could she invite such people to her own home, for they might return the invitation and she would be embarrassed by having to refuse it. The basic fear was a fear of strangers, which was fueled by phobic reactions to memories of mother's warnings about strangers and the fantasies these warnings evoked. Until this fueled phobia was reduced, no progress could be made in removing the cat phobia.

A phobia may be reinforced in that it allows the person to avoid situations which may lower his self-esteem or challenge an unrealistic self-image. "If it were not for my fear of flying I would have that top level executive job." "If I were not frightened of sex I would be freer to socialize with women and would be a really cool type of guy." In each instance the person may be aware on some level that he does not have the skills necessary for the maintenance of that image, and the phobia provides an excuse for not putting it to test.

The gain may also be in the maintenance of other, long-standing habits that may influence many areas of his life. Most obvious is when the phobia maintains a passive, dependent, or withdrawn style of life which, in turn, is maintained by still other aspects of the organization. Or it may be used to maintain a series of irrational beliefs about the world and the people in it when challenging these beliefs would set up a state of dissonance and its consequent anxiety.

In these instances, the gains must be considered in a treatment program. However, they are not easily recognized at the outset of treatment. Even if there appear to be obvious gains, these may be by-products rather than maintainers of the phobic reactions. Not infrequent among agoraphobic people are very obvious dependency needs. The agoraphobia appears to be in the service of these needs. However, many times, when the agoraphobia is removed, these needs simply vanish. It is only when problems arise in removing the agoraphobia or other phobia that the reinforcing gains are to be sought.

Social Organization

Phobias occur not only within the contexts of biological and intrapsychic organizations but also within the context of a social organization. These social organizations may provide reinforcers for the phobia, situations that superficially appear to be simple but which, upon analysis, are often quite complex. They may directly provoke the phobia. They may prevent the removal of the phobia through the inertia to change that is found in social situations. Finally to be considered is the special social situation provided by the therapeutic dyad.

Socially reinforced phobias

Behaviors may be maintained by the reinforcing attention paid to it by other people, be that attention manifested by caring or by irritated behavior on the part of the other. (This is also true of many other disturbed behaviors such as depression or obsessions.) In such an instance the therapist works at reducing the phobia while the other person constantly reinforces it. Progress is often slow and sporadic. However, once the situation is identified, the required treatment is obvious: instruct the other person to ignore completely the phobic behavior but to pay much attention to new nonphobic behaviors. With the withdrawal of the reinforcement, phobic reduction will be easily accomplished. Or will it?

In actual practice such an approach often turns out to be quite difficult to carry out. The reinforcing person often has a stake in the patient's phobic reactions. That is, the reinforcing person himself gains something from the patient's phobia. The person has his own problem habit patterns, his own fears and anxieties, his own skill deficits, and the patient's phobia may help him to avoid situations that provoke these. Hence, as the patient improves, the person may become more anxious; as the patient retrogresses, he becomes more comfortable again. In these instances aversion-avoidance reinforces the phobia-reinforcing behaviors in the other person.

The reinforcing person may have his own phobic response to the patient's phobia. The attention he pays, whether concern or irritation, may itself be automatic, persistent, and out of deliberate control. Often such a phobic response is more indirect. A common form of this is an automatic guilt reaction to the patient's phobia. The person then becomes hypervigilant to the possible appearance of any signs of a phobic reaction and inadvertently reinforces the earliest signs of anything that may lead to the phobic reaction.

The interaction between the two people may sometimes become quite complicated, each person reinforcing the other. Fensterheim and Kantor (1980) report several such instances. In one case the man presented with the problem of sexual impotence based on a fear of sexual impotence. The woman involved, because of her own past experiences, was phobic to the possibility that he might become impotent, and it was her anxiety that initially set off the process. He reacted to her anxiety; as his reaction exacerbated, her anxieties increased still further, exacerbating his phobia. Desensitizing the woman to her fears broke this cycle and relieved his sexual dysfunction. A similar phobic interaction, in this instance maintaining a depression, is also reported by Fensterheim (1981).

Beyond these person interactions, social systems themselves do have an inertia to change, be the social situation a dyad, a family, or some other grouping. Therapists are quite familiar with this. No matter how much a husband wants his wife to lose weight, when she starts to do so he often feels threatened and begins to sabotage the very change he wants. During the treatment of premature ejaculation, the wife often panics at the first signs of success, no matter how much she wants the change. Family therapists see firsthand how the families they work with tend to maintain the very same destructive equilibrium they had entered therapy to change. So it is with phobias. The inertia of the patient's social system may make change difficult or may provide the contingencies for the relearning of phobic responses.

Phobias in treatment

Phobias other than those selected as treatment targets may be at work within the social context of the therapeutic dyad. They may lead to noncooperation on the part of the patient. Among the common phobias we have noted that may interfere with treatment progress are phobic reactions to instructions, fear of change, and automatic reactions of various kinds to the therapist as an authority figure. When such reactions are present, they may make it difficult for the patient to carry out assignments or even to follow relatively simple procedures in the office. At times the manifestation of this latter may be quite subtle, such as an unidentified source of anxiety during relaxation procedures. Sometimes such phobias are reduced during the course of work on other phobias;

sometimes they must be identified and treated before other therapeutic work can be undertaken. Although many behaviors may lead to non-cooperation, as has been shown in the analysis of this by Goldfried (1982), phobic reactions are very frequently involved.

Behavior therapists often label such noncooperative behaviors as "resistance," and it is in the consideration of resistance that one of the main differences between behavior therapy and behavioral psychotherapy becomes obvious. Jahn and Lichstein (1980) and Goldfried (1982), in their need to define resistance in phenotypic terms rather than in terms of processes involved, focus on noncompliant behavior. However, the process of resistance, in its commonly used meaning, has two characteristics these writers ignore: 1) It is unconscious, i.e., performed without the patient's awareness, and 2) it is defensive, i.e., it protects the patient from anxiety-eliciting information. In traditional psychotherapy such insightful information is considered to be the core of the change process. Hence resistance may interfere with the course of treatment. In the behavioral approaches, however, such information is needed mainly for the selection of target behaviors; insight, although it may bring with it cognitive reorganizations, usually emerges after the main behavioral change is accomplished. Hence, from the behavioral psychotherapy perspective, resistance must be considered when selecting target behaviors and when planning treatment rather than during the ongoing course of treatment.

Indeed, resistance may lead to a great deal of cooperation. It may lead to the patient who follows all assignments, is a pleasure to work with, but who shows only minimal improvement. A patient has a phobic reaction to dissatisfied authority figures. Further, he becomes extremely anxious when he allows himself to realize this. Over the years he has developed a coping pattern which not only avoids dissatisfied authorities but also keeps him from being aware of so doing. This phobia and its attendant coping pattern play a definite role in the patient's presenting problem and treatment cannot be considered to be complete until it is identified and treated. Because of just these patterns, the patient is cooperative in treatment and relates well to the therapist. However, they also lead to change that is either limited or temporary. How is the therapist to identify this key target area? One way is, once the therapist realizes that something is missing from his formulation, to use the methods of traditional psychotherapy: dreams, fantasies, slips of the tongue, apparently irrelevant associations and feelings emerging during the behavioral treatment procedures, and just clinical feel and intuition. Many of the failures and the relapses of behavior therapy occur from the lack of consideration of this aspect of resistance.

SUMMARY

This detailed consideration of phobias illustrates how the behavioral psychotherapy approach integrates the thinking styles of behavior therapy and of the traditional psychotherapeutic approach. Like behavior therapy it aims at identifying very specific target behaviors and systematically and rigorously attempting to change them. There is a constant clinical evaluation of whether changes are indeed taking place and whether they are bringing about the desired changes within the life situation.

Like the psychoanalytic approach, great attention is paid to the processes (although not necessarily psychodynamic ones) involved and to the organizational contexts (biological, intrapsychic-behavioral, and social) in which these processes occur. This has allowed us to broaden the concept of phobic reactions so that a powerful therapeutic method may now be applied to areas where it was not previously considered. More important, it gives us a systematic basis for selecting target behaviors for treatment and for determining the order of treatment. As previously noted, behavior therapy provides no basis for such a determination. It also provides a number of approaches to be considered systematically when treatment difficulties arise.

REFERENCES

Ellis, A., and Harper, R. A. *A Guide to Rational Living*. Hollywood: Wilshire, 1962.

English, H. B., and English, A. C. *A Comprehensive Dictionary of Psychological and Psychoanalytical Terms*. New York: Longmans, Green & Co, 1958.

Eysenck, H. J. A theory of the incubation of anxiety-fear responses. *Behavior Research and Therapy*, 1968 6: 309-321.

Eysenck, H. J., and Eysenck, S. B. G. *Manual of the Eysenck Personality Questionnaire*. London: Hodder & Stoughton Educational, 1975.

Eysenck, H. J., and Rachman, S. *The Causes and Cures of Neurosis*. San Diego, CA: Robert R. Knapp, 1965.

Feather, B. W., and Rhoads, J. M. Psychodynamic behavior therapy. *Archives of General Psychiatry*, 1972, 26: 496-502.

Fensterheim, H., and Kantor, J. S., The behavioral approach to sexual disorders. In B. B. Wolman and J. Money (Eds.), *Handbook of Human Sexuality*. Englewood Cliffs, NJ: Prentice-Hall, 1980.

Fensterheim, H. Clinical behavior therapy of depression. In J. Clarkin and H. Glazer (Eds.), *Depression: Behavioral and Directive Intervention Strategies*. New York: Garland Press, 1981.

Freud, S. (1909) Analysis of a phobia in a five-year-old-boy. In *Collected Papers*, vol. 3. New York: Basic Books, 1959.

Goldfried, M. R. Resistance and clinical behavior therapy. In P. L. Wachtel (Ed.), *Resistance: Psychodynamic and Behavioral Approaches*. New York: Plenum, 1982.

Jahn, D. L., and Lichstein, K. L. The resistive client: A neglected phenomenon in behavior therapy. *Behavior Modification*, 1980, 4: 303-320.

Lum, L. C. The syndrome of habitual chronic hyperventilation. In O. Hill (Ed.), *Modern Trends in Psychosomatic Medicine*, vol. 3. Boston: Butterworths, 1976.

Lum, L. C. Respiratory alkalosis and hypocarbia. *The Chest, Heart & Stroke Journal*, 1978/1979, 3: 1-4.

Morgenstern, F., Pearce, J., and Rees, W. I. Predicting the outcome of behavior therapy by psychological tests. *Behavior Research and Therapy*, 1965, 2: 191-200.

Mowrer, O. H. A stimulus-response analysis of anxiety and its role as a reinforcing agent. *Psychological Review*, 1939, 46: 553-565.

O'Leary, K. D., and Wilson, G. T. *Behavior Therapy: Application and Outcome*. Englewood Cliffs, NJ: Prentice-Hall, 1975.

Rahman, M. A., and Eysenck, S. B. G. Psychoticism and response to treatment in neurotic patients. *Behavior Research and Therapy*, 1978, 16: 183-189.

Rhoads, J. M., and Feather, B. W. The application of psychodynamics to behavior therapy. *American Journal of Psychiatry*, 1974, 131: 17-20.

Sunwit, R. S., Bradner, M. N., Fenton, C. H., and Pilon, R. N. Individual differences in response to the behavioral treatment of Raynaud's disease. *Journal of Consulting and Clinical Psychology*, 1979 47: 363-367.

Ullmann, L. P., and Krasner, L. (Eds.) *Case Studies in Behavior Modification*. New York: Holt, Rinehart and Winston, 1966.

Watson, J. B., and Rayner, R. Conditioned emotional reactions, *Journal of Experimental Psychology*, 1920, 3: 1.

3

Basic Paradigms and Behavioral Formulation

Herbert Fensterheim

The logic of behavioral psychotherapy requires systematic attempts to change carefully chosen target behaviors. The target behaviors are chosen through the behavioral formulation, an attempt to depict the organization of behaviors for that person. The change methods to be used are selected on the basis of the basic paradigm into which the target behavior falls. The determination of applicable paradigms and the formulation of behavioral organization are crucial areas of behavioral psychotherapy.

THE BASIC PARADIGMS

A limited number of specific paradigms appears to emerge repeatedly in the course of clinical work. Each of these paradigms strongly suggests a given set of treatment tactics and a given change technology to be considered. The major paradigms we have so far identified are: general disturbance, automatic emotional reactions, obsessions, assertive difficulties, behavioral deficits, and unwanted behaviors. It must also be noted that a number of special paradigms for such specific conditions as stuttering have also emerged. However, these latter will not be discussed here.

We have already presented in some detail the paradigm of automatic emotional reactions (phobias). The discussion will now center around the remaining paradigms and, as in the book as a whole, will be oriented mainly to the practical-clinical rather than to the theoretical-experimental.

General Disturbance

A major cause of problem behaviors appears to be a constant, or almost constant, state of bad feelings. These are most frequently experienced as tension or anxiety but also may be experienced subjectively in a variety of other ways such as anger, depression, or fatigue. The subjective experience may in part depend on the temperamental characteristics of the nervous system or on the impact of life experience as revealed by the presence of a fueling phobia. It is because of the wide variety of subjective experiences that we prefer the term "general disturbance" rather than the more usual behavior therapy term "general tension."

The patient often presents with this disturbance as the major problem. However, he may present with completely different problems which only careful investigation shows to be set off by the general disturbance. A constant feeling of anger or irritability may markedly interfere with interpersonal relations. A constant fatigue may interfere with the marriage. Difficulty in falling asleep is a common symptom. Regardless of the subjective nature of the disturbance, onset is usually slow and gradual. The condition may have been building up over a long period of time, often years, before the person seeks help.

Only rarely is the intensity of the disturbance the critical variable. Rather, it often comes down to the question of who is in control: the disturbance or the person. After all, under certain life situations, we do experience fairly intense anxiety but we retain control and do what we have to do, minimizing as much as possible the attention we pay to the disturbance. However, with our patients, the disturbance brings on strong feelings of helplessness, of not being in command. In most instances, it is these feelings, not the disturbance itself, that must be the target.

A number of behaviors may feed into the feelings of helplessness. The person may assume a passive orientation towards the increasing disturbance and so let it build up without any attempts to gain control. Or the person may have the concept but may not know how to gain this control. In both these cases the treatment to be considered is relaxation training of some type and its application to life situations. Gold-fried's coping desensitization (1971), where the person is trained to relax under anxiety conditions, is often helpful. Again, it is stressed that these methods may be considered whatever the subjective experience of the disturbance: anxiety, anger, depression, etc.

There may be cognitive or automatic response elements that serve to maintain the state of continual disturbance. The person may label himself as "nervous," "neurotic," or some other pejorative term. This last may lead to a self-fulfilling prophecy wherein his prediction that he will be nervous does indeed come true. Here, challenge and dispute (Ellis and Harper, 1962) may be needed to supplement the relaxation training program. He turns every situation into a test situation—Will I get anxious? Am I getting anxious?—rather than using it as a practice situation for gaining increasing control over the disturbance. The secondary automatic emotional responses to the disturbance, the fear of being frightened, the *Angst von Angst,* may lead him to pay much attention to the disturbance and so to reinforce and to maintain this state. Desensitization to the disturbed feelings themselves may be considered. We have reported elsewhere (Fensterheim, 1981) that depressive reactions that fall under this rubric may be markedly helped through taped desensitization exercises to be used at home.

There are times, however, when the feelings of helplessness are justified, when the person truly has no control over the disturbance. This most usually occurs when the intensity of the disturbance is at a very high level. Here the disruption may be so great and so pervasive that no control over it is possible and no other target behaviors can be used constructively. However, similar situations have been encountered with the lower levels of disturbance. We have seen individuals where the disturbance level, whether continuous or intermittent, was at the level of 20, 15, or even 10 subjective units of disturbance (suds), and where the person had no control over it at all. Indeed, attempts to lower that level even by a small fraction often led to frustration and increased disturbance. With these lower levels, desensitization to the feelings of disturbance can be tried and sometimes may be helpful. However, frequently with these, as well as with the higher levels, some form of medication must be considered as a first step towards gaining control over the condition.

Whenever the intensity of the disturbance remains high, does not appear to be elicited by specific stimuli (such as obsessive thoughts), and does not respond to intensive treatment, biological variables should be investigated. Among these may be hypoglycemia, endocrine dysfunction, or even a chronic low-grade infection. One such variable that we believe will be of increasing clinical importance is habitual chronic hyperventilation (Lum, 1976).

Habitual chronic hyperventilation (HCH) differs from the commonly recognized acute hyperventilation which is the consequence of anxiety. HCH instead precipitates the anxiety. It is a habit of incorrect breathing, apparently acquired during childhood, where the person constantly throws off too much carbon dioxide. This leads to a continual state of hypocarbia, and the person is either always symptomatic or at risk for symptoms to develop under mild stress. Diagnosis is based mainly on observing the breathing pattern (lower thorax should expand three to four times as much as upper thorax) and noting the presence of typical hyperventilation sighs (Lum, 1976). Not only anxiety, but also a variety of somatic symptoms and other disturbances may be brought on by this condition. It has been suggested that depression may be a direct product of such faulty breathing (Gibson, 1978) or an indirect one (Fensterheim, 1981).

Thus, within the paradigm of general disturbance, the type of subjective experience is relatively unimportant. Among the most frequent behavioral variables to be investigated and treated are the self-control behaviors, possible biological variables, and the presence of a state of habitual chronic hyperventilation.

Obsessions

Obsessive thoughts are those unwanted thoughts that intrude upon a person, bringing fear, depression, or some other disturbance in their wake. *Intrude* is the operational word, for they thrust themselves unwantedly on people despite attempts to control them. Following Solyom, Zamanzadeh, Ledwidge, and Kenny (1971), we find it helpful to place obsessions into one of three groups: "horrific temptations," chronic indecisiveness (*folie de doute*), and ruminative obsessions which may or may not be accompanied by compulsions. The ruminative obsessions are the most commonly seen in an office practice and will be discussed in some detail. First, however, some things must be said about the other two forms of obsessiveness.

The "horrific temptations" are sudden intrusions of unacceptable thoughts that set off high levels of fear or anxiety. Usually they involve unacceptable sexual activity ("I am really homosexual") or fear of harm to someone close ("My wife will be killed in an accident"). The suddenness of the intrusion leads to sudden high levels of disturbance.

Often no direct elicitor of the thought may be determined. It feeds back upon the general psychological organization in terms of anticipation ("When will it happen again?") and in terms of its meaning to the person (" I must really want that to happen. There is something really sick about me"). The first treatment approach is usually an aversion relief desensitization combined with teaching the patient to relax out the secondary anxieties when the thoughts do come. This seems to work often enough, but other approaches such as flooding or satiation may have to be attempted. Usually in the course of treatment other important psychological problems emerge and, in turn, must be formulated and treated. It is not unusual to find a fueling phobia involved.

The obsessive indecisiveness is the one that we find most difficult to treat. The person with this condition has a flat or mildly depressive affect and very often has assertiveness problems. Assertiveness training is usually necessary to crystallize the points of decision-making before the obsessiveness can be approached directly. However, the obsessiveness itself may interfere with any course of treatment, and so progress is slow and often unsuccessful.

In ruminative obsessions, clinically the most important of this group, thoughts intrude over and over, bringing anxiety and/or depression in their wake. The content of the thoughts, except for their direct consequences, are usually irrelevant for gaining an understanding of the patient's general psychological organization. Indeed, they tend to mask other problems even more frequently than they reveal them.

An important variable is the presence of a compulsion. When this is present, whether in the form of a ritual such as handwashing, an avoidance of certain areas or objects, or a series of questions for reassurance, it functions as a negative reinforcer. The obsession elicits disturbance which is reduced by the compulsive act. That is, the compulsion subtracts the anxiety and thereby, although it gives momentary relief, reinforces and so maintains the entire process. To remove such reinforcement it becomes necessary to control the compulsive acts through the array of response prevention methods available (Marks, 1981; Beech and Vaughan, 1978).

Ruminative obsessions without compulsions tend to be maintained through positive reinforcement. Again the obsessive thought brings on disturbance. In this instance the disturbance causes the person to pay attention to the thought (i.e., attention is added to the situation), which serves as the reinforcer to maintain the entire process. The target behavior chosen here may depend upon the intensity of the disturbance. If the disturbance is relatively mild, the thought itself may become the target, and a method such as thought stopping may be effective. However, once the intensity of the disturbance reaches a moderate or higher level, it is the disturbance itself that must become the target. Here flooding and satiation methods (Marks, 1981; Rachman, 1976) are usually the methods of choice, although aversion relief desensitization may sometimes be effective.

Even after the obsessiveness is cleared up, cognitive characteristics of the obsessiveness may remain and interfere with many aspects of the person's life. These must be sought out and the need for specific treatment evaluated. Illustrating such characteristics are the lack of a hierarchical organization where there is no criterion for what is important and what is trivial, and the presence of Aristotelian thinking where things either are or are not, rather than existing to some degree. These cognitive characteristics may impede the initial treatment of the obsessiveness, but even if they are not evident during that phase of treatment, the therapist at some point must search for them. If they are truly present to any great degree, their influence on the person's life may be quite pervasive.

Should the therapist be successful in reducing the obsessive process to the degree where it is manageable and no longer dominates the person's life, a brief vacation from treatment is usually indicated. This allows the person time to integrate such changes into his daily life, and it allows time for psychological reorganization to occur. Thus, with the removal of the obsessiveness, there may be a great increase in self-esteem which, in turn, influences still other behaviors. Following such a vacation, there should be a thorough reexamination of the person and his then current life. People with obsessive disorders often have other severe problems requiring treatment, and these other problems may be neither evident nor accessible until after the removal of the masking obsessiveness.

Direct treatment of the obsession is not always effective; other of our basic paradigms may be maintaining the obsessive state. Treatment of these other variables may be the necessary first targets for change. General disturbance is frequently one such paradigm. It may act directly on the obsession; obsessiveness tends to increase with general disturbance. Or it may act indirectly on it as it does, for example, by causing sleep disturbance; obsessiveness tends to increase with overfatigue. Many years ago, Jacobson (1929) reported that complete relaxation of certain key muscle groups controls obsessiveness, and one of our own faculty members (Gordon Ball) confirms this through his clinical experience with biofeedback relaxation. Thus, there are instances when tension reduction must be carried out before control of the obsessive state can be achieved. However, this is a most difficult determination to be made at the outset of treatment. Such consideration is usually not given until and unless marked difficulties are encountered in treating the obsessiveness directly.

There are also times when the obsessive-compulsive state is maintained by the characteristics of the general psychological organization. Jacobson (Chapter 5) reports on a man with disabling checking behavior. As the case was eventually formulated, these checking behaviors at once protected the patient from a feeling of helplessness and also allowed him to play the role of "the sick one" within his family. Direct treatment of his compulsions through response prevention precipitated a depression so severe that hospitalization was necessary. Hence, the helplessness and the family role had to be the target behaviors rather than the checking itself.

The very opposite may also be true: There are times when a complex behavioral organization may have a disguised or minimal obsessive process as its core. The patient may present with depression, disturbed interpersonal relations, creative blocks, sexual problems, or any other set of difficulties imaginable, and these may have a hidden obsession maintaining them. Such obsessions are not always identifiable during the initial formulation but may become obvious through careful reformulation during the process of treatment. Fensterheim (1981) reports one such instance with a depressed patient. The core of the depression was formulated as centering around assertive difficulties associated with a learned helplessness. Obsessive fears of losing his job were believed to be a by-product of the depression. However, when the case was reformulated because the treatment was not working, the obsessive fears were placed at the core. An aversion relief desensitization to the ruminative obsession of losing his job led both to an amelioration of the depression and to the disappearance of both the assertive difficulties and the helplessness.

Thus, in the treatment of obsessions a number of target behaviors are available. These include: the thoughts themselves, the compulsions or the disturbed feelings that may be maintaining them, some other problem fueling the obsession, or some gain (reinforcer) achieved by the obsession. Obsessions tend to be fairly complicated, and many times there exists a mixture of these targets. The target behavior to be treated is selected on the basis of the behavioral formulation with the distinct realization that this formulation will probably change during the course of treatment.

Assertive Difficulties

The area of assertion is more often easier to treat than to define. It has been noted that there are about as many different definitions of assertion as there are therapists who practice assertiveness training. For practical clinical purposes we ourselves define assertive behavior as the ability deliberately to act to maintain or increase self-respect. Difficulties, according to our definition, stem from the lack of necessary skills or from incorrect cognitions. What disturbances, fears, or obsessions may be present stem from the assertive difficulties rather than cause or maintain them. These difficulties are most usually to be found in the interpersonal areas. Hence, examination to investigate these problems focuses on social behavior.

Much information can be gathered about assertive difficulties during the ordinary course of the general examination. The patient will probably give details of his social life and his personal relations which may alert the therapist to the possible presence of such difficulties. However, a more systematic examination is usually needed. Such an examination will cover both different situations where difficulties may appear and the specific behaviors that may be involved.

We identify three general areas of social function to be examined: the work situation, superficial social relations, and close personal relations. Although these areas often shade off into each other, they are sufficiently different in their goals and the criteria for appropriateness to warrant the distinction. The goals in the work area are to move toward short- and long-term career objectives, to keep interpersonal relations in a manner that will aid this, and to give personal feelings a low level of priority. The close personal relationship is the exact opposite. There, feelings come first, and the goal is the ever increasing sharing of the most personal feelings. The goal of the superficial social relationship is to make things pleasant and interesting for all concerned, to be appropriately self-revealing and to invite others to be the same. Patients may be completely competent in two of these areas but have sufficient difficulty in the third to bring on marked disturbance. When this is the case, what may be involved is either a misunderstanding of the requirements of that type of situation or a specific phobic response rather than an assertive skill deficit.

We also investigate three levels of assertive behaviors: basic assertion, basic social skills, complex social skills. The basic assertion includes such behaviors as appropriate eye contact, loudness of voice, latency of response, posture, gestures, emotional expression conveyed, etc. These can usually be noted during the course of the interview. However, sometimes the difficulty is situation-specific, and the patient must always be questioned about these behaviors.

The main behaviors to be investigated in the area of basic social skills are: the ability to say "No," making requests and asking favors, the appropriate expression of positive and negative feelings, the ability to start, maintain and end conversations, and the ability to respond to hostile criticism or "put-downs."The first four of these were suggested by Lazarus (1971), and we have found the last to be of particular clinical importance. Although these appear to be most important, other basic social behaviors, such as the ability to accept compliments, must also be examined. Systematic search for difficulties with these skills in the three areas of social functioning should be part of every examination. Usually, direct questions supplemented by a questionnaire (Figure 1) are sufficient to alert the therapist to possible difficulties.

The complex social skills involve such activities as forming a social network, striving for career advancement, moving from superficial to close relations. Each of these involves a series of specific skills. Forming a social network may involve the skills of being a good host or a good guest, the art of meeting new people, and a variety of others. The command of the basic social skills may or may not be a problem. Many of the difficulties here lie with misconceptions and lack of proper understanding, and treatment is an educational program.

Following these general procedures will yield a great deal of data concerning possible assertive difficulties. However, two further questions must be addressed:

1) *Are the problems noted truly problems of assertion?* The behavioral difficulties noted may be the result of one of the other paradigms we describe. In other words, the patient may have the necessary skills and concepts in his repertoire, but the use of these may be inhibited by general disturbance, by automatic emotional reactions or by obsessions. Often when assertive difficulties are present, we also find these other difficulties, and it becomes a question of which is the cart and which is the horse. Do these difficulties bring on the assertive problems, or do the assertive problems bring on these difficulties? History is often helpful in making this distinction. However, many times no clear answer is available. Or often the behaviors so interact and feed into each other that they cannot be disentangled. In those instances it probably is best to rephrase the question in action terms: If I use the methods of asser-

Figure 1
Questionnaire used to survey basic social skills.

Grade yourself in each of the following areas:
A = Few Problems
B = Some Problems
C = Many Problems
D = Inadequate
1. Ability to say "No" when you want to say "No"
   At work ———
   In social situations ———
   In a close relation ———
2. Ability to make requests and ask favors
   At work ———
   In social situations ———
   In a close relation ———
3. Ability to express appropriately positive feelings
   At work ———
   In social situations ———
   In a close relation ———
4. Ability to express appropriately negative feelings
   At work ———
   In social situations ———
   In a close relation ———
5. Ability to start, maintain, end conversations
   At work ———
   In social situations ———
   In a close relation ———
6. Ability to handle put-downs (hostile criticism)
   At work ———
   In social situations ———
   In a close relation ———
7. Other
   At work ———
   In social situations ———
   In a close relation ———

---

tiveness training, is there a reasonable chance that we will make progress? If so, start such a program as much for testing the formulation as for attempting to bring about the desired change. Patients are quite willing to accept the fact that this is an experimental approach to achieve those purposes.

2) *Is the assertive difficulty ego syntonic?* Although this question may be asked of any difficulty, it appears to be especially relevant to the area of assertion. We are not referring here to the impact of changes in

assertiveness on the social environment, that people close to the patient, no matter how much they want the patient to change, may actually sabotage and punish increased assertion. Rather, we are referring to the situation where the patient, whatever his complaints, just "feels more comfortable" by not being assertive. Psychodynamic variables such as conflicts about dependency, fears of aggression, and masochistic needs may be at work here. We have seen several patients who had obvious problems in assertion but with whom long-term and varied assertive treatments yielded no results until these psychodynamic problems were uncovered and behaviorally treated. Fried's book *Active/Passive* (1970) provides some helpful concepts along these lines, although we differ with her on the course of treatment to which these lead. Such formulations cannot be made during the initial stages of treatment. Rather, the possible presence of such a situation should be noted to be considered if and when unusual difficulties appear in the course of treatment.

One final word is needed in this area. Due to the publicity through the media that assertion has received, many people present with the complaint that they have assertive problems and need assertiveness training. These complaints should never, never, be taken at face value; a complete examination is always indicated. Even if it does turn out that the patient is correct, and often he is not, much information is necessary to plan the highly individualized program so characteristic of both behavior therapy and behavioral psychotherapy. Routinely placing the patient into a prepackaged group program is completely antithetical to both approaches (Barlow, 1980; Wolpe, 1981).

Behavioral Deficits and Unwanted Behaviors

These two paradigms will be discussed together because each involves autonomous habits or behavior patterns, and each such habit tends to carry along with it a secondary organization of disturbance. In the behavioral deficit paradigm the person has not learned, or learned but lost, skills necessary for coping with life. Deficits in the areas of work habits, promptness, self-care, and orderliness may be sufficiently great to have marked consequences in life; they may lead to depression, anxiety, low self-esteem, and other characteristics stemming from a feeling of not being in control. The unwanted behaviors refer to behaviors that are compulsive, ritualistic, and out of voluntary control. This area most often refers to the sexual variant behaviors, tics, and to the addictive and overeating behaviors. They, too, carry an organization of disturbance with them.

Once the specific behavior deficit is identified and the absent component parts of it pinpointed, a fairly straightforward program of habit change can be devised. This usually involves schedules, self-monitoring and record keeping, and perhaps reinforcement. The major clinical difficulty is to keep the patient working on the program. Two frequent sources of difficulty involve sabotage, however unwitting, by others and a generally passive attitude on the part of the patient. When difficulties in treatment arise, these are the first areas to investigate. Similarly, unwanted behaviors can often be brought under control through establishing counterhabits or through directly suppressing the behavior itself by aversion (Maletsky, 1980) or thought stoppage (Fensterheim, 1974) or some other indicated method. In general, good results may be expected.

This, of course, assumes that the behaviors are autonomous, as they often are. However, this is not necessarily so. Sometimes the behavior may involve an anxiety avoidance area that is so strong that the approach behaviors of the training program must be inhibited. Thus, overweight may be in the service of avoiding sexual anxieties, and as the person loses weight, anxiety is precipitated and the motivation to stick with the program is diminished. Sometimes the behaviors (or lack of them) are in service of some deeper need, fantasy or conflict. We have seen lateness stemming from power needs, work procrastination from a grandiose self-fantasy, and voyeurism from a conflict involving a desire to be and a fear of being sinful. In these three instances, the psychodynamic forces were sufficiently strong to prevent the success of the behavior change program.

Once again, it is difficult to identify these forces and their effects during the early stages of treatment. They become increasingly important as obstacles and difficulties arise during the treatment program. However, even when the program is successful and goes smoothly, when there are indications that such forces may be at play, they must be taken into consideration. Although they may not be interfering with this aspect of treatment, they still may influence the patient's life in many ways. They must be evaluated, and a therapeutic decision must be made whether or not an attempt to treat them is warranted.

The trap to avoid in this paradigm is one of overcomplication. Behavioral deficits and unwanted behaviors carry along with them their own organization of disturbance. These may be direct disturbances such as depression, low self-esteem, or social inhibitions. Indirect disturbances may be brought on by the consequences of the behaviors on the life situation, such as loss of job or being put in jail. The tendency to be resisted is that of regarding these disturbances as the precipitators or the maintainers of the behavior difficulties, rather than as their by-products. The best principle to follow is that, unless there are clear indications to do otherwise, the initial treatment attempt should focus on the specific behavior involved; then the outcome of this attempt should be evaluated. Only then, if indicated, should complications be introduced.

THE BEHAVIORAL FORMULATION

While the behavioral paradigms determine the tactics of treatment, the behavioral formulation determines the strategy of behavioral psychotherapy. This formulation is an attempt to place the problem behaviors within the context of the relevant psychological organization. Its main purpose is to provide the basis for a reasoned and systematic selection of key behaviors which become the targets for change. A specific illustration will clarify how this is done.

Illustration

The behavioral formulation to be presented concerns a hypothetical young woman and has previously been published and discussed in some detail (Fensterheim, 1975). The patient, Marion, is described as having an obsessive-compulsive personality and presenting with the complaints of depression and of unsatisfactory relationships with men. Among other symptoms were bodily malfunctions attributed to tension, lack of spontaneity, and obsessions. Based on this and the other material provided about Marion, a formulation of the relevant psychological organization was made and presented in schematic form (Figure 2).

In this formulation the core of the organization is a series of ruminative obsessions to which she reacts with helplessness and passivity. This, on one hand, feeds into a fear of losing control, which in turn inhibits her spontaneity and leads towards her depression. On the other hand, it feeds into a neurotic problem with men, the root of which is her fear of being hurt by men—a fear she may have learned in her father's dental chair. This fear leads to her assertive problems, which are also maintained by her fear of losing control. The guilt, inferiority, low self-esteem and depression are behaviors that emerge from this organization.

Target behaviors are selected from the formulation. It is obvious that the depression, guilt, and low self-esteem cannot be the initial targets. Because they are emergent characteristics, any direct change of them

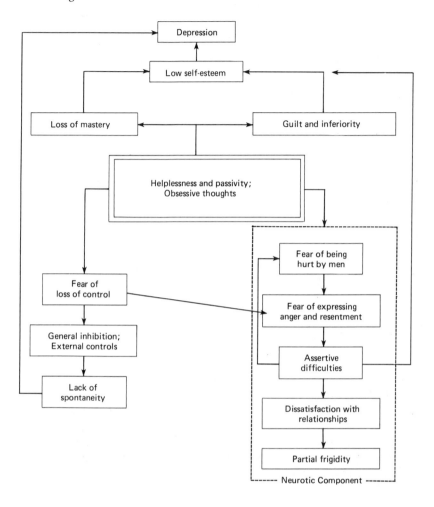

Figure 2. Behavioral formulation of Marion, an obsessive-
compulsive personality with a neurotic component
concerning her relations with men (Fensterheim, 1975).

will be at best transitory. It is the organization that must be changed in order to bring about more permanent ameliorations of these symptoms.

Two main target areas were selected for initial treatment. One concerned the behavioral organization overall, and the other concerned the neurotic component. For the first area, rather than a direct approach to the obsessive thoughts, her generally passive and helpless orientation was chosen. She would be taught self-control methods such as thought stoppage and relaxation primarily for the purpose of instilling an active orientation, with the control of the obsessions and tensions being only a secondary purpose. If this could be brought about to any degree, it was predicted that her fear of loss of control would diminish and that she would become somewhat more spontaneous. For the neurotic component, the targets chosen were her fear of expressing anger and resentment (to be treated through systematic desensitization) and her assertive problems. Assertiveness training, it was expected, would both reinforce the development of an active orientation and also weaken the fear of being hurt by men. This latter fear may eventually require more direct treatment and a fueling phobia may be involved. However, this cannot be determined at the early stage of treatment. Success in the two main target areas should lead to a behavioral reorganization, and the emergent behaviors such as low self-esteem and depression should disappear without themselves being treated directly.

One further note should be made of this formulation. The symptom of partial frigidity has been placed within the neurotic component but no relation to other aspects of this organization has been indicated. At this early stage it could not be formulated whether it is an emergent characteristic of the organization, whether it is an integral part, feeding into and helping to maintain that organization, or whether it is a separate problem relating to an aspect of the behavioral organization not considered in this formulation. Information relevant to making this distinction probably will emerge during the course of the planned treatment. For the moment, this partial frigidity is considered to be trivial, i.e., peripheral to the first main thrust of treatment.

Characteristics of the Behavioral Organization

The case of Marion shows some of the characteristics of the behavioral organization. The ones we will discuss here are its hierarchical organization into systems and subsystems, the functional relations among behaviors, and the possession by each of the systems of its own characteristics, beyond those of its component behaviors.

Hierarchical organization

Behaviors do not stand alone as if in a vacuum but are integrated with each other. This integration is such that some behaviors are dominant and some subordinate, some more central to the organizational structure and some more peripheral to it. In the illustration of Marion it was formulated that helplessness and passivity were more central than the fear of loss of control. Hence, successful reduction of the fear of loss of control would not be expected to reduce the passivity, whereas the converse, successful treatment of the passivity, would be expected to reduce the fear of loss of control. Further, each system or subsystem tends to have a core, a focal point, around which the main aspects of the system are organized. This core tends to color and to influence the expression of the other (subordinate) behaviors that compose the system. If the core can be modified, the entire behavioral organization and the manifestation of each component would be expected to change. Hence, where possible, the core is usually one of the main targets selected for initial treatment.

Thus, the concept of a hierarchical structure implies that all behaviors are not equal, that some are more important than others. Modifying those more important behaviors would be expected to lead to more generalized and more permanent changes in that area. One of the main purposes of the behavioral formulation is to identify such behaviors.

Functional relation

Within the behavioral organization, the different components stand in a functional relation to each other. This goes beyond the mere associational or reinforcing impact of one behavior on another, beyond the mere facilitation or inhibition of a given behavior by others. Functional relationship is used in its mathematical sense: "a relationship between two or more variables such that the value of one is dependent on the value of others" (Wilson, 1972). Thus with Marion, her assertive behavior is a function of her fears and of her social skills, both magnified by her passivity. A change in any one of these variables should bring about a change (not merely an increase or decrease) in the others. Indeed, the thrust of the entire subsystem may change qualitatively. By changing the fears and the social skills, there should not only be an increase in assertive behavior, but the central motive of that system would be expected to change from one of self-protection to one of self-fulfillment.

There is an interesting corollary to this that relates to psychodynamic variables. Changes in one behavior not only may qualitatively influence other overt behaviors but also may influence unconscious aspects such as defense mechanisms and conflicts. Thus, for example, in the course of desensitizing a simple phobia, insights may emerge or cognitive reorganizations take place.

Emergent behaviors

Each system or subsystem tends to possess characteristics of its own that go beyond those of the behaviors that compose it. This is essentially the Gestalt or organismic approach which holds that the whole is greater than the sum of its parts. The main implication of this point of view in the present context is that certain behaviors may emerge from the organization itself rather than being freestanding behaviors in their own right. In other words, certain behaviors may be by-products of a condition, neither precipitating nor maintaining that condition. For example, earlier (Chapter 1) I argued that helplessness and negative thoughts were such behaviors emerging from a depressive organization, while in the illustration of Marion I indicated that low self-esteem and depression were emergent behaviors.

One of the major purposes of the behavioral formulation is to identify such emergent behaviors. These behaviors cannot truly be changed except as the organization itself is modified. Thus, to treat Marion's depression directly through changing her negative thoughts would be successful and permanent only to the extent that it influenced the organization centering around her passive orientation. Were the organization formulated in a different way, the very converse might have been true. Thus, it might have been formulated that the content of the obsession precipitated and maintained a depressive organization and that the passivity and helplessness emerged from that organization. Under those conditions, treatment of the passivity would not be indicated. Rather, some tension reduction approach to the content of the obsessions would have been the first treatment strategy.

Rules for the Behavioral Formulation

Drawing up a behavioral formulation is a clinical art. A subtle point must be understood about this formulation: It is not primarily about the patient and his behavioral organization. Rather, it is a way of helping the therapist to organize his own thoughts about the patient's behavioral organization, a method of helping him to make sense out of a mass of complex and disparate data about the patient and his life situation. The aim is not to verify hypotheses about the patient; even if the treatment plan is effective it does not mean that the formulation upon which it was based was correct. Instead, the aim is to furnish a blueprint for action leading to a series of planned and integrated therapeutic interventions. Hence, at this stage in the development of behavioral psychotherapy, the formulations are made on a case by case basis with "clinical judgment" as the major criterion for its adequacy. The main question is whether the formulation leads to a plan of action that appears to be promising in terms of everything the therapist knows.

Despite the seeming vagueness of this clinical orientation, several rules for drawing up a behavioral formulation have been devised. Those to be discussed here include the evaluation of phenotypy, emphasis on current status, and the use of the law of parsimony.

Phenotypy

This rule states that no behavior can be considered solely in terms of its phenotypic characteristics but must be placed into the context of its behavioral organization. The rule appears to be self-evident. Behaviors may possess very similar phenotypic characteristics and yet stem from very different organizational structures. Chronic lateness may serve as an example of this. In one patient such lateness may be a blind habit to be treated through a self-monitoring operant program. In a second, it may be part of a pattern of the avoidance of anxiety situations and treatment should center around tension and phobic reduction methods. Finally, in a third patient the chronic lateness may be behavior emerging from psychodynamic conflict concerning authority or power. In this instance, the lateness would not be a target selected for initial treatment. Hence, no matter how obvious the problem may appear to be, a careful formulation of the organizational substructure is always necessary.

Under this rule we are not concerned only with the possible effectiveness of the treatment intervention. We are also concerned with the potential impact of such change on other aspects of the patient. Of special concern must always be the chance of actually bringing about harm. In Chapter 1 we have illustrated how the removal of a symptom appears to have made the patient worse. Other examples may be cited. In the case referred to in the discussion of obsessions (Chapter 5), the use of response prevention in a patient with compulsive checking behavior led to a depression so severe that hospitalization was deemed necessary. In this last instance we can see that a proper formulation of the behavioral organization did eventually lead to some control over the symptom. This possibility of bringing about harm makes it imperative that the behavioral organization always be formulated.

Current status

The behavioral organization is formulated as it is functioning in the present. Thus, emphasis is placed on maintenance rather than on genesis, on the variables that keep the organization going rather than on those that led to its original formation. The conditions under which the organization was first formed, the variables or psychodynamic forces then at work, may not be active in the present. The problem organization as a whole, for example, may have become autonomous from other aspects of the patient's organization. This appears to be what often happens with sexually variant behaviors. Hence, with these behaviors, the psychoanalytic methods (which emphasize genesis) are not often successful, whereas the behavior therapy methods (which emphasize maintenance) report remarkably good results (cf. Maletzky, 1980). Childhood memories, for example, are important only to the extent that they elicit disturbance or defenses in the present. Genesis becomes important only as it suggests for investigation characteristics that may be functioning in the here-and-now to maintain a given behavioral organization.

Law of parsimony

This fundamental law of scientific logic basically states that when alternative explanations of a given phenomenon are available, that explanation requiring the fewest assumptions should be chosen, provided it meets the facts adequately. A corollary to this is Morgan's Canon, which states: "In no case may we interpret an action as the outcome of the exercise of a higher psychical faculty, if it can be interpreted as the outcome of the exercise of one which stands lower in the psychological scale" (quoted in Aronson, Tobach, Rosenblatt, and Lehrman, 1972). This law and its corollary have a number of implications for the behavioral formulation.

Purposive or teleological behaviors such as those stemming from psychodynamic forces are the exercise of a higher psychical faculty than is the acquisition of a conditioned response. The human being is quite capable of behaving at either level. The law of parsimony requires that we choose the simpler conditioning formulation over the purposive one unless compelling reasons exist to do otherwise.

Fensterheim and Kantor (1980) illustrate this point with the symptom of a sexual dysfunction. A consequence of such a symptom may be feelings of self-humiliation or the frustration of the partner. The achievement of such consequences may be the motive that maintains the dysfunction. People are indeed capable of behaving in such a purposive manner. However, the dysfunction may also be the product of the automatic conditioned reaction of anxiety to sexual stimuli. People are certainly capable of acquiring such conditioned responses. The self-humiliation or partner frustration may be by-products of this conditioning. The principle involved here states that unless there are compelling reasons to do otherwise, the simpler conditioning explanation should be used in the behavioral formulation.

A second application of the principle of parsimony involves the ability to discern when problems are independent of each other. In medicine, when several symptoms are present, it is usually considered most parsimonious to consider them as stemming from a single root cause. Such an approach applied to the behavioral formulation may force the therapist to assume the exercise of a higher level psychical faculty than would otherwise be necessary. Hence it would violate Morgan's Canon. Unless otherwise indicated, it is most parsimonious to assume the problems are independent of each other.

An example may be cited of a woman who presents with two problems: a dysfunction of sexual arousal and a fear of authority (Fensterheim and Kantor, 1980). To see these two problems as stemming from a common cause (such as an Oedipal conflict regarding father) requires the assumption of a series of conative mechanisms and may lead to an unnecessarily complex formulation and to a cumbersome treatment strategy. To consider them as two independent problems, each a conditioned anxiety response to a given class of stimuli, makes fewer assumptions and leads to a simpler formulation and treatment strategy. Hence, this last formulation would be preferred when all other things are equal. There will be many times, however, when the more complex formulation best fits the information about the patient and, at those times, it would therefore be the approach chosen.

Continual Revision

So far we have been discussing the initial behavioral formulation. However, that is not an end product set for all time. As new information becomes available through outside sources, through discussion with the patient, and through the treatment process itself, the therapist's understanding of the patient changes and the behavioral formulation must be revised. The final revision occurs when termination is being considered. At that time the formulation must answer the question of whether the behaviors in the problem area have been reorganized to the extent that the return of the symptom or the development of other symptoms is unlikely. Even prior to this, particularly when there are problems in treatment, constant reformulation must be carried out. One of the characteristics of most of the cases to be presented is this process of continual reformulation on the part of the therapist.

SUMMARY

The therapist receives much information about and from the patient. This includes his own firsthand observations, feelings, speculations, and "clinical instinct." The behavioral formulation helps him to organize this multitude of data in a manner that leads to a reasonable and systematic strategy for treatment. The basic paradigms provide the basis for selecting the specific change tactics to be attempted. By keeping these two areas constantly in the forefront of his thinking, the therapist himself constantly maintains an active orientation to the ongoing treatment and truly assumes responsibility for the therapy.

REFERENCES

Aronson, L. R., Tobach, E., Rosenblatt, J. S., and Lehrman, D. S. (Eds.) *Selected Writings of T. C. Schneirla.* San Francisco: W. H. Freeman & Co, 1972.

Barlow, D. Behavior therapy: The next decade, *Behavior Therapy*, 1980, 11: 315-328.

Beech, H. R., and Vaughan, M. *Behavioral Treatment of Obsessional States.* New York: Wiley, 1978.

Ellis, A., and Harper, R. A. *A Guide To Rational Living.* Hollywood: Wilshire, 1962.

Fensterheim, H. Behavior therapy of the sexual variations, *Journal of Sex and Marital Therapy*, 1974, 1: 16-28.

Fensterheim, H. The case of Marion: Behavior therapy approach. In C. A. Loew, H. Grayson, and G. H. Loew (Eds.), *Three Psychotherapies.* New York: Brunner/Mazel, 1975.

Fensterheim, H. Clinical behavior therapy of depression. In J. Clarkin and H. Glazer (Eds.), *Depression: Behavioral and Directive Intervention Strategies.* New York: Garland Press, 1981.

Fensterheim, H., and Kantor, J. S. The behavioral approach to sexual disorders. In B. B. Wolman and J. Money (Eds.), *Handbook of Human Sexuality.* Englewood Cliffs, N. J.: Prentice-Hall, 1980.

Fried, E. *Active/Passive: The Crucial Psychological Dimension.* New York: Grune & Stratton, 1970.

Gibson, H. B. A form of behavior therapy for some states diagnosed as "affective disorder." *Behavior Research and Therapy*, 1978, 16: 191-195.

Goldfried, M. R. Systematic desensitization as training in self-control, *Journal of Consulting and Clinical Psychology*, 1971, *37*: 228-234.

Jacobson, E. *Progressive Relaxation*. Chicago: Chicago University Press, 1929.

Lazarus, A. A. *Behavior Therapy and Beyond*. New York: McGraw-Hill, 1971.

Lum, L. C. The syndrome of habitual chronic hyperventilation. In O. Hill (Ed.), *Modern Trends in Psychosomatic Medicine*, Vol. 3. Boston: Butterworths, 1976.

Maletzky, B. M. Assisted covert sensitization. In D. J. Cox and R. J. Daitzman (Eds.), *Exhibitionism: Description, Assessment, and Treatment*. New York: Garland Press, 1980.

Marks, I. M. *Care and Cure of Neuroses: Theory and Practice of Behavioral Psychotherapy*. New York: Wiley, 1981.

Rachman, S. The modification of obsessions—a new formulation, *Behavior Research and Therapy*, 1976, *14*: 437-444.

Solyom, L., Zamanzadeh, D., Ledwidge, B., and Kenny, F. Aversion relief treatment of obsessive neurosis. In R. D. Rubin, H. Fensterheim, A. A. Lazarus, and C. M. Franks (Eds.), *Advances in Behavior Therapy*. New York: Academic Press, 1971.

Wilson, D. G. Function. In H. J. Eysenck, W. Arnold, and R. Meili (Eds.), *Encyclopedia of Psychology*. Volume 1, New York: Herder and Herder, 1972.

Wolpe, J. Behavior therapy versus psychoanalysis, *American Psychologist*, 1981, *36*: 159-164.

4

Basic Procedures

Herbert Fensterheim

Dominating the initial stages of behavioral psychotherapy are the first selection of target behaviors, the development of a treatment plan, and the selection of specific intervention technologies. Dominating the on-going stages of behavioral psychotherapy are the testing of the intervention methods, the evaluation of change, and the reformulations and changes of target behaviors as problems arise and as new information becomes available. The final step is, of course, the decision to terminate.

THE INITIAL STAGE

The first true contact with the patient is the initial interview. It usually is not the very first contact. In an office practice particularly, this is usually preceded by a telephone call from the patient and/or a call from the referring professional. However, at this point the aim is to minimize the information. If the call is from the patient, the idea is to screen out completely inappropriate referrals. If you treat only adults, you want to make certain that the patient is not an adolescent. If you do not treat substance abuse, you want to be certain that substance abuse is not the patient's problem. Further information from the person at that point not only is usually unhelpful but may actually be detrimental in that it may mislead the therapist or may create an inappropriate set on the part of the patient which he then brings into the initial interview. The same holds true when talking with a referring professional. During the initial telephone call the therapist does not know what to listen for or what questions to ask. We find it best to form our own initial impressions after meeting the patient and then to contact the other professional. Where possible, appropriate questionnaires are sent to the patient prior to the initial interview.

The goal of the initial interview is twofold. First, it is to set the ambience, the tone, of the therapeutic situation as a collaborative, working-together procedure. Second, it is to gather the necessary information in a systematic way. The information concerns the presenting problem, life history, diagnosis, behavioral paradigms, behavioral formulation, and finally, treatment plan. These last two are discussed with the patient. Usually this information can be gathered in one or two interviews, but sometimes it may take a number of exploratory sessions.

Presenting Problem

The formulation of the presenting problem is an important first step in selecting the initial target behaviors for change. It usually represents the matters of greatest concern to the patient at this time and the specific reason he is now seeking treatment. Relieving this problem, regardless of any other problems that may be present, often improves the patient's functioning and makes these other problems more accessible to treatment. At times, the presenting problem may be quickly and easily formulated; at other times, considerable effort must be exerted to do so.

Patients present their problems in a variety of ways. Some patients present with one or two or three clearly delineated and clearly described problems. Others present with vague dissatisfactions, depressions or anxieties, with no awareness of cause. Still others are completely overwhelmed by a series of major dysfunctions which they are completely incapable of sorting out without help. There are also patients who present pseudoproblems. These are the people who talk of a relatively trivial problem because they are too ashamed or too anxious to talk about what really bothers them until the therapist has won their trust. Finally, there are the people who come under pressure from others and do not truly believe that they have problems sufficiently severe to require treatment.

The problem must be formulated in specific behavioral terms as it exists in the present. Until this is done, the therapist does not know what to listen for in the history. The best way to obtain this information is to ask for specific recent illustrations of the problem. Most patients are able to do this, although many will need help in describing it objectively without confounding interpretations and opinions. For each illustration, the therapist attempts to obtain a clear picture of the antecedents and the consequences, of the overt actions of the patient, and of his covert reactions such as feelings, physical sensations, and thoughts. Attempts by the patient at this point to give the history or his understanding of the problem are discouraged as being confusing.

When the therapist believes he has a clear understanding of the problem, he reflects this understanding back to the patient. One purpose of this is to allow the patient to provide corrections and supplements to the therapist. An equally important reason is that it sets the atmosphere of task orientation, collaboration, and nonjudgmental attitude that is so characteristic of this treatment. "Okay," the therapist is saying, "we see the problem in the same way. It is a pretty specific one, so let's just roll up our sleeves and work together to solve it."

First, however, more information about the problem is needed, and at this time a history of it should be taken. Some of the questions that might be explored are:

•When did the problem start? What was going on in the patient's life at that time? What were the exact circumstances under which it first occurred? (Fensterheim, 1972)
•How has the symptom fluctuated over time? When was it worst? When was it best? Did it ever disappear entirely?
•At this time, too, the patient should be asked about his understanding of the problem, about how he explains it to himself. If he has had previous treatment, he should be queried about how he perceived the problem during that treatment and about how he thought his therapist perceived it. (Note that, when appropriate, the previous therapist himself will be contacted directly.)

The patient's description and history of the presenting problem, of course, cannot be taken at face value. The therapist is not the passive recipient of this information but is constantly weighing, speculating and formulating his own conception of the problem. Most obvious are the times when the patient sees a series of unrelated problems, and the therapist sees a series of related problems, all of which are expressions of a common basic paradigm. Or, also not uncommon, what the patient perceives as the main problem, the therapist may perceive as the by-product of some different problem area. These perceptions are not sufficiently well founded at this stage of the examination to base a treatment plan on them. Rather, the purpose of gaining a clear picture of the presenting problem is to structure areas for further examination.

Life History

The therapist is now ready to gain a wider perspective of the patient. He has some idea of the things to listen for in the story of the patient's development. However, we would not advise undertaking the two-, three-, or four-session history-taking that some therapists recommend. We find that a life history questionnaire, supplemented by a few questions to clarify specific points and by what the patient himself believes to be important, is usually sufficient. The relevant history will emerge in the course of behavior change attempts. The history must be sufficiently complete to allow for proper diagnosis.

The history is also where the therapist begins to test his speculations and hypotheses derived from considering the presenting problem. Should he suspect the presence of a separation anxiety, he will ask a series of questions about experiences while beginning grade school, going to summer camp, leaving home for college, reactions to death of a significant person or to divorce of parents, etc. Should he suspect an assertiveness problem characterized by a lack of certain social skills, he would explore the opportunities the patient had had both within and outside the family to learn these skills, the assertive models present during his development, the bad experiences he may have had, and the misconceptions and incorrect attitudes he may have learned. In the course of such history-taking the therapist strengthens, rejects, or modifies his earlier speculations. He also becomes sensitized to possible pervasive and important problem areas the patient had not discussed.

A further word must be said concerning the inadvisability of taking too detailed a history during the initial interview. It not only may be an uneconomical use of time, but also may be actually detrimental to achieving an adequate formulation of the case. Too much material of unknown relevance may create such interference. Beyond that, especially if the patient had been previously in an unsuccessful or partially successful treatment, the focus may be on the wrong information and so distract the therapist from the correct course. Hence, history-taking is a limited collection of basic information about the patient, a limited testing of hypotheses and speculations, and a limited exploration for other important problems.

Psychiatric Diagnosis

Accurate diagnosis is extremely important in planning treatment. Fensterheim (1972) noted the clinical observation that in using desensitization procedures with hysteric patients, relatively few broad categories may be used in the hierarchy, whereas obsessive patients often require many highly defined categories, several different desensitization hierarchies, and perhaps even an *in vivo* supplement to achieve the same result. We have seen several patients with Tourette's Disorder who had previous "successful" behavioral treatment for tics (Shapiro, 1976). Many other obvious examples may be cited, and as our knowledge of disorders increases, more meaningful and treatment-related diagnostic categories will come about.

A sound knowledge of clinical psychopathology is essential. Knowing the usual age of the onset of various disorders, for example, may often provide an essential cue. Evans (1970) reports on an exhibitionist where the variant behavior started at age 30, a time of life when such variant behavior tends to diminish rather than to start. Alerted by the unusual time of onset, he proceeded with a careful examination, which revealed a hypoglycemia leading to periods of confusion, when the patient exhibited himself. The target behavior then became the hypoglycemia rather than the disrupted behavior. Recently we have seen a man with a typical clinical picture of agoraphobia with panic. The first attacks, however, occurred at about five years of age, a rather atypical age of onset for this disorder. The patient was successfully treated for habitual chronic hyperventilation exacerbated by severe fears of separation.

Proper diagnosis may also serve to alert the therapist to the need for medication. There are a number of disorders now identified where the first approach should be a pharmacological intervention, and only after that has been successfully achieved is psychological intervention indicated. The model for this approach, particularly useful with some of the psychoses (Hersen and Bellack, 1976), is to control the psychotic manifestations through medication and, since adaptive social behavior cannot be expected to emerge spontaneously on its own, to use the appropriate psychological methods to train these adaptive behaviors. The affective disorders may be similarly treated with a combination of psychopharmacotherapy and psychotherapy. During the past number of years several patients presented with "assertive problems," and examination of current functioning did reveal deficits in this area. However, upon taking a history of the presenting problem it became evident that there had been periods where adequate assertive behaviors had indeed been present. The problem was not an assertive one but rather a cyclical depression; some patients even showed signs of a bipolar condition. In most of these instances, pharmacological intervention by itself was a sufficient treatment without any psychological treatment being indicated.

The original diagnosis may change in the course of treatment as further information becomes available. Many times, as specific changes are brought about, the pathology is far less severe than it initially had appeared to be. The patient presented by Sands (Chapter 7) was so severely disabled over so long a period by her agoraphobia, fears of loss of control, and passive attitudes, that a diagnosis of borderline personality had to be seriously considered. However, as these characteristics changed with treatment, psychological strengths emerged and such a diagnosis could then be rejected. At other times the presenting problem masks a more severe pathology. For example, we have seen several patients presenting with fairly severe agoraphobia with panic, where the lack of social life appeared to be a by-product of the fear of panic. However, as the agoraphobia was relieved through treatment, it became clear that a schizoid personality disorder was also present.

Finally, there are those conditions that have been brought on by the presenting problem but that are now autonomous and require separate treatment. An illustration of this is the young man who presented with a severe stutter. When cured of this, when he was able to speak well, it turned out he had nothing to say. The stutter had so severely restricted his social life that he had not had the opportunity to learn conversational and social skills and was also dominated by a series of social phobias. A long-term and rather complicated treatment program, both individual and group, was eventually successful.

In arriving at a diagnostic formulation, a mental status examination is often helpful. Psychological tests, where indicated, may also be helpful. In this regard we have found the Minnesota Multiphasic Personality Inventory and the Maudsley Personality Inventory most useful. In certain instances, special instruments such as the Beck Depression Scale can also supply important material. However, the results of these procedures cannot be taken at face value but must be interpreted in light of the entire examination. There is no substitute for a thorough knowledge of psychopathology and for trained clinical acumen.

Basic Behavioral Paradigms

The basic behavioral paradigms to be considered have already been discussed in detail (Chapter 3), as have the major methods for investigating them. This investigation should be carried out within the framework of a functional behavioral analysis. That is, these processes must be evaluated in terms of what controls them, of the stimulus context within which they occur. This means a careful search for the antecedents and the consequences that surround fluctuations in the activity level of the behaviors being explored. The stimulus context may be external in that it involves events or the behavior of other people. It may be internal and involve feelings and thoughts. Or it may involve a combination of the two, often in the form of a chain of behaviors. The personal history of the patient is important at this point only as it serves to alert the therapist to possible stimuli that might otherwise be overlooked. Care should be taken to assess these in terms of what actually happens, rather than in terms of some preconception of what should happen. Such an analysis is extremely individualized and tailored to take into account each patient's idiosyncrasies. As Glazer, Clarkin, and Hunt (1981) note, one person's reward may be another person's punishment.

Such an analysis, while necessary and important, is in itself not sufficient, for it has a major theoretical and clinical limitation. It assumes that all symptomatic behaviors are "freestanding" behaviors under the control of the stimulus context in which they occur. It has no place for behaviors emerging from the psychological organization, nor does it have any method for differentiating those behaviors which are by-products of a disturbed reaction from the reaction itself. The application of a functional behavioral analysis to the area of depression may serve to illustrate and to clarify this point.

Glazer, Clarkin, and Hunt (1981) do perform just such an analysis, and they note the functional relationship between depression and various aspects of the learned helplessness model. They note that depressed patients lack positive reinforcement, expect to have insufficient control over events, to get rewards due to assumed defects in themselves, and a number of similar characteristics. Their therapeutic strategy is to change the learned helplessness aspects. Thus, they would attempt to increase the flux of positive reinforcement, to alter cognitions and expectations, and to undercut the hopelessness and helplessness through rational confrontation. The assumption is that, however it had developed, the learned helplessness is the maintainer of the depressed state. There is no consideration given to the possibility that the learned helplessness may be a behavioral phenomenon emerging from the depressed state rather than maintaining it.

That depressions can come about through biochemical dysfunctions is now a generally accepted finding. These depressions, too, are characterized by aspects of the learned helplessness constellation, although in this instance no one would argue seriously that helplessness either precipitates or maintains the depressed state. Changes in the biochemical functions through appropriate medication may relieve both the depression and the helplessness. An even clearer example concerns thyroid dysfunction. MacCrimmon, Wallace, Goldberg, and Streiner (1979) report that in the presence of hyperthyroid malfunction, cognitive deficits and emotional disturbances appear, including depression. In the very few patients we have seen with this condition, along with the depression was the hopelessness and helplessness, Upon control of thyroid functioning, upon the establishment of a state of euthyroidism, these symptoms disappear without any direct treatment of them. In these instances neither the depression nor the learned helplessness is a freestanding behavior; but rather, both emerge from the context of the biological organization. No amount of functional behavioral analysis will lead to appropriate treatment.

As depression and its attendant learned helplessness phenomena can emerge from the biological organization, so, too, is there evidence that it can emerge from psychological processes and organization. Wolpe (1979), for example, presents evidence that depression can stem from a conditioned anxiety and can be successfully treated as such. Recently, Lewinsohn, Steinmetz, Larson, and Franklin (1981) provide evidence that the depressive cognitions accompany the depression rather than preceding or following the depression. Fensterheim (1981) has expanded on Wolpe's approach and has argued that not only conditioned anxiety but also the other paradigms we consider here can lead to depression. He presents one case where the learned helplessness was so dominating that it was chosen as the target behavior for modification. It did not respond to treatment but did completely disappear when, after reformulation and a choice of new target behaviors, obsessive processes were successfully modified. Thus, the learned helplessness appeared to be a set of behaviors emerging from the depressive organization rather than a freestanding behavior in its own right.

This argument concerning the limitations of a functional behavioral analysis does not detract from the necessity of making such an analysis. Each of the behaviors being examined must be carefully placed within its stimulus context. The stimuli, internal as well as external, that precede and that follow fluctuations in these processes must be teased out and explored. However, in the behavioral psychotherapy model this is not sufficient, and other investigations must also be carried out.

Before proceeding to the nonbehavioral aspects of the examination, one further behavioral problem must be considered. Having performed such a functional behavioral analysis, the therapist usually has sufficient data to form at least a supposition of the significant behavioral variables involved in the problem area. However, there are occasions when this is not true, when some important bit of information appears to be missing. On those occasions a supplementary behavioral examination must be performed. This examination must also be systematic, approach the patient from a somewhat different perspective, and so bring to the fore aspects of behavior that may have been overlooked or underestimated.

One supplemental examination that has proven to be useful is to be found in the multimodal behavior therapy approach set forth by Lazarus (1977). Drawing heavily on the therapeutic experiences not only of behavior therapy but also of rational-emotive and Gestalt therapy, as well as others, Lazarus has designated seven modalities for examination. The acronym BASIC ID is used to cover these: behavior, affect, sensation, imagery, cognition, interpersonal relations, and drugs. Each of these areas is systematically investigated and dysfunctions therein noted. The definitions of each area, as well as modes of examining and of treating each, may be found in Lazarus (1977). The system is partially based on the belief that the more modalities treated, the more complete the treatment and the less chance for relapse. However, we are offered no rules for the order in which the various dysfunctions are to be approached.

Much of the data needed for this supplementary examination will have already been gathered during the prior examination. At this point the information is reorganized, and areas not yet covered become obvious. The data so obtained may then be reassessed in terms of the basic behavioral paradigms, and, hopefully, the gaps in the behavioral material will be filled in.

For example, a woman presented with agoraphobia with panic. She had previously undergone group behavioral treatment for this condition, as well as appropriate medication. Although these treatments brought about only slight changes in the frequency of the panics, they did restore her approach behaviors in most situations. She had also been well trained in relaxation procedures and was able to control her secondary reactions during panic attacks and so did not escape from these situations. Thus, while she appeared to be doing everything necessary, her condition had not improved over a period of close to two years. The behavioral psychotherapy examination of the basic paradigms yielded no information that may have been relevant to this lack of progress, nor could a suitable behavioral formulation be drawn up. No other phobias (including paired and fueling phobias) appeared to be feeding into this area. The problems in the areas of general tension and of assertion appeared to be minor. She denied any obsessive material other than a mild to moderate ruminative anticipation of panic attacks. Nothing in her social interactions appeared to be maintaining it. In other words, this examination did not appear to provide the behavioral information necessary to formulate the maintenance of the agoraphobia. Hence, a supplemental behavioral examination was carried out.

Each of the seven modalities composing the BASIC ID was examined in turn. The clue came during the examination of the imagery functions. Here, following Lazarus (1977, p.31), she was asked: "What 'mental pictures' or images are bothersome to you so that you would like to erase them?" At this point she related recurring fantasies of panic attacks in a variety of situations where, in each instance, she would collapse to the ground feeling helpless and ashamed. She appeared to be covertly rehearsing her panic attacks and so maintaining them.

This finding was then evaluated in terms of the basic behavioral paradigms, two of which appeared to be involved. One was a phobic process. The feelings of helplessness and shame were automatic emotional reactions to the images. These in turn caused her to pay great attention to the images and so to reinforce them. A second and less important element concerned assertion. She had a mild difficulty in expressing anger in close relations and had learned instead to turn it against herself. Upon questioning, it was revealed that there was a great increase in the frequency of images following some situation where she did not adequately express anger, whereas there was only a slight increase under other conditions of stress. This analysis proved to be crucial in drawing up an almost completely successful treatment plan.

In the practical clinical situation, there are times when even with a supplemental examination there still appear to be gaps in the behavioral examination. However, further investigation along these lines may appear to be time-consuming and of doubtful success. Here, a deliberate therapeutic decision must be made: to investigate further or to start treatment. In making this decision, three questions must be considered:

1) Is enough information present to make a start on treatment? The therapist must consider whether he knows enough about the behaviors that may be involved in the problem area to draw up even an

admittedly highly speculative behavioral formulation, but one which suggests a starting point for treatment that makes clinical "common sense." In this the therapist's comfort and his own tolerance for ambiguity become variables in the decision-making process. If such a start is made, it is assumed that further relevant information will become available during the treatment attempts and that the therapeutic strategies will be adjusted accordingly.

2) How urgent is the need for immediate relief? The patient may be in great distress, or some practical situation may exist where time for a leisurely investigation is not available. Under these conditions the therapist has to go with what he has and to do what he can. In the extreme, for example, when the patient presents in a great panic, even the basic examination may have to be foregone. In this decision, the clinical judgment of the therapist must dominate.

3) How pessimistic and despondent is the patient? Some patients do appear to believe that treatment holds little hope for them. This is particularly true of patients who have previously undergone an unsuccessful course of treatment. Often, if too much time is spent on exploration, the patient will tend to see this as just some more of the same fruitless approach and to drop out of treatment. This feeling will be somewhat allayed by the task-oriented nature of the examination. The therapist's attempts to delineate specific problem patterns carries the implication that once they are defined and properly analyzed, they can be solved. However, this can be carried only so far, and actual problem-solving attempts must be made. Even if the attempt is premature and based on admittedly inadequate information (and this is conveyed to the patient), the attempts tend to give the patient the feeling that he is doing something constructive and so to differentiate it from his previous treatment.

The task chosen to test a behavioral formulation must be selected with care. It must make sense to the patient within the therapist's incomplete understanding. Usually assignments that are primarily for the purpose of providing information, assignments concerning the monitoring of given behaviors, for example, do not fill this need. The best tasks for this purpose are most often those which attempt to bring about some crucial behavior change and which, even if the attempt fails, will provide useful material for further planning. The task should have a reasonable chance for success but not be so easy that the patient does not regard it as a challenge. Should the patient be unable to perform the assignment, the constructive handling of this by the therapist to formulate another meaningful task generally takes the sting out of the failure.

Nonbehavioral Processes

Important though it is, the behavioral examination by itself is not sufficient for planning treatment. Further information must be obtained about the patient as a person. This involves the area of psychodynamics, whether or not specific psychoanalytic concepts are used—or if they are, whether or not they stem from Freud, Horney, Sullivan, some other school, or an eclectic combination of these. The therapist will use those concepts in which he has been trained and towards which he has gained a theoretical predilection. What is under consideration is how the behavioral paradigms described fit together within the person, their impact upon him as a person in terms of his motives, values, conflicts and self-concept. His most characteristic defenses must also be taken into consideration.

One goal of this part of the examination is to place the function of the symptomatic behavior within a dynamic context. The dysfunctions may be syntonic with motives or with teleologic goals of which the patient is unaware. Unassertive behaviors may be "in the service" of strong dependency needs. Sexual anxieties may be "in the service" of controlling unacceptable sadistic impulses or of achieving a masochistic self-humiliation. Social anxieties may stem from a Rankian-type goal conflict between conforming and expressing individuality. Often these aspects cannot be formulated with certainty during the initial examination, but the therapist has been alerted to them should obstacles arise during the course of treatment.

Much of the information concerning the nonbehavioral processes is gathered during the course of the examination. It may be supplemented by a series of inquiries concerning the impact of the problems and their consequences on the patient's self-concept, how he himself explains the problems, and through his fantasies and dreams. The difference between this part of the examination and the behavioral examination is not only in the data and material sought, but also in the style of thinking used. In the behavioral examination, inductive thinking tends to predominate, and empirical verification is sought wherever possible. In the nonbehavioral examination, deductive thinking predominates, and verification is usually in terms of a logical internal consistency, as, at best, only indirect empirical verification is possible.

Behavioral Formulation

The data gathered in the course of the examination are organized into a behavioral formulation. This formulation, along with some of the rules for making it, is discussed in Chapter 3. It basically is an attempt on the part of the therapist to picture the organization and interaction of behaviors and the psychological characteristics of the patient in the major problem areas. The formulation is usually drawn up in the form of a chart showing the behaviors and characteristics involved. Arrows between the behaviors are used to show how they facilitate or inhibit each other, how they reinforce or feed into each other, and how they tend to modify each other. The attempt is to indicate the interactions as they exist in the present. The purpose of the formulation is to indicate key targets for therapeutic modification. Essentially it is an hypothesis about the patient and is subject to constant reexamination and change as new information becomes available or as treatment difficulties emerge.

The formulation, whether actually drawn in the form of a diagram or roughly worked out in the therapist's thoughts, is discussed with the patient. The manner of presentation, the amount of detail given, depends, of course, on the therapist's own style as well as the characteristics of the patient. Clinical judgment must be used. If the patient presents in a panic, he may not be able to tolerate an explanation. However, another patient in a similar panic may gain a good deal of support from having a detailed formulation given him; he gets the reassurance that he is in good hands, that the therapist knows what he is doing. Giving such an explanation to the patient serves a threefold purpose: It allows the patient to make corrections and to bring in relevant material that had not yet been told. It presents the problems in a task-oriented, and hence nonjudgmental and nonpejorative manner, which further encourages the patient to talk about difficult material. Most important, such a discussion makes the patient aware of why a specific target behavior has been chosen for initial treatment and what changes may be expected if the hoped-for behavioral realignments take place.

Very often a tentative behavioral formulation can be made at the end of the initial interview. Indeed, the very style of the interview is constant formulation, goal-directed data collection, and reformulation. From the very first presentation of the disturbing symptoms, the therapist's thoughts are constantly at work in this mode. The patient states that his problem is constant and severe anxiety that interferes with his functioning in all areas of life. The therapist begins to wonder whether this is truly anxiety or whether it may be a variety of other things ranging from hyperventilation to Tourette's syndrome to agoraphobia. He asks for the physical sensations as well as the subjective sensations of the anxiety, their patterns of variation during the day and during the week, the cues that increase and decrease the anxiety sensations. In this manner, the therapist takes a major step towards his formulation. The entire interview is conducted in this manner so that it is quite possible to arrive quickly at the formulation.

A major characteristic of the formulation, however, is that it is tentative and subject to constant change and modification. One of the major sources necessitating revision is the fact that the patient often is not completely free and revealing during the initial interview. Not common, but certainly known to every clinical practitioner, is the patient who, once trust is established, states that his major problem was not the one he had presented but really a quite different one. Recently this writer was consulted by a young woman who had been under a two-year behaviorally oriented biofeedback treatment where she had received a good deal of help. However, all throughout this period she was well aware that her major problem was in the sexual area. She not only was too ashamed to bring it up but actually denied any such problems when the therapist inquired about them. More common are the patients who during the second or third session do bring up the more relevant problems.

Another source of error involves inadvertently withheld information. Either the patient does not think of it or believes it to be meaningless and does not mention a vital bit of information; or else the therapist, not being omniscient and having much other data to gather, does not think of inquiring. An unusual and dramatic illustration of this concerns a patient who presented with a problem of insomnia, a difficulty in falling asleep. Upon inquiry, he denied taking any medication or substance prior to going to sleep. Several sessions later, upon a good deal of pressing by the therapist, he did reveal what he truly believed to be an irrelevant bit of information: he had a sinus condition, and every night he would thoroughly douse himself with neosynephrine, a stimulant. Removal of the stimulant resolved the sleep problem. It must be noted that he did not deliberately withhold this information; he just did not consider it worth mentioning.

One source for an early modification of the first formulation is the patient himself. At the close of the examination, the therapist usually summarizes his impressions and his tentative formulation and offers the patient a chance to correct it. At this time the patient may correct misimpressions of the therapist, may give a different perspective of his problem, or may bring in new and important information. For example, a formulation centering around the fear of rejection was presented to a patient who responded that he was not as afraid of rejection as the therapist appeared to believe. Rather, the patient stated, his main concern was that people would be nice to him because that meant that they pitied him and did not regard him as an equal. Following the patient's correction and working with him, a reformulation in terms of a fear of closeness was derived. Sharing the formulation with the patient thus provides a structure that makes it easier for the patient to provide important data.

There are other reasons for sharing the initial (or any other) formulation with the patient. For one, the patient has the right to know what the therapist is attempting to do, if only for the reason that he can give a truly informed consent for the procedures to be undertaken. Also, such sharing makes each individual procedure more meaningful to the patient and, hence, influences his motivation to cooperate with the program. Beyond that, and perhaps more important, it sets the tone for the cooperative and mutually sharing atmosphere of the therapist-patient relation of behavioral psychotherapy.

There are, of course, times when the therapist is stuck, when he cannot form a working behavioral formulation or when he cannot decide between two or more very different but equally reasonable formulations. A common example of the latter is when the choice lies between an assertiveness problem, a social phobia or an interaction between the two. These difficulties are also to be shared with the patient. At times the patient may be able to throw light on certain issues, helping the therapist resolve his difficulties. At other times the patient and therapist may decide on a need for further exploration. Or else they may agree to start work to modify some apparently crucial behavior and to see what develops. At still other times, the therapist may simply tell the patient that he has to study the data and that he will attempt to present a formulation to the patient at the next session. One of the things the therapist can do during this interval is to attempt to formulate the patient in psychodynamic terms. If he can do so, he can then reformulate these concepts back into behavioral action-oriented terms and present this to the patient for comments. This does not mean that dynamic material is not to be presented. What it does mean is that the dynamic material is presented within a behavioral, action-oriented frame of reference.

Whether a tentative formulation can be derived or not, it usually is important for the patient to leave the first session with an assignment to perform. The assignment often is a simple exercise. It may be the completion of a questionnaire, bibliotherapy, or the monitoring of specific situations or behaviors for the purpose of providing more systematic information. The feeling that he is "doing something," that he has already started on a program to resolve his difficulties, is often very supportive. Further, it strengthens the work-oriented, action-oriented atmosphere of behavioral psychotherapy, as well as bringing home to the patient that treatment is concerned with the life situation outside of the consultation room.

Care must be taken and a clinical judgment may be required. There are some patients for whom this is exactly the wrong kind of approach. These are patients who would be too frightened by rapid movement, by a quick initial formulation, by assignments given at the first session. Usually these are people who have a need to talk and share their problems, who need to experience some kind of nonpossessive warmth, empathy, and trust before they feel safe in their attempts to understand or to try to change. If the therapist attempts to move too fast with such people, most often they quietly listen while in the consultation room, phone to cancel the next appointment, and drop out of treatment. Moving too fast is probably the most common reason for early dropouts in behavioral psychotherapy. We can present no certain way to recognize such patients; we can only encourage the therapist to be aware of the problem and to use his "clinical feel" to identify them.

Choice of Procedures

Once the initial target behaviors have been selected, the therapist is faced with the determination of which methods and techniques he should use to modify them. Usually an entire array of possible techniques is available, and the therapist must choose from among them. So simple a procedure as teaching the patient to relax can serve to demonstrate this. There are some people who can deliberately relax upon self-command but just never think of doing so. To these people, specific instructions to relax by any means at their disposal may be sufficient to bring about the desired change. Others may not know how to relax and may need a fairly complicated training program involving different relaxation methods to be practiced during treatment sessions and at home. Still others are able to relax but are frightened to do so for any of a variety of reasons. Here, the therapist may have to choose between encouraging the person to move through the fear, to use a covert reinforcement method, or to desensitize him to the fear. Usually (but not always), support and encouragement by the therapist are sufficient.

Sometimes technical features are the determining element in the choice of change methods. If a patient cannot prevent himself from neutralizing his thoughts, then a flooding or satiation method using imagery cannot be used. If a person is too frightened of a group situation to even agree to participate in one, then initial assertiveness training may have to be carried out on an individual basis (assuming phobic reduction to groups is not indicated at that time). Or the technical problem may be the therapist's: Group assertiveness training may be indicated, but no appropriate group may be available at that time. Because of these technical difficulties, second choice methods may have to be used. However, it must be noted that there are times when the time taken to assess and to remedy these technical difficulties is apparently warranted. This is a deliberate clinical decision that must be made.

A major feature to take into consideration in the choice of techniques is its meaning to and its effect on the patient. Fishman and Lubetkin (1980), for example, note when considering the use of relaxation procedures:

> For these clients who have pan-anxiety mediated by a fear of losing control, along with interpersonal anxiety, techniques such as differential progressive relaxation (see Jacobson, 1929) would be contraindicated. Such methods suggest that clients focus attention on the body and musculature, when de-emphasising such self-focus is crucial. Various distraction and externalization methods would be more appropriate (p. 87).

Of vital importance is whether the person sees the technique as something being done to him, by him, or by him in conjunction with the therapist. At times a technically inferior method must be used to stimulate the person's feeling that he himself is making something happen. The above-cited instance of a person with pan-anxiety illustrates this. Although Fishman and Lubetkin's statements concerning the use of differential progressive relaxation are certainly true for most of these patients, there are exceptions. Sometimes it becomes more important to fortify the person's concepts of his own active attempts to change than it is to lower his anxiety. In these instances it may be more important to use relaxation procedures to lower disturbance by even one percent than it would be to train him away from a focus of attention on body and musculature. Usually the behavioral and the dynamic formulations serve as a basis for making such a clinical decision.

Most behavioral methods do require work, practice and application on the part of the person. His contribution to success is usually evident. An exception to this is the desensitization procedures used in the office, especially when they work well. Regardless of the explanations of the therapist, many patients look on these methods as magic. All they really see is that the therapist performed a strange ritual and somehow they feel better. Sometimes they note changes in areas seemingly having no direct connection with the specific subject of the desensitization, and this increases the sense of magic. To counter the latter, the therapist keeps referring back to the formulation; eventually this sinks in. To counter the former, as a matter of routine procedure the therapist continually stresses the difficulty of the task being performed by the person, the calling up and the pushing away of specific images, and how well the person appears to be doing it. Questioning the person about the conditioning further adds to the feeling of participation as well as often supplying important data.

The potential efficacy of a given change method for a given set of behaviors, of course, remains primary. However, it must be modified by such considerations as technical difficulties, longer range goals and the meaning of the procedure to the person. The aim is to change the person (i.e., aspects of the psychological organization), rather than a specific behavior in a vacuum.

Treatment Problems

Many times treatment proceeds smoothly and according to plan. We have determined the target behaviors through a behavioral formulation which proves adequate as the treatment goes on. We have selected the change technology most applicable, the predicted changes occur in life, and the person "gets better." Many times, however, problems arise due to technical difficulties in the application of the change technologies or due to inadequacies of the initial formulation. Many of these difficulties stem from the goal of assuming responsibility for the entire person rather than limiting ourselves to removing a specific cause of distress. In these instances the actions of the dynamic defense mechanisms often may be recognized.

The concept of "resistance" is valuable in that it helps the therapist focus his attention on the difficulty. However, the specific processes active in such resistance must be formulated. The most common processes involved are phobic avoidance or the search for certain specific reinforcers.

Phobic avoidance is often manifested in the defense mechanisms of denial or repression. As an illustration of denial we present the young woman who stated: "Yes, I do have these other problems but they don't really disturb me and they're not very important. I'm really only concerned with my panics." Under the gentle persuasion of the therapist, a desensitization to the "other problems" was undertaken, and the first products of this procedure were increased feelings of anger and rage to the images being used. It was the phobic avoidance of these feelings that led to the initial denial.

The more difficult problem is when the phobic avoidance is such that there are few cues to the existence of the problem. When the problem begins to enter the person's thoughts, anxiety is elicited. To avoid the increasing anxiety, the person stops thinking of that subject and, hence, never is able to bring it up. The entire process may be so automatic and so rapid that the person is not even aware of its occurrence. In this way, neither therapist nor patient may become aware of an important area for investigation.

One area where this becomes especially important is in the relationship between therapist and patient. Many examples of this may be cited, but a clear one concerns the person who has a fear of criticism. In the treatment situation he acts in such ways as to avoid the therapist's criticisms, and all the therapist may perceive is a cooperative person who is making good progress. The person himself may not be aware of the phobic avoidance that is taking place. Yet this very fear may be active in many areas of the person's life where it has a subtle, unrecognized, but important influence. The attempts to identify and to treat such fears may complicate treatment (after all, the patient had been making good progress), but it may also lead to more pervasive and more permanent changes.

Constant examination of the ongoing relationship becomes important in the recognition of such phobic avoidances. All too often when "things are going well" the behavior therapist himself begins to avoid potential disruptions of the treatment. This is understandable from the behavior therapy point of view. The behavior therapist is trained to search for increasing strengths and for positive changes so that he may reinforce them and so increase the progress of such change. The dynamically oriented therapist, on the other hand, is concerned not so much with changing specific behaviors as with changing the person as a whole.

Recognizing that people are quite complex, he is constantly searching for new understandings, new areas of problems for potential exploration. Consequently, all too often he fails to reinforce, even to notice, the positive changes that come about. In behavioral psychotherapy, we attempt to strike a balance between these opposing perspectives. Although attending to positive behavioral change, because of his constant awareness of the need to revise his behavioral formulations, the behavioral psychotherapist is also on a continual search for new understandings and possible new problem areas for exploration. Hence he is on the alert for signs of such resistance.

The person's dreams may be an important source for identifying areas of phobic avoidance. Associations to and discussion of dreams may alert the therapist to such areas. Recurrent dreams or dreams with a disturbing element may be desensitized and sometimes yield insight into the meaning of the dream. Such insights are often helpful where the symptom is unresponsive to treatment, where it appears to be reinforced but where it is impossible to determine specific reinforcers. One example:

A young woman presented with a series of problems where an inability to act assertively appeared to be the core. However, extended treatment involving both individual and group assertiveness training, desensitization to the performance of assertive acts and to social fears, and a cognitive approach yielded at best only transitory change. There was much discussion concerning the possible reinforcers that maintained her helpless and dependent behaviors, but no specific reinforcers could be found. The person then reported a series of dreams which suggested that the inhibiting behaviors helped to avoid aggressive fantasies which, further, she associated with being masculine. It was the fear of being masculine that appeared to be the phobic area she was avoiding. Work along these lines had barely started when the person proclaimed herself much improved, no longer needing treatment, and terminated against advice.

Not all difficulties in treatment stem from phobic avoidance. Many other variables may be at work. A person may be given therapeutic assignments to carry out in life situations and do them incompletely, incorrectly, or not at all. Lazarus (1971) points out a number of possible processes that may contribute to this. The assignment may be irrelevant, premature or too anxiety-provoking. It may be sabotaged by others close to the person. It may mean giving up secondary gains. However, phobic avoidance remains one possibility to be considered. Sometimes the phobic core is quite subtle. We have seen several people with difficulty in carrying out assignments who turned out to be phobic to discipline, whether externally or internally imposed. A desensitization to accepting discipline usually brought about a rapid change.

Thus, when resistances arise, an exploration must be carried out for the purposes of identifying the specific behaviors involved and formulating these difficulties in behavioral terms. Dynamic concepts may be extremely useful in helping the therapist to do this but must eventually be translated into behavioral terms. Even when the treatment appears to be proceeding smoothly and according to plan, the therapist must constantly search for new understandings and possible new and important areas for treatment.

Course of Treatment

The course of treatment may be regarded as a living, changing series of events. Following the evaluative process and the explanation to the person, systematic work begins on the initial target behaviors. Sometimes this proceeds smoothly, evenly, and successful termination of treatment soon follows. Most often this is not the case. Even in the least complicated treatment, progress tends to ebb and flow, and the patient should be prepared for this. Technical difficulties arise or various forms of noncooperation may provide obstacles which the therapist must understand and treat. Life circumstances may provoke a series of problems unrelated to the chosen main target behaviors where the person needs immediate help. The behavior of others, the social contingencies surrounding the person, may be sabotaging treatment. The initial formulation may prove to be incorrect, or the initial presenting problem may prove to be trivial compared to others, as increased information about the person becomes available. Hence, treatment is often a series of formulations and reformulations with specific target behaviors changing and being worked on systematically.

Obstacles that arise during the course of treatment must always be evaluated in such a manner that target behaviors whose change may remove these obstacles are identified. These obstacles may stem from patient characteristics. The patient may be passive or may be phobic to the pressure he perceives as emanating from the therapist's instructions. These may have to be modified before the initial target behaviors can again be approached. The obstacles may stem from the therapeutic relationship or the therapeutic atmosphere. Or the obstacles may be iatrogenic; the therapist may have chosen an incorrect target behavior, may have an unrealistic evaluation of the patient's capabilities, or may just have given inappropriate assignments. The behavioral formulation of such obstacles often indicates that therapeutic changes must be brought about before the presenting problems can be treated.

Therapeutic Atmosphere

As with any form of individual psychotherapy, behavioral psychotherapy aims at setting an ambiance of warmth, trust and understanding. Many times this is difficult to establish because of the characteristics of the patient. For example, people who tend to be hostile and uncooperative as shown by high scores on the psychoticism scale of the Eysenck Personality Questionnaire tend to make poor progress in treatment (Rahman and Eysenck, 1978). In these instances the therapist must identify, formulate and attempt to modify the patient behaviors that may interfere with treatment.

However, because of the active, directive role of the behavioral psychotherapist, great attention must be paid to the possibilities that his own behavior may be providing or contributing to the problems in the therapeutic atmosphere. Countertransference problems may emerge, as when the patient's problems or behaviors set off phobic reactions in the therapist. Or he may bring to the session his own cognitive sets of behavior patterns which, although they may be generally appropriate and helpful with most patients, interfere with his relationship with that specific individual. Hence, the therapist must always evaluate his own behavior and reactions, as well as those of the patient, whenever difficulties in this area arise.

One obvious way of getting relevant information for this evaluation is to ask the patient about it directly. A simple question such as "What can *I* do differently to make things easier for you?" may lead to a productive discussion. However, a more systematic approach to this problem is available.

With several patients we have found the Lazarus and Fay (1975) Therapist-Selection Questionnaire most helpful. The items of this questionnaire are shown in Figure 1. Although the authors also provide a scoring system, we do not use it for the present purpose. We have the patient complete this questionnaire and then discuss it with him item by item where difficulties appear. This discussion considers what both the patient and the therapist can do differently to alleviate the problem. Also helpful at times is for the therapist himself to complete the questionnaire as he believes the patient would do it. Discrepancies may emerge that challenge the honesty of the patient's report (e.g., there may be a phobic

Figure 1

Items from Therapist-Selection Questionnaire (Lazarus and Fay, 1975; reproduced with permission).

1) I feel comfortable with the therapist (T).
2) T seems comfortable with me.
3) T is casual and informal rather than stiff and formal.
4) T does not treat me as if I am sick, defective, and about to fall apart.
5) T is flexible and open to new ideas rather than pursuing one point of view.
6) T has a good sense of humor and a pleasant disposition.
7) T is willing to tell me how s(he) feels about me.
8) T admits limitations and does not pretend to know things s(he) doesn't know.
9) T is very willing to acknowledge being wrong and apologizes for making errors or for being inconsiderate, instead of justifying this kind of behavior.
10) T answers direct questions rather than simply asking me what I think.
11) T reveals things about herself or himself either spontaneously or in response to my inquiries (but not by bragging and talking incessantly and irrelevantly).
12) T encourages the feeling that I am as good as s(he) is.
13) T acts as if s(he) is my consultant rather than the manager of my life.
14) T encourages differences of opinion rather than telling me that I am resisting if I disagree with him or her.
15) T is interested in seeing people who share my life (or is at least willing to do so). This would include family, friends, lovers, work associates, or any other significant people in my environment.
16) The things that T says make sense to me.
17) In general, my contacts with the therapist lead to my feeling more hopeful and having higher self-esteem.

---

avoidance of the therapist's displeasure) or that challenge the perceptions of each of the participants. Such a procedure may help to identify crucial areas for the change necessary to facilitate treatment.

Termination

Nevertheless, somehow, treatment progresses and we come to a time when a group of apparently meaningful target behaviors have been changed, and this change carried over to the life situations. At this time we expect more than a change in just these behaviors and their specific consequences. We would expect a more generalized change, a reorganization of at least some part of the person's psychological organization. The extent of the change would depend upon the central or peripheral nature of the modified target behaviors. However, these changes are not immediate, nor are they automatic. The person needs time to integrate the changes brought about by the modification of the target behaviors in order to allow such reorganization to take place. Unless there are important other behaviors requiring immediate work, this is a good time for a vacation from treatment.

Besides allowing for integration, such vacations have another importance. They give the person the legitimate feeling of doing things on his own, of testing his own strengths, of using by himself the skills he has learned in the course of treatment. In this way they also reduce the dependency on the therapist. We usually set such vacations from four to six weeks' duration and then evaluate the next steps of treatment, if any, to be taken. During the vacation period the person would contact the therapist if 1) there is a setback that he attempts to handle but cannot; 2) if another problem arises that he wants to discuss; or 3) if he becomes aware of some area where it would be constructive to begin work. It may well be that the removal of a set of problem behaviors may bring on a new set of difficulties. We have seen stutterers who, when cured of the stutter, had nothing to say; agoraphobes who, when cured of the panics or the fear of panics so that they could travel, had nowhere they wanted to go; young people who, when cured of a fear of dating, became aware of a previously unknown fear of closeness or of sex. Problems such as these may emerge during the vacation and serve as the basis for a new behavioral formulation and for the next step in treatment.

Termination is usually handled as an extended vacation. According to our formulation, the major target behaviors have been modified and there are good indications that the major problems have been (or are in the process of being) resolved. Often some contact is maintained with the person by telephone or through the mail for a short period of time. The person may consider the therapist as his "doctor" in much the same way he views his family physician. Some come back after many, many years with new sets of problems on which they want to work. Others come back every few years for "check-ups." This may be true not just with successful treatment but also with people where treatment has been only partially successful or even an outright failure. Posed in this way, and because of previous vacations, we find no special preparation is needed for termination.

SUMMARY

The description of the basic procedures of behavioral psychotherapy shows how the model set forth in the first chapters is implemented. The stress throughout is on evaluation and reevaluation. Information is sys-tematically gathered not merely about the stated presenting problem but about all aspects of the person and of his life situation. The patient's response to the specific therapeutic interventions, the therapeutic in-teraction, and the subjective reactions of the therapist are important sources of data. The behavioral formulation, a means of organizing the therapist's understanding of the patient, is the core of treatment plan-ning. This formulation is subject to constant revision as the therapist's understanding deepens.

Evaluation is not limited to the organization of behaviors in the prob-lem area. Should obstacles arise in the course of ongoing treatment, each such obstacle must be formulated and the treatment adjusted in the light of this formulation. Should the patient have difficulty in performing his assignments, this difficulty may be formulated in terms of passivity, phobic reactions to "demands," or inappropriate assignments being given. Whatever the formulation, the therapist will take the necessary steps to counter the difficulty. Should there emerge an unsatisfactory therapeutic atmosphere, the therapist may formulate the difficulty in terms of patient characteristics but must also examine his own possible contribution to this. Only then can he decide upon the necessary course of therapeutic action. The concepts used in such formulations may stem from the biological, social or psychoanalytic areas as well as the more strictly behavioral. In all instances, the formulation must be reduced to the specific identification of target behaviors to be modified in order to make treatment more effective.

Thus, it is the responsibility of the therapist to maintain the effec-tiveness of the treatment program. Many times behaviors not directly relevant to the presenting problems may have to be treated before an effective treatment program for those problems can be established. Even when treatment appears to be proceeding smoothly and according to plan, the therapist must be ever alert. Resistance on the part of the patient, the process through which without his awareness of doing so he tends to avoid important but anxiety eliciting information about him-self, is always possible. The alert therapist is often able to identify such areas, to change his treatment plan accordingly, and so to effect more complete change in the patient.

When changes in important behaviors are accomplished, a vacation from treatment should be considered. This allows for the integration of these changes into the general life of the patient and also provides him with the opportunity to gain the legitimate feeling of using his own newly acquired strengths. When the changes occur in areas that have been formulated to be the core of the problem behavioral organization, termination may be considered. Termination, however, is regarded as an extended vacation with the patient being expected to return as new areas for change become apparent.

REFERENCES

Evans, Dr. R. Exhibitionism. In C. G. Costello (Ed.), *Symptoms of Psychopathology: A Handbook*. New York: Wiley, 1970.

Fensterheim, H. The initial interview. In A. A. Lazarus (Ed.), *Clinical Behavior Therapy*. New York: Brunner/Mazel, 1972.

Fensterheim, H. Clinical behavior therapy of depression. In J. Clarkin and H. Glazer (Eds.) *Depression: Behavioral and Directive Intervention Strategies*. New York: Garland Press, 1981.

Fishman, S. T., and Lubetkin, B. S. Maintenance and generalization of individual behavior therapy programs. In P. Karoly and J. I. Steffen (Eds.), *Improving the Long-Term Effects of Psychotherapy*. New York: Gardner Press, 1980.

Glazer, H. I., Clarkin, J. F., and Hunt, H. F. Assessment of depression. In J. F. Clarkin and H. I. Glazer (Eds.), *Depression: Behavioral and Directive Intervention Strategies*. New York: Garland Press, 1981.

Hersen, M., and Bellack, A. S. Social skills training for chronic psychiatric patients: Rationale, research findings and future directions. *Comprehensive Psychiatry*, 1976, *17*: 559-580.

Jacobson, E. *Progressive Relaxation*. Chicago: Chicago University Press, 1929.

Lazarus, A. A. *Behavior Therapy and Beyond*. New York: McGraw-Hill, 1971.

Lazarus, A. A. *Multimodal Behavior Therapy*. New York: Springer, 1977.

Lazarus, A., and Fay, A. *I Can If I Want To*. New York: William Morrow, 1975.

Lewinsohn, P. M., Steinmetz, J. L., Larson, D. W., and Franklin, J. Depression related cognitions: Antecedents or consequence? *J. Abnorm. Psychol.*, 1981, *90*: 213-219.

MacCrimmon, D. J., Wallace, J. E., Goldberg, W. M., Streiner, D. L. Emotional disturbance and cognitive deficits in hyperthyroidism. *Psychosomatic Medicine*, 1979, *41*: 331-340.

Rahman, M. A., and Eysenck, S. B. G. Psychoticism and response to treatment in neurotic patients. *Behavior Research and Therapy*, 1978, *16*: 183-189.

Shapiro, A. K. The behavior therapies: Therapeutic breakthrough or latest fad? *American Journal of Psychiatry*, 1976, *133*: 154-159.

Wolpe, J. The experimental model and treatment of neurotic depression. *Behavior Research and Therapy*, 1979, *17*: 555-565.

PART II

The Cases

5

Behavioral Psychotherapy of Obsessional Checking: Treatment Through the Relationship

Marie Edwards Jacobson

Mr. B., a 40-year old single male, applied for help with his obsessions and compulsive checking. Ten years earlier, while working as a locomotive mechanic, he developed a severe compulsion to check and recheck all his work on the locomotive. This need became so intense that he was unable to carry out his duties. The precipitating factor appears to have been a near crash of one of the trains on which he had worked, due to mechanical failure. The compulsion grew to pervade every aspect of his life, in and out of his home. To take a bath became an all-day project and Sundays were devoted to this one endeavor. Although he tried to work part-time for a relative as a bartender, he was unable to continue and became increasingly isolated and depressed. He had sought treatment in a private psychiatric clinic and over the past 10 years had a wide variety of treatment modalities. These included traditional individual and group psychotherapy, various forms of medication, and 60 electric convulsive shock treatments for depression; once he had been hospitalized for a period of one month with severe depression. At the time of referral to our clinic, Mr. B. was still severely depressed, obsessional checking was severe, and self-esteem was extremely low.

PAST HISTORY

Mr. B.'s family consists of two single older brothers who live nearby with their 78-year-old father and two married sisters who live away.

Mr. B. was the middle child and distinguished as being the "sickly" one in the family. From about age five he had severe asthma and a large part of his growing years was spent "lying around" and being cared for by his mother. He also had acne which caused considerable shame during his adolescence and left his face scarred. It was very difficult to get a picture of the interactional patterns within the family, not because of Mr. B.'s withholding, but because he actually was not aware of their ways of relating. He saw his father and brothers as hard workers in the restaurant business and his mother as taking care of the house. His mother died eight years before Mr. B.'s obsessive checking started, but he believed this had no relevance to his emotional difficulties. Efforts to explore this area were unfruitful.

Mr. B. finished high school, where he was an average student. He then attended a vocational school for locomotive mechanics where he excelled. He described with pride how later he was able to solve mechanical problems on trains that others could not and how he won a special commendation. During this period he occasionally dated, but most of his socializing was with a group of young men his own age who went bowling and attended sports events together. He said he felt he had "always been afraid of girls," and had never had sexual intercourse. He denied that this bothered him.

Both of Mr. B.'s brothers have a history of psychiatric illnesses but neither had been hospitalized. Mr. B. could only say that they became "nervous," and they were treated at the same clinic Mr. B. had attended before coming to Payne Whitney. A year before referral to the Payne Whitney Clinic, Mr. B. moved from the family home to his own apartment nearby because his obsessive checking caused much family conflict. However, at the time of referral, he still went home each day for his evening meal, and this was the primary focus of his day. The remainder of his day was spent checking and rechecking his apartment or attending to taking baths and personal cleanliness. He was supported by social service assistance for the disabled.

OTHER BEHAVIORAL DATA

One of the striking aspects of Mr. B.'s life was his extreme isolation from other people. He had no friends at all, and his only social contact was within his family. Even his men friends from earlier days "seemed to have gotten lost somewhere." Mr. B. had severe assertiveness problems. He was unable to make any distinction between assertiveness and aggressiveness. He passively accepted a great deal of contempt and put-downs from his brothers with occasional ineffective outbursts. One of his brothers had named him "The Mouse That Roared." Bodily tensions were so high that often under stress his left hand would tremble. Also, at times, his vision would become distorted and surfaces would tend to appear wavy or unsettled. The latter could be precipitated merely by his not having "counted enough" or "looked at something long enough," even when alone in his own apartment. Unwanted behaviors included vacillation between neatness in appearance and being quite unkempt.

One special note must be made concerning his checking behavior: It was completely under his control. He could stop it at any time and keep from checking for long periods. The problem was that when he did this he became extremely depressed. One previous therapist had used response prevention, and Mr. B. was able to refrain from checking behaviors for an entire month. However, the depression that came about at that time was so severe that his one hospitalization was deemed necessary. When the checking behavior was deliberately resumed on that therapist's instruction, the depression was ameliorated.

FIRST BEHAVIORAL TREATMENT

When first referred to our unit, Mr. B. was treated by another therapist. At that time he was diagnosed as having a severe obsessive-compulsive neurosis with depressive and schizoid features. The behavioral formulation (see Figure 1) centered around an obsessive need to control and treatment centered around attempts to lessen these obsessions. In order to lessen the need for checking and the obsessiveness in general, an attempt was made to bring down his general level of anxiety. Mr. B. was taught the Jacobson (1929) method of relaxation. In order to encourage practice, a tape of the exercises was given to him. As the checking seemed to be a source of pleasure for him as well as reassuring him of control, a systematic effort was made to have him seek other sources of pleasure. Included were such activities as enjoyable snacks or movies. In order to increase self-esteem he was to do one thing each day that might make him feel better about himself. As an example, he chose to do some painting on his father's house, and he did indeed do a little of this.

This first therapist perceived Mr. B. as being superficially cooperative

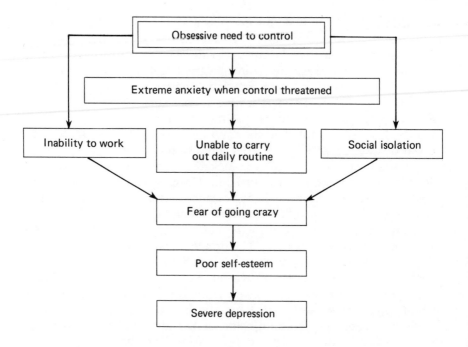

Figure 1. Initial behavioral formulation with the obsessive need
to control as the core of the problem organization.

but as actually carrying out the treatment plan only to a minimal degree. Unfortunately, after six months of treatment, this therapist had to leave the clinic suddenly and was unable to prepare Mr. B. for this change.

TRANSFER TO PRESENT THERAPIST

State of the Problem

The status of the problems which Mr. B. presented at the time of transfer was essentially the same as described at original intake. Nothing basically had changed.

Behavioral Data

The same was true of the behavioral data available, with several additional factors now to be considered. At this point it was known that

Mr. B. handled his anger by taking a strong passive-aggressive stance while operating under a rigid defense system of denial. Since this not only interfered with his social relationships in general but kept his treatment at a standstill, this pattern was of crucial importance. It was also believed that underlying this anger was an intense fear of any situation that elicited feelings of helplessness. It was the opinion of the present therapist that Mr. B.'s early history of illness as an asthmatic child who was kept in a dependent position by his family had entrenched his fears of abandonment and helplessness, even though these fears were not available on a conscious level at this time. It was formulated that a phobic reaction to these feelings of helplessness provoked an entire defensive system, which included an excessive need to feel in control.

At this point the diagnosis and formulation for treatment were changed. On Axis I he was diagnosed as Obsessive Compulsive Disorder (DSM-III 300.30). In addition, his longstanding difficulties in a variety of ego functions were taken into account. Considering the pervasive impairment of object relations, social isolation, inability to work, poor self-esteem, and the ease with which he regressed to a state of helplessness under slight stress, he was diagnosed on Axis II Borderline Personality Disorder (DSM-III 301.83) with passive aggressive and schizoid features. A psychological examination done at this point confirmed the diagnosis.

Revised Behavioral Formulation

The new behavioral formulation placed at its core the phobic reaction to helplessness (Figure 2). The other aspects of disturbance were hypothesized as flowing from this core difficulty. His checking behavior, for example, was avoidance behavior. Because it gave him some feeling of control it helped to avoid helplessness and the constellation of feelings associated with helplessness. This formulation helps us to understand how the response prevention method led to so severe a disturbance that hospitalization became necessary.

Revised Treatment Plan

Based on this reformulation the new focal target became the phobic reaction to helplessness. It seems appropriate here to give some clinical basis for this shift. The crucial aspect of this state of helplessness has been described by Guntrip (1964) from a psychoanalytic point of view, and by Seligman (1975) from a cognitive and behavioral perspective.

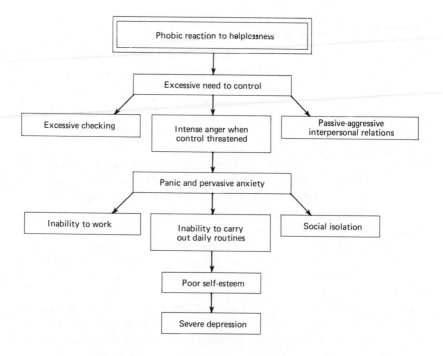

Figure 2. Revised behavioral formulation with a phobic reaction to feelings of helplessness as the core and the need to control deriving from that.

Guntrip, in his earlier work, describes the difference between the primary fear of the withdrawn or schizoid personality and that of the neurotic:

> These phenomena, so different from the guilt-producing conflicts, have their roots in fear: not fear of disapproval as a secondary result of trouble over bad impulses, but fear in a primary sense, the fear of the small helpless human child at the mercy of a bad environment (p.61).

He goes on to describe the "bad environment" as not just being physical but rather as the helplessness of the child to effect a warm, nurturing, emotional environment around him. Such helplessness then leads the person to withdraw from any attempts even to reach out for the kind of interpersonal exchange so necessary for a feeling of well-being. Some aspects of this phenomena were described much earlier in the well-known studies of Spitz on anaclitic depression (1946).

Seligman (1975) describes this same theme from a behavioral and cognitive point of view. He suggests that it is not only deprivation of nurturance and lack of emotional stimulation that cause damage to the ego but also what he calls the lack of established consistency between responding and feedback. "The notions of ego strength and competency are related to mastery over events. I suggest that synchrony between responding and its consequences is crucial to healthy development" (p. 7). He goes on to describe in repeated studies how once either an animal or human being "learns" that he is helpless in repeated situations he will later not be able to use the tools available to him even if he is no longer actually helpless. His description of how both can "relearn" to cope in more effective ways and extricate themselves from this supposed helplessness seems to be one of the more hopeful and efficacious means of helping persons who are fixated on this level deal with anxiety and depression.

It is maintained that too often the assumption is made with the patient who is fixated in an obsessional state that repressed anger is the primary source of anxiety. In actuality, if the diagnosis is borderline rather than neurotic, the client is often regressed to the deeper level of helplessness, and the anger is not experienced or is not available to him. This is more than a repression of anger into the unconscious, but rather a splitting of the ego where the client sees himself as completely lacking in strengths and effectiveness. This he experiences in all its painfulness and despair. Until this state of helplessness is focused on and dealt with, it is rare that the client feels understood and that a therapeutic working alliance can be established. Such a phenomenon has been beautifully described in Goulding and Goulding (1978). Although their approach is primarily from a transactional and Gestalt point of view, it is helpful for any therapist who hopes to avoid power struggles with those clients who need desperately to be in control and to avoid further experiences of helplessness in the hands of the therapist.

The application of this discussion, of the relation between anger and helplessness in a borderline person, was clear from the outset. It had been noted that the change of therapists was fairly sudden and without adequate preparation of the patient for the change. It would have been understandable if Mr. B. had shown some anger or at least recognized that anger might have been an appropriate response. Instead, he not only denied this but stated: "They tried very hard to help me." His discussion centered around his difficulties: "So maybe you can help me." He was clearly taking a very passive position in relation to his own therapy, and this was interpreted to be a defense against his own feelings of helplessness.

Hence, the major thrust of treatment was to be aimed at his helplessness and at the constellation of behaviors that surrounded it. The therapeutic relationship was formulated as being crucial in this. In past treatment, his use of passivity to avoid the feelings of helplessness had doomed his treatment to failure. The aim was to use the current therapeutic relationship to provide him with legitimate feelings of competency that would change this aspect of his behavioral organization.

ONGOING TREATMENT

With this in mind, Mr. B. was asked if there was anything he could envision that would make him feel better. Mr. B. said he wished he could get out of the house without it taking all day. It was suggested that he pick an area where he had the least anxiety, which happened to be the kitchen, and to see if he could speed up his checking in that area just a tiny bit each day. It was also suggested that he record his time each day so he would know if he was making any progress. Mr. B. returned the next week to say that doing this made him feel worse instead of better, that it was impossible to keep a record because he became obsessed with the record keeping, and that it took him longer to get out of the house. Asked if he could think of anything other than working directly on the checking that would make him feel better, Mr. B. said he would like very much to go to a Christmas party that was being held in his building but that he thought he would be too anxious to do so. He was told that if this was something he wanted to do just for fun and not for his "mental health," that possibly there was an exercise that might help him—and again maybe not. This tack was taken with Mr. B. because of his passive-aggressive patterns and because of the suspicion that defeating therapists' well-intentioned interventions over the last 10 years may have given Mr. B. one of the few experiences of warding off helplessness that he had available to him.

His goal of wanting to go to a party was a particularly pertinent one at this point because in Mr. B.'s eyes it did not directly focus on his "problem." However, it was important that the therapist not be too enthusiastic about this or any intervention being offered. He was told that some people had found an exercise for deep breathing quite helpful in mastering anxiety, but that again *he* might not find it helpful. We would take the time to teach him this method only if he wanted to give it a try. Mr. B. decided to try it "just in case." This method had been chosen because the therapist had noticed that when Mr. B. seemed anxious, such as when he first arrived at the therapy sessions, he tended to breathe mainly with the upper part of his chest. There was the possibility that he was hyperventilating, which would increase his anxiety. However, he was more apt to work on his breathing in relation to the party, rather than as a "problem" in itself. Mr. B. was taught the deep breathing exercises as described by Lum (1976) and again cautioned that only he could tell whether it would be of help to him or not. This was repeated to make certain that Mr. B. did not see the therapist as having an investment in the exercises being successful and therefore need to defeat it.

The therapist was to be away for the Christmas holidays; she made sure Mr. B. was told well in advance and set an appointment immediately afterwards. Although Mr. B. had denied any separation anxiety, it was felt that this was an important factor in his feelings of helplessness and that it was important to build a feeling of trust if at all possible. Mr. B., of course, denied any fantasies that she would not return. He asked jokingly if she would send him a Christmas card, the first indication that a connection had been made and his first assertive gesture towards getting himself out of his isolation. He was told that she would like to do that and would like to have a Christmas card from him. She suggested that perhaps there were others to whom he might wish to send cards, and Mr. B. decided to send cards to several members of his family. During the holidays the therapist did send him a card, adding a note that she hoped he had fun at the party and reconfirming the date of the next therapy session.

After the holidays, Mr. B. came in saying he had indeed gone to the party and that, although it was very difficult because of his anxiety, he had been able to stay longer than he expected. At one point when he was talking to a young woman, he had become very anxious, went to the bathroom where he did his breathing exercises, and returned. He hastened to tell the therapist that he modified the exercises to do them *his* way, however. The therapist congratulated him and told him that he had been the one to make it work and that she knew how much determination that had taken on his part.

The passive-aggressive aspect of his personality was also demonstrated in how he handled his therapy sessions. Mr. B. came late for every session, saying that his checking took so long that he just couldn't get there on time. He indicated that the former therapist had "felt sorry for him" and had given him extra time at the end of the session. Exploration of any feelings of annoyance or rejection that the current therapist was not also doing this was met with absolute denial. He did say that he had a history of being late all his life. With glee he told of how his high school teacher "tried to get me out of it but he never won!" It was felt that being on time for appointments that other people set touched on Mr. B.'s fear of helplessness. The therapist asked Mr. B. if he would like to say when his session would begin and how long it would last. Mr. B. said he would like that but wasn't sure what to set up. It had been noted that Mr. B. was quite consistent in his lateness, always being between 12 and 15 minutes late. It was suggested that the therapist would be there at 12 minutes after the hour the following week. At the next session the therapist got there just as Mr. B. walked in, and he exclaimed, "You just got here?" He was reminded of the agreement and he looked slightly displeased, but he again denied any angry feelings. After two such sessions Mr. B. said he would like to go back to the regular time, and this was agreed. This time he came five minutes late, and the comment was made that he seemed to be finding the time that was best for him. It was suggested that our next session start at five after the hour. It only took a few more sessions for Mr. B. to settle into a regular 45-minute session with almost no lateness at all.

One might say this is not treatment on a "deep" level; however, just the opposite is true. For a client fixated in this helpless position it is absolutely crucial that he go through a testing period of whether he or the therapist will be in control and that the therapist be genuinely willing to be the helpless one in this aspect of treatment. Those of us who have worked with emotionally disturbed children who have not been able to navigate successfully the separation-individuation phase of their development have seen similar results. If the child was not able to separate from the mother appropriately and go on to explore effectively and to master his world, he remained stuck in the state of helpless dependency or in a constant state of defiance as an attempt to ward off helplessness. The issue of control becomes one of crucial importance. Seligman, in his work on helplessness, points out repeatedly how he sees the drive to resist compulsion as the drive to resist helplessness. In this respect he refers to the work of Kavanau with wild mice:

> Kavanau has postulated that the drive to resist compulsion is more important to wild animals then sex, food or water. He found that captive white-footed mice spent inordinate time and energy just resisting experimental manipulation. If the experimenters turned

the lights up, the mouse spent his time in turning the lights down. If the experimenter turned the lights down, the mouse turned them up (1976, p. 55).

With this in mind, there was always the danger with Mr. B. of his seeing the therapist as needing to mastermind his therapeutic progress and make him well. An example of how easily the therapist can fall into this trap took place at this point in treatment. One cold morning Mr. B. appeared at his therapy session with mucus running out of his nose. He said that this happens often because he can't blow it. If he tried to blow his nose he would become so obsessed with the checking procedure that he then couldn't do anything else. His feelings of helplessness and despair about this seemed quite intense. The therapist had been hoping for an opportunity to do some *in vivo* exercises on his checking compulsion and thought this was the opportunity. In order to help him relax, she suggested that he do his breathing exercise and add the words "calm and relaxed" as he exhaled. She also hoped to use visual imagery as described by Lazarus (1977). Without attempting to blow his nose, he was to go through the visual image of blowing his nose, and when he reached any stage that he was anxious, we would stop and do the breathing exercise again. This was to be repeated until in imagery Mr. B. could complete blowing his nose. Only then would he try in actuality to slowly blow his nose, again stopping and relaxing if he became anxious.

Mr. B. cooperated well in this exercise and was actually able to blow his nose. Since our central focus at this point was in reducing Mr. B.'s sense of helplessness, this seemed quite an achievement. The therapist was quite enthusiastic and genuine in her praise of Mr. B.'s efforts. However, the next week Mr. B. came in rather surly and announced that he never wanted to do that again and that he had become quite compulsive in his checking of everything afterwards. The therapist acknowledged that Mr. B. was probably right, that she, the therapist, had been trying too hard and that understandably he was quite angry with her. He denied any anger and added, "but what am I to do about blowing my nose—people look at me like I'm crazy." This time the therapist threw him the ball. He was told that it is true that people will look at him as if he were crazy because this is one of his crazy-acting behaviors. However, the therapist was convinced he wasn't crazy, the psychological examination showed that he wasn't crazy, and a piece of him knows that he isn't crazy. Therefore, he himself will have to decide when he is ready to stop misleading people. Although he never brought it up again, neither the therapist nor anyone else ever saw him with a runny nose after that time. Later in the therapy, Mr. B. told the therapist that he thought the visual imagery had helped him master other situations. Nevertheless, it demonstrated to the therapist once again how her therapeutic zeal must be tempered not to arouse Mr. B.'s sense of helplessness.

This experience later helped to control another instance of his fear of "being crazy." Mr. B. told of how he tried to help by sweeping the walk in front of his father's house. He then described how a woman neighbor would stand on her porch and watch "as if he were crazy." When Mr. B. detailed the compulsiveness with which he swept the walk over and over, he was told that his behavior did make him look crazy and that it was understandable that the neighbor saw him that way. Mr. B. said defiantly that this was the only way he could sweep it, almost daring the therapist to try to change him.

The therapist commented that it was interesting that this took place repeatedly outside his father's home, whereas he had been quite careful that his own neighbors should not observe his checking compulsion. It was pointed out to him that although his two brothers had a history of psychiatric treatment, he and his family seemed to have a pact that he, Mr. B., would play the role of the emotionally disturbed one. In this way he protected them from facing their own emotional disturbance. She commented that he was truly cooperating in this project and that she doubted that this dedication to them would be changed in the near future. The subject was then dropped. Several weeks later Mr. B. commented almost as an aside that he thought the breathing exercises had helped him "to sweep a little faster." Here, for the first time, he had voluntarily used a coping exercise to control a compulsion. Doing so, incidentally, also took him a step in the direction of changing his family-assigned role of being the "crazy one." The nonhostile paradoxical intervention, because it did not activate his helplessness, made this change possible.

At this point an attempt was made to communicate some intellectual understanding of his difficulties to Mr. B. It was explained that when he was a little boy and ill with asthma, he was indeed quite helpless and unable to function as did his brothers and friends. During that time his family, for various reasons, acted towards him in ways that inappropriately increased his feelings of helplessness. Mr. B. remembered that when he tried to do different things at home his family would hasten to discourage him and that he did indeed feel weak and helpless. The concept of learned helplessness was described to him. Because Mr.

B. could relate to ideas more easily than to feelings, he became intrigued. It was further proposed that perhaps his reaction to the near crash of the train was so stressful that he went back to functioning as he did when he was a helpless little boy, ill with asthma. It was pointed out that his obsessive checking made him feel less helpless and more in control, thus temporarily making him feel stronger.

In the next phase of treatment, as Mr. B. built up more trust that the therapist would not render him helpless, he told her about a woman in his building who had acted friendly toward him and said he would like to talk to her. He wondered if deep breathing and visual imagery could help. He agreed to setting up a hierarchy of the different stages of approaching her. A desensitization using visual imagery and deep breathing for relaxation was conducted. We also later role-played what he would do if she gave a negative response, so he would hopefully not be thrown into despair if she rejected him. Actually she did say "No," but very soon after Mr. B. met another woman while sitting on a park bench, a woman who responded by showing considerable interest in him. Mr. B. immediately decided she was too old for him; she was two years older than he. His brothers and father also thought she was too old for him. This was discussed with him as a fear of closeness; with closeness his need for absolute control would certainly be threatened, and he would then feel helpless and overwhelmed. Perhaps, it was suggested, it would help his changing role within the family were he to introduce her to his brothers. Then, joining the resistance to minimize his feelings of helplessness in treatment, it was noted that it might be too early for either him or his family to accept such a step. This allowed him to become assertively possessive; she was his girlfriend.

This relationship appeared to present an opportunity for therapeutic growth and change. He wanted to invite the woman to his apartment. However, the very thought brought on a cold sweat. His fear was that she would expect sexual relations and that she might become pregnant. If that happened he would have to marry her and so become trapped. This, of course, would bring on the very state of helplessness that he so feared. He knew little of contraceptives and it was believed that he would not accept the woman's controlling its use. Hence a therapeutic-educational program was devised that included a homework assignment. He was to buy a box of condoms and every day to masturbate, ejaculating into a condom. This was one assignment he carried out with spirit. Incidentally and probably connected with this, soon after starting this homework he reported a remarkable decrease in the time he needed to shower. Although he did not eventually have intercourse, he was able to progress to the point where he could lie nude on top of the woman and ejaculate while wearing a condom. He also learned to get satisfaction in giving her pleasure through oral sex—though on one occasion he swore that the pubic hair gave him an asthma attack. Just as important, he gained confidence in other aspects of the relationship. Once he was able to fix her car after she had done a favor for him, and he was very proud of this. The relationship did not last very long before she broke it off, but it was the closest he had ever been to a woman.

Mr. B. was depressed for a short period after the breakup but soon began to have fantasies of meeting other women. At this point he said that what embarrassed him the most with his woman friend and with others was his inability to work, but he thought the checking was still too intense for him to hold a job. This once more made him feel helpless and demeaned. It was explained to him that there was a sheltered workshop where persons with emotional problems could gradually get used to working again. Unfortunately, it was in another area of the city and would require about two hours' travel time on the subway each way. Mr. B. was doubtful. Although the traveling was bothersome, his worst fear was that he would be with people who might be quite disturbed and he would again start calling himself crazy. This anticipatory anxiety proved to be the biggest obstacle to his trying to go to the sheltered workshop.

In essence, what Mr. B. anticipated was that upon contact with very disturbed persons at the workshop he would then conclude that he was automatically as disturbed as they were. He would be flooded with anxiety, would panic, and then indeed would function as a very disturbed person, thus fulfilling his original fearful prophecy. From an analytic point of view the basis of Mr. B.'s anxiety was his diffuse ego boundaries. He was actually unable to conclude that being around severely disturbed persons did not make him either more or less disturbed. Anyone who has tried to make an interpretation to a patient struggling with this fear will know how completely unhelpful such an interpretation will be, no matter how well it is timed and phrased. Something more is called for than an understanding of what is setting off his anxiety. In this particular situation it was of crucial importance to give the patient some tools with which to cope with his anticipatory anxiety. Fensterheim and Baer (1977, p.81) discussed a behavioral approach to dealing with anticipatory anxiety. "If you learn to control your thoughts and images, your anticipatory anxiety will decrease and you will be in a better position to cope with the frightening situation itself. You can do this in three ways:

"Thought Stoppage: You keep yourself from thinking dire thoughts.
"Thought Switching: You practice thinking 'I will cope' thoughts instead
of 'I will fail' thoughts until the former become so strong that they
replace the anxiety thoughts.
"Success Rehearsal: You change the images from scenes of failure to scenes
in which you manage the feared situation successfully."

This was the model used to approach the problem. In teaching Mr.
B. to apply thought stoppage he was asked to close his eyes and to
imagine a scene where he is in the workshop with a very disturbed co-
worker. When the thought intruded that he was like that person, he
was to raise his finger. At this signal, the therapist shouted, "STOP!"
Mr. B. was then taught to shout this word inside his own head as soon
as such a thought started. He was then instructed to do his breathing
exercise, saying "calm and relaxed" as he exhaled, and to imagine a
scene in which he felt emotionally strong (switching from crazy to
emotionally strong). For this latter, he used the scene of working on his
girlfriend's car. We practiced this many times during the sessions and
Mr. B. also practiced at home. However, as often happens in family
dynamics, as Mr. B. came nearer to applying to the workshop, his family
began pulling the other way. His sister called from another state saying
she had just put in a new swimming pool and urging him to come for
the summer; he could go to work later. His father and brothers became
adamant against it, insisting that too much time would be required in
traveling. They stressed what a come-down this would be from his
original job; besides he would probably get mugged on the subway. The
therapist also realized that she would soon be going on vacation and
would not be available to support him in this venture. Hence, it was
agreed that any attempt to go to the workshop would be held in abeyance
until after her vacation.

In September he was still quite anxious about the workshop but
wanted very much to go. We rehearsed all the previously learned coping
behaviors, and it became clear that Mr. B. hoped that somehow the
therapist could make him "well" without his actually having to risk this
anxiety-producing situation. He was told gently but firmly that if he was
to go further he would have to make a choice. He could stay home and
live out the image of the damaged one, as he had for the last 10 years,
or he could go toward the goal he had set for himself where he would
indeed probably have some discomfort.

Mr. B. came back the next week saying that during the week he had
decided to make a "trial run." He had gone on the subway to the

workshop without going in. He had found the subway was not nearly as bad as his family had warned him. For the first time he was excited about the prospect of working. We rehearsed the next step, which was to go inside and look over the place, always knowing that he could choose not to stay, i.e., that he was not helpless if he gave it a try. Mr. B.'s reaction to the workshop itself was more positive than anticipated. There were, of course, some severely disturbed people there, but this had the effect of making him feel more intact by comparison. Also, when he saw the machine shop he felt "it was like coming home," and he discerned quickly that he was more highly skilled than most of the people there.

The therapist had spoken to the supervisors in charge of the workshop and prepared the way for Mr. B. to be given as much choice as possible as to what he did there, even to the point of leaving immediately. This was again to counteract his feelings of helplessness, which continued to be our chief target area.

Mr. B. was able to stay at the workshop the rest of the day. Just as he had spiraled downward from one problem to another when he had originally been unable to work, his self-image now began to strengthen in many areas. He wisely chose to remain in the machine shop area where he felt least anxious. At first he found the coffee breaks difficult because he anticipated rejection by the other workers, but he was able to employ thought stoppage. Soon he found a group who invited him to join them. From time to time his hand shook from anxiety and his checking resurged, but he found deep breathing helpful. As he found his mechanical skills returning, he actually became elated. A further boost to his self-esteem came when the supervisor enlisted his help with some of the less skilled men. One day he did have quite a setback. A spark flew out, hit his hand, and he began checking so obsessively that he couldn't work for a while. However, he went into the bathroom where he used his coping mechanisms (thought stoppage, deep breathing and positive imaginary scene), and soon he was able to go back to work.

Mr. B. has been doing well at the workshop. Since he has been there he has not been late once. He recently made friends with a shy, frightened young woman who is a co-worker in the workshop. Mr. B. stated that he thinks he is less anxious with her because "she has been hospitalized twice and I have only been hospitalized once." Mr. B. sees himself as the strong one in this relationship and actually has been much less narcissistic than in his previous relationship. He sees himself as being the needed one, rather than the needy one, and he has responded to this. Because she needs to be taken somewhere in a car, Mr. B. has been practicing driving, extending the time and length gradually. Recently he was able to make the drive to her house through the heart of New York City traffic. This was his first drive of any length in 10 years. It was indeed a big accomplishment for him and increased his feeling of mastery. She appears to be even more afraid of sex than he is, and he has become the gentle initiator of exploratory sex between them. Recently when one of Mr. B.'s brothers made a put-down remark to him, he replied, "You know I've realized that I am the one man in this family who is both working and has a girlfriend. I think I'm the healthiest one of the bunch!" That remains to be seen, but Mr. B. is certainly changing the image of the damaged, helpless one.

It has been six months since Mr. B. began at the workshop, and recently he was questioned by the psychologist there as to why he thinks he is doing so much better than some of the others. Mr. B. replied, "Maybe they don't know about thought stoppage, deep breathing, and visual imagery." He said the psychologist looked at him as if he had never heard of that stuff. The therapist jokingly told Mr. B. that he had better watch the talk about that "stuff" or the psychologist might think he's crazy. Mr. B. laughted heartily and said, "He probably does," and then added, "No, I doubt it. I was the only one who knew how to get his car started the other day, including the supervisor."

Mr. B. does not plan on trying to go back to work on locomotives, but hopes to take a course in electrical appliance repairs if he continues to do well in the workshop. He can now shower in 45 minutes and get out of the house in two hours in all. This may seem like a long time to someone without Mr. B.'s difficulties, but to him it is a source of great pride. He has been seen by this therapist for a total of a year and a half; however, we do not anticipate termination in the near future, as this progress is not yet consolidated.

SUMMARY

This man had been treated for 10 years with a variety of traditional treatment approaches. These included individual, group, various medications, electroconvulsive therapy, and hospitalization, all resulting in no improvement. In the current therapy the diagnosis was first reevaluated. The behavioral formulation based on this diagnosis was formed and a treatment plan based on this formulation initiated. The new target area was his "phobic reaction to helplessness," and his relationship to the therapist was considered of prime importance. Time was spent in building a relationship of trust, and techniques such as joining the defense kept the therapist out of a power struggle with the client. Interpretation of the family dynamics helped the client see his role as the "sick" one in the family and mobilized his determination to fight that role, rather than fighting the therapist. With this accomplished to some degree, the client was then more open to learning behavioral coping mechanisms to help him deal with his anxiety. These skills gave him a greater feeling of mastery and his ego functions were able to strengthen. At present he attends a sheltered workshop daily and works regular hours; he is functioning much more as an equal member of his original family; he has a tentative relationship with a young woman; and his obsessional checking has diminished to where he can carry out his daily routine within a reasonable amount of time.

REFERENCES

Fensterheim, H., and Baer, J. *Stop Running Scared*, New York: Rawson Associates, 1977.
Goulding, R., and Goulding, M. *The Power is in the Patient*, San Francisco: TA Press, 1978.
Guntrip, H. *Healing the Sick Mind*, London: Unwin Books, 1964.
Jacobson, E. *Progressive Relaxation*, Chicago: University of Chicago Press, 1929.
Lazarus, A. A. *In the Mind's Eye*, New York: Rawson Associates, 1977.
Lum, L. C. The syndrome of habitual chronic hyperventilation. In O. Hill (Ed.) *Modern Trends in Psychosomatic Medicine*, Vol. 3. Boston: Butterworths, 1976.
Seligman, M. E. P. *Helplessness: On Depression, Development, and Death*. San Francisco: W. H. Freeman, 1975.
Spitz, R. Anaclitic depression. *The Psychoanalytic Study of the Child.*, Vol. II. New York: International Universities Press, 1946, pp. 313-342.

6

A Modified Behavioral Psychotherapy Approach in the Treatment of a Schizophrenic Adolescent

Mary FitzPatrick

Therapy is not a static experience, for either the patient or the therapist. The following case illustrates how changes in the theoretical orientation of the therapist can lead to a reformulation of core problems and intervention strategies. The patient is a 19-year-old girl who was in treatment with me for four-and-a-half years. Her current psychiatric diagnosis is Schizophrenia, Paranoid Type, in Remission (DSM-III 295.35). She was initially referred for treatment following an acute aggressive outburst at age 13. When treatment began, I used a standard psychotherapy approach consisting of some interpretation of symbolic material and supportive counseling regarding day-to-day problems in functioning. In the third and fourth years of treatment, I received training in behavior modification and behavioral psychotherapy which involved developing special skills, as well as the perspective of thinking in terms of a behavioral formulation for each patient, with core areas and their interactions, and planning a subsequent behavioral treatment plan. My patient's problems, as well as my treatment of these problems,

The therapy described in this chapter was carried out at the League School and the Carl Fenichel Community Services Day Treatment Centers in Brooklyn, New York could then be reformulated in behavioral terms, and dynamic factors incorporated into the second, more behavioral approach.

The patient's psychotherapy was carried out as part of a total treatment in a therapeutic day treatment center. Treatment involved a team approach consisting of therapeutic teaching, individual psychotherapy, close support and treatment for the family provided by the team social worker, and psychiatric supervision of medication.

BACKGROUND AND PRESENTING PROBLEMS

Ann was a pretty, sensitive, and outgoing 19-year-old girl who used the therapeutic help provided to her in an extraordinary manner to overcome the profound emotional problems which brought her to the attention of the school and day treatment center where she was seen for therapy.

When referred for placement in this program, Ann had not attended school for over one year. She had refused to return to her public school following an aggressive outburst. She was described by clinicians in her school as a frightened youngster who was unable to cope with the demands of a regular school program. She was immature and fearful of her own impulses and of attack by others; she used withdrawal as a coping mechanism. At her initial psychiatric interview in this setting, Ann was described as a severely obese (212 lbs., 5'3") female who cried and expressed fear of being thrown out of the program if she could not control herself. She spoke openly of her difficulties in controlling herself and about her auditory and visual hallucinations, the latter including seeing people who made threatening gestures toward her. She was oriented in all spheres. Affect was agitated and somewhat depressed. Psychiatric diagnosis on admission was Schizophrenia, Paranoid Type. Diagnosis was later changed to Schizophrenia, Residual Type and Schizophrenia in Partial Remission.

Throughout Ann's treatment, she continued to be placed on a variety of medications. At various times, trifluopenazine (Stelazine), chlorpromazine (Thorazine), fluphenazine (Prolixin), and molindone (Moban) were prescribed for the management of the psychotic disorder. Clorazepate (Tranxene) was administered as an anti-anxiety medication, and benzatropine (Cogentin) was taken to control extrapyramidal disorders, a possible side effect of the other medications.

BACKGROUND OF PSYCHIATRIC PROBLEMS

Ann's psychiatric problems began when she was 12 years old and in the seventh grade in an intermediate school. At that time an incident occurred which led to her eventual placement in the school and day treatment center for children with severe emotional problems where I conducted my therapy. Ann became agitated in her classroom and it became necessary to call the police to bring her home. She was taken for a psychiatric evaluation at a large municipal hospital where she was diagnosed as having an acute schizophrenic reaction. She was released on an outpatient basis, medication was prescribed (Stelazine, 2 mg. bid), and she was referred for group therapy. At that time, her mother reported that for the preceding year Ann had been concerned about developing a disease like a tumor, reported visual hallucinations, and expressed a desire to remain at home. Ann was followed in group therapy for one year and in individual therapy for six months following the dissolution of the group. She was described as initially suspicious and uninvolved but she eventually became a cooperative participant.

After admission to the day treatment center, Ann had one additional acute psychotic episode and was hospitalized at a nearby psychiatric hospital. Prior to this hospitalization, she became aggressive in school and overturned furniture; four staff members were required to subdue her. The following day, she appeared enraged, her hallucinations increased, and it became necessary to hospitalize her for a two-week period. At that time, it was discovered that she was not taking her medication. Once it became possible to regulate her medication, further hospitalizations were averted in spite of periods of acute anxiety.

DEVELOPMENTAL AND FAMILY HISTORY

Developmental history, as provided by Ann's mother, was normal in every way. Early fears included the dark, being lost, doctors and fires. These fears, while normal in a young child, remained with her through her teenage years and became a focus of our therapeutic intervention. Ann was hospitalized twice, once at age 10 for an eye injury, and a second time at age 12 after she was hit by a car and injured her arm.

Ann is the oldest of six children in an intact family. She was raised in an inner-city neighborhood where poverty and violent crimes are commonplace. The family has experienced multiple emotional and financial stresses. Ann's mother has a history of psychiatric illness similar to Ann's. She was hospitalized frequently while Ann was in treatment, and she was often depressed. Two of Ann's siblings attended special classes within the public school system. Another was in a program for the gifted. Ann's father was in and out of work, with the result that they would go on and off welfare. Often, because of delay in welfare payments, they were on the brink of eviction from their apartment for nonpayment of rent, or they lacked sufficient money for food.

Their perilous financial situation caused realistic stress for this family who found it difficult to plan beyond their immediate day-to-day existence. Despite these multiple problems, there was a great deal of warmth and humor within the family and they obviously loved and supported each other. This gave Ann a source of strength and support at times in her life when she was particularly upset. In addition, the family became very involved in a local church group, which served as an outside source of affiliation, support, and social activity.

TREATMENT

When Ann was first seen for treatment, a behavioral formulation was not made. She was viewed as a schizophrenic teenager who was extremely anxious about losing control and whose daily visual hallucinations resulted in confusion and anxiety regarding reality-testing.

During this period, the main issues discussed with her were the exact nature of her emotional disability; her fear of losing control, going crazy and being rehospitalized; control over anger; her day-to-day problems in getting along with parents, siblings, teachers and classmates; and ways of dealing with her many somatic complaints. The latter included stomachaches, headaches, backaches, blurred vision, seeing dots in front of her eyes, and various aches and soreness of muscles.

In spite of her multiple mental problems, Ann had many strengths which helped her to profit from all programs she entered. She was aware and sensitive to the needs of others. Even at her worst moments, she had developed a keen sense of humor which she used to gain perspective on her many problems. Ann was very direct both in looking at herself and in dealing with others. For this reason, she was very open to help from others. Prior to the advent of her psychiatric problems, Ann's life had been quite social; she therefore had developed good social skills which she could not use initially, but which she could draw on in later treatment.

During the first two and a half years of treatment, therapy was primarily supportive and tied to day-to-day functioning. The initial goal of therapy was to establish a supportive, consistent relationship with Ann, to serve as a stable adult to whom she could turn to separate reality from illusion. Although she was generally seen one to three times a week for individual sessions, with the number of sessions based on need, she was seen daily during particularly stressful periods. For example, initially it was necessary to schedule five minutes at the beginning of the day following her arrival after taking public transportation (bus) to the school. The trip was harrowing for her. The bus was crowded and she became frightened over what she would do to others or what they would do to her. Often, she would experience others turning into manikins and waving their arms at her. She would turn to me for assurance that this could not really happen. I would affirm her judgment and we would discuss what she could do to ignore others and tell herself that what she saw was not real. At the same time, she continued to have visual hallucinations at home. As we explored her feelings at such times, she expressed anger at her siblings, who teased her and engaged her in frequent physical fights. Her hallucinations were tied to experiences where she felt anxious, angry, or in danger of losing control. When her medication was regulated, the hallucinations stopped.

Much of our time together was devoted to solving real life problems, such as how to avoid fights with her siblings and how to avoid people who made her feel anxious, as well as to developing coping strategies to use when she became upset. Ann was extremely dependent on and identified with her mother. A goal of therapy was to help foster a sense of separateness and a realization that Ann and her mother had different needs and ideas, as well as different emotional problems.

In her therapeutic classroom, there was ample time to discuss experiences, feelings, tasks, and assignments in detail. All activities were broken down into simple steps which could be readily understood and accomplished. In this milieu, Ann learned to think in a logical, detailed manner. This cognitive skill was later used in the behavioral intervention.

Socially, at this time, Ann made no friends outside of her family and class. She rarely left her house once she arrived home and then only in the presence of a family member. She was afraid to be alone and slept on the living room couch rather than in her bedroom. In her day program, however, gradual changes were apparent over a two-year period. Ann entered into the daily program and became a cooperative member of her class. Following her hospitalization, she religiously took her medication and became quite active in seeking help when she became upset. In therapy, she actively monitored her emotional state and would report periods of stress so that her medication could be increased. At this time, Ann's fear of rehospitalization was so great that she became extremely vigilant. She felt that control was possible only if she remained in touch with adults who could help her to monitor her daily state. For example, during vacations, no matter how short, Ann remained in touch with me, often coming to the Center to report on how she felt. A long-term goal of treatment at that time was gradually to help her to feel more in control of herself. During this period, Ann's family was informed of all treatment plans. They were given ongoing help in managing Ann's behavior at home and in understanding her emotional needs and problems.

During the final two years of treatment, I formulated Ann's problems in a different way. Until this time, much of the treatment had involved changing specific obvious behaviors as they manifested themselves, and presenting myself as a consistent, supportive adult whom Ann could always turn to. The treatment program helped Ann to relax while in the program, to begin to participate and learn while in school, and to bring her psychotic symptoms under control through the consistent use of appropriate medication. However, other problem areas remained unchanged. At home, she remained isolated. Her numerous fears kept her at home, dependent on family members whom she could not leave even at night, as she was afraid to sleep alone. She had a persistent fear of loss of control and rehospitalization.

A behavioral approach appeared to be the most effective treatment model to intervene in the still remaining areas of chronic tension and phobias and to enhance feelings of self-control. I had begun training in behavioral psychotherapy and therefore had a new perspective at my disposal. The case was reformulated in the manner designated by the behavioral psychotherapy approach and an integrated treatment plan emerged. During this second stage of treatment, behavioral data were obtained and grouped into the broad categories described by Fensterheim (Chapter 3) in the following manner:

General Tension

Ann described herself as "having anxiety" much of the day. Her heart would pound, at times she would have trouble breathing, her head felt funny, her skin would crawl, and she complained of tension in her neck, arms and legs. She associated these feelings with seeing and hearing things. Ann had other somatic complaints, including headaches, dry mouth, vision problems where she would see dots in the visual field, and mild stomach upset. She would experience some type of unpleasant bodily sensation daily. Her somatic complaints were due to multiple factors, including tension, side effects of medications, and manifestations of the psychotic process. It was important during the course of therapy to teach Ann to differentiate between probable causes of symptoms and to then take appropriate action to alleviate the symptoms (i.e., changing medication, using relaxation procedures).

Phobias

Ann had a number of fears. We compiled the following list of situations which she found very upsetting.

1) Getting attacked
2) Death
3) Her house
4) Going outside
5) The dark
6) Closets
7) Dark rooms or halls
8) Her room
9) President on TV
10) War and nuclear power on TV
11) Brother jumping out at her
12) Being alone
13) Getting sick again
14) Bridges
15) Doctors
16) Mean people
17) Killing insects
18) Dead animals
19) TV violence
20) Violence in the streets
21) Men in the streets

Ann's overwhelming fear was of losing control—of going crazy and being sent back to the hospital or of becoming angry and injuring someone. Maintaining control and avoiding aversive stimuli absorbed most of her attention.

Obsessions

While Ann was preoccupied with thoughts of losing control or being harmed, it was my hypothesis that her thoughts were a result of her fears. Her core problems appeared to be related to phobic avoidance, not obsessive thoughts.

Assertion

Again, Ann's problems in this area seemed closely tied to her fear of loss of control. She withdrew from situations to avoid this. However, at other times, when she felt calm and at ease, she demonstrated the ability to express feelings, communicate her needs, and make requests.

Habits

Ann's emotional problems led to behavioral deficits. She could not maintain concentration long enough to develop academic skills commensurate with potential. Likewise, she did not have appropriate functional skills (i.e., cooking, shopping, etc.). However, again it was hypothesized that her skills would improve once she became less phobic. It was essential to assess if deficits were the result of an inhibitory process rather than a true skills deficit.

BEHAVIORAL FORMULATION

The behavioral formulation drawn up (see Figure 1) contains two major components: a psychotic component and a neurotic one. The psychotic component takes into consideration the schizophrenic condition and its direct consequences. These latter include her difficulties in concentration and other thought disorders, and also her bizarre thoughts, hallucinations, and extreme mood swings. It was this component that was the target for the first stage of treatment. The schizophrenia was brought somewhat under control through medication and a full-time, structured program. The educational program helped somewhat to improve her concentration and her ability to think in a logical and problem-solving manner. Emphasis could now be placed on the neurotic component.

The core of the neurotic component was her fear of loss of control, which was experienced as a fear of becoming angry or of "going crazy." Any sign of disturbance elicited this fear and led to series of mainly

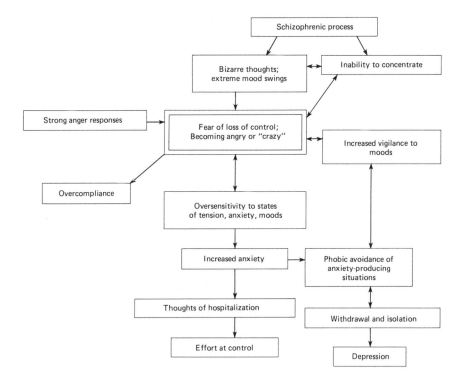

Figure 1. Behavioral formulation showing the process fueling the fear of loss of control, the core of the neurotic organization.

inadequate coping behaviors. One of these involved attempts to withdraw from the situation, which in turn led to isolation and to depression. Another set of coping behaviors led to her seeking help from adults and to a general overcompliance in her social interactions in school. Both of these avoidance patterns, although making her more comfortable for the moment, tended to maintain the core fear of losing control.

Three major fueling sources for this core phobia were also formulated. One source was the consequences of her schizophrenia. The peculiar sensations and the extreme mood swings stemming from this condition did signal a real threat of the possible loss of control. Her frequent and strong anger responses, especially in the home situations, formed the second fueling source. Finally, the secondary anxiety about feeling disturbed, her state of hypervigilance, caused her to pay much attention to even the smallest signs of disturbance and so to reinforce them. The entire phobic area was made worse by her inability to differentiate among the different feelings—her inability to distinguish between the schizophrenic symptoms which posed a true threat and the neurotic feelings which could be brought under a more deliberate control.

One further point may be noted concerning the behavioral formulation. Her oversensitivity to disturbed feelings, despite the fact that it helped to maintain the core phobia, did have a positive consequence. It did lead to fear of rehospitalization, which led to greater efforts to achieve control in order to prevent this from happening. This was an important motive for her cooperation with the treatment program.

TREATMENT PLAN

The main target behavior chosen from the behavioral formulation was the core fear of loss of control. It was believed that if this could be reduced, many of the other elements of the neurotic organization would change and more adaptive behaviors would replace them.

One extremely important step to control this core fear was to teach her to differentiate different kinds of disturbances. If she could learn to recognize the schizophrenia-derived disturbances, she could take the appropriate actions of consulting with her psychiatrist to have her medication adjusted. If she could learn to recognize the neurotic disturbances, she could realize that they posed no real threat to her control and could use adaptive coping behaviors to counter their effects.

Part of the treatment program, therefore, had to be to teach her adaptive coping methods. It also had to be aimed at more directly reducing the fear of loss of control, so that she could control her need to avoid anxiety-provoking situations and so eventually rid herself of the many fears that led to her confined life situation. Finally, she had to be taught to use positive behaviors such as social skills, many of which appeared to be in her behavioral repertoire but which she had little opportunity to use. Specific areas of focus were to include training in anxiety management through a combination of relaxation and cognitive techniques, desensitization to anxiety-provoking situations and feelings, and practice in assertion and social skills. It was predicated that the outcome of such a program, combined with the proper management of medication to control the psychotic manifestations, would bring about an adaptive change of her entire life-style.

A first step was to help Ann learn ways to decrease her level of anxiety. This would in turn reduce her fear of loss of control, reduce the number of avoidance responses, and ultimately free her to invest energy in more productive and satisfying activities.

When we began, Ann's most effective way of dealing with anxiety was to seek help from a supportive adult. While this action helped to reduce the effects of the psychotic component, it reinforced the neurotic component. While this was a type of avoidance response, the adult also would serve as a source of external control while she reoriented herself. It was explained to Ann that we would be working on ways that she could learn to calm herself, ways that she would be able to use when she became upset at home and could not receive the support she had come to rely on in her program, where staff were always available.

To accomplish this, it was necessary to begin a gradual sorting out of her different anxiety states, to separate psychotic states from nonpsychotic anxiety reactions. Ann had to learn that the experience of anxiety, no matter how severe, did not necessarily result in the advent of a psychotic process. She gradually became able to label different states, to say when she was "feeling off" or "having anxiety" or "feeling depressed." At times she would experience feelings of dissociation, and the degree and speed with which she could reorient herself helped us to decide whether to discuss a need for more or different medication or to simply work on reducing her anxiety level. Initially, the act of discussing a feeling state increased her level of anxiety and she would then try to avoid the topic. As a result, it took months to discuss her feelings in detail.

As Ann became more aware of subtleties in feeling states, it was possible to alter and reduce her fear of "going crazy." A first step was for her to label her feeling states, and to differentiate feelings, moods and tension states. It was essential that she not label all states as "crazy." Rather, Ann gradually came to learn that it is normal to experience uncomfortable and intense feelings, both positive and negative. She learned to separate feelings of anger, depression, and anxiety from experiences that could indeed be labeled as psychotic or crazy. As Ann learned to identify her internal states, she became more comfortable expressing them; by doing so, she learned that expression did not necessarily lead to escalation into psychosis.

As she gained a cognitive understanding of herself, it became possible to explore hypothetical situations. Thought, deed, and feelings were no longer indistinguishable for her. Prior to this, Ann feared that if she discussed her fears, they would occur. Now, she was able to think about feared situations, to follow events to their logical conclusions, and to evaluate the results in thought rather than in action. For example, as we explored what it meant to her to "go crazy," in contrast to what actually happened, it became apparent that Ann's psychotic experiences were actually of short duration. The two breakdowns which she had were acute and were rather quickly controlled by medication. Her daily periods of dissociation were also short and she could refocus herself quickly, generally by speaking with another person about how she was feeling. In contrast, the more neurotic processes—her fear of loss of control, efforts to avoid anxiety and anger-producing situations, and resultant coping behaviors, pervaded her thoughts and actions. As she became better able to understand the difference between the schizophrenic symptoms and the neurotic responses, she understood that she could learn to bring the latter under control through directly working to change her behavior and her reactions when in threatening situations. This awareness gave Ann the necessary motivation and courage to try new and frightening experiences and to tolerate the level of anxiety which they produced.

In the course of our therapy, Ann became able to remember details of her hospitalization. This period had been a very painful one for her which in the past she could not speak about as she would become too upset and anxious to continue. She now was able to describe her fear and anger over specific events, including her anger at me for my role in the process. Once she began to express her thoughts and feelings, Ann could then evaluate what had occurred without being overwhelmed by her anxiety. She began to see the need for hospitalization at that time. Ultimately, we could discuss the worst possible event that could happen to her: rehospitalization at the same hospital. She could articulate that if this occurred, she would stay for a few weeks, reevaluate her medication, return home, and go back to school. Since our program was located within sight of the building where she had been, she could discuss her fears while looking at the hospital, and she was able to walk by it each day on her way to the program.

As Ann became able to separate a more psychotic process (when she felt she was losing contact with reality) from an anxiety attack (where there were more fear and somatic responses) and to learn that both states could exist simultaneously, we worked on helping her to learn to relax and/or to seek medical help to control the psychotic manifestations or extreme levels of anxiety.

At first, Ann strongly resisted speaking to the staff psychiatrist. She was afraid that if she spoke to him in a manner that was in any way different or "crazy," he would hospitalize her. This association stemmed from a reality experience of being hospitalized by this same staff psychiatrist while in a psychotic state. It was necessary, through lengthy discussions, to articulate her exact behaviors when hospitalized and to compare them to her current behaviors in an effort to further differentiate and label feeling states and behaviors. Next, a series of graded appointments was set up to give Ann the direct experience of talking to the psychiatrist without being hospitalized. She learned to observe her physical and emotional states, to verbalize them to another person, and to form questions about side effects, dosage, and medication changes. At the initial meetings, Ann and I discussed what we wanted said and she sat in the room while I spoke for her (prior to our interviews, the course of the conversation was discussed with the psychiatrist). Next, Ann spoke while I sat in the room. Ultimately, after months of careful behavior rehearsal, Ann was able to see the psychiatrist alone and then report back to me. It was essential that she learn this skill for a number of reasons. Because of the nature of her emotional illness, Ann's moods could shift dramatically and it was quite probable that she would need to take medication on and off throughout her life. While she was in such a supportive, structured environment, it was possible to build the skills she would need to advocate for herself; at no other time in her life would it be possible to engineer such a careful rehearsal. Also, it was essential to break the association she held of seeing physicians only when she needed hospitalization. Gradually, through this educative experience, she was able to learn that it was possible to recognize changes in mood and level of anxiety and to seek a medication change to ward off a possible breakdown. Gradually, Ann learned to recognize changes at earlier points and to seek help more and more in advance. At one point, Ann began to manifest the symptoms which had put her in the hospital before—inability to control aggressive impulses, suspiciousness, feelings of dissociation, and extreme anxiety. However, this time, by seeking help at an earlier point, she was able to receive a high enough dosage of medication to sustain her through this difficult period without hospitalization.

A second goal was to teach Ann to relax when anxious. Initially, a standard muscle relaxation procedure (Goldfried and Davidson, 1976) was taught to her. During the training period, Ann reported that when she began to feel relaxed, she experienced her body differently and had intrusive thoughts. It seemed that for Ann, relaxation was not totally positive. For her to maintain control over psychotic thought processes, it was necessary for her to remain somewhat vigilant; if she became too relaxed, this was not possible. Our goal than became a modified one of teaching her to relax enough to gain relief but not enough to become psychotic. Fishman and Lubetkin (1980) report similar experiences with clients who have pan-anxiety mediated by a fear of losing control, stating that relaxation techniques which focus attention on the body should be replaced with distraction and externalization methods.We finally developed a very modified, highly personal relaxation procedure using breathing and imagery which she found especially helpful at home.

Ann was taught to attend to her breathing, to try to breathe slowly and to breathe from her belly. When upset, she would imagine a pleasant scene and concentrate on her breathing. In addition, she would repeat to herself "Mary wouldn't like it if I ————————." In this manner, she brought me into the procedure. This act seemed to provide a bridge between external and internal control. In addition, as Ann was quite religious, she also began to read the Bible to calm herself.

Throughout therapy, efforts were made to teach Ann to record her levels of anxiety at home or to keep a record of anxiety-producing or anger-producing situations, complete with her feeling states and responses. This was largely unsuccessful. Only in school, where plans could be outlined in sequential steps by staff members, were any records kept.

As Ann's treatment became more behavioral in orientation, this approach was extended to her classroom to help her to overcome her numerous fears which kept her homebound and with few friends. In this way, skills which we worked on in therapy could be shaped and reinforced on a daily basis. In this approach, the focus was geared toward altering the neurotic component illustrated in the behavioral formulation by decreasing her phobic avoidance of anxiety-producing situations. Once this could be accomplished, it was expected that she would become less withdrawn and isolated, and consequently, less depressed. Success in this area would affirm a sense of increased control and thus affect the core of the neurotic component.

The two main target areas approached in the classroom involved efforts to overcome phobias by helping her to sleep alone in her bedroom at night and to leave her house. One important effect of her fears was to increase Ann's dependence on her parents. By helping her to separate from them, an important secondary effect was to facilitate emotional growth in a more age-appropriate direction toward expanded peer contact and independence. The success of this effort was demonstrated by Ann's eventual expressed wish at 19 to leave home and find her own apartment or live with members of her church group. Both target areas—sleeping alone and leaving the house—took well over one year to accomplish.

To help Ann learn to stay alone in her room, a check system was set up to reinforce reaching a daily goal which both Ann and her teacher planned. Ann was involved in setting up a detailed hierarchy with a time limit in which to accomplish each step. Each day her progress was reviewed by her teachers; in the process, she received an enormous amount of support and attention for her efforts. As part of an earlier classroom program, Ann had been taught the steps in problem solution as well as the verbal skills necessary to conceptualize a problem and its solution. As her therapist, I consulted with her teachers on at least a weekly basis at first, and later every two to three weeks. Ann knew that we were working together and this gave her program a continuity for her. The checks that she earned could be turned in for a reward, first on a weekly basis, then every 5, 10, and 15 days until she was able to wait one month for her reward. Rewards were generally social and included activities such as taking a walk with a favorite teacher or having lunch with me. Every Monday, the plan was revised with smaller steps added if necessary. The hierarchy essentially consisted of:

Staying close to her room
Walk in once a day
Walk in twice a day
Go in the room during the day and spend time in a relaxing activity such as drawing
Increase time spent in the room (here she used relaxation procedures and cognitive restructuring to manage anxiety)
Spend time in the room during the day with the lights off
Sit in the room at night with the lights on but continue to sleep in the living room
Try to spend one entire night, then two successive nights, then five successive nights in the room

After approximately a nine-month period, Ann was able to sleep by herself. The secondary gains of this accomplishment were extremely important. By becoming able to go to her room, she no longer was as dependent on family members to allay her anxiety. Because she was no longer in the constant presence of her siblings, she fought less and had less occasion to worry about losing her temper. When she did become excessively angry, Ann had the option of going to her room, thus gaining a sense of increased control over the situation. This was especially important for her because when she became angry at home, she frequently had impulses to pick up a knife or to throw objects. This frightened her very much, as she felt that she might injure herself or another. Being able to escape from the situation that produced these feelings was a great source of relief for her. Also, at this time, Ann was placed on a new medication, Moban, which relieved her anxiety and helped her to sleep at night. She found the experience of mastery and the social praise such powerful reinforcers that she frequently forgot to collect her rewards.

A second area which she also chose involved going outside, first with family members and then by herself. Although the active intervention program lasted approximately 18 months, the problem had been a long-standing one which coincided with her first breakdown. Learning to tolerate the anxiety which occurred when she tried to leave her house allowed her to begin to develop a social life. It then became apparent that Ann was very adept socially. She had a good sense of humor, warmth, and a sensitivity to others which made her popular with both peers and adults. As she began going out, Ann became more concerned about her looks. She lost a great deal of weight and, although still quite heavy, she began to dress in an attractive manner and became very popular with men. After years of withdrawal, Ann handled the intricacies of dating with remarkable skill. Because Ann was so motivated to become more social, she did not need to receive any kind of check or reward for achieving the steps in the hierarchy which she and her teacher created:

Staying directly outside her house with a family member

Going to a phone booth a block away with a family member

Going for a walk in the neighborhood with a friend

Going for a walk near the school with another student (later this was changed to going to a store by herself)

Going to a point outside of the immediate neighborhood with a friend or relative

Going on class trips and traveling home by herself

Going on a weekend trip with her church group with no family members present

As Ann began to travel, fears emerged which we had not known about before, including a fear of going over bridges and being in subway tunnels. By this time, however, Ann had developed a system to relax while anxious, and if this did not work, she had developed the realization that her anxiety attacks, though very painful and frightening, would pass and would not result in her becoming psychotic. This was in part a result of the more detailed relabeling of her feeling states which she had learned before.

At this time, Ann became very active in a church group whose members were available to work with her, travel with her, and offer emotional support. As Ann became more involved in activities outside of her home, she became less preoccupied with her internal states and more focused on events outside of herself. She learned to distract herself from an uncomfortable inner state by concentrating on something happening outside of herself.

Initially, Ann assumed that remaining with her family at all times would provide a structure in case she became psychotic. When she spent her first weekend away from home with a church group, we carefully planned how she would act, what she would say and do if she became upset, and what learned coping skills she could use if she got into trouble. As might be expected, Ann feared that she would act in a manner that others would label as unusual. It was necessary to explore in detail how she appeared to others, how others might interpret her behaviors, and to rehearse in advance what she could say or do if she became upset. The success of this weekend tremendously increased her confidence and motivated her to begin to go out on weekends. As she learned to travel independently around the city, Ann was able to get a part-time job and to earn money. Becoming a member of the work force again changed her self-concept and increased her motivation to leave home.

In a recent interview, Ann was given the Fear Survey Schedule (Wolpe and Lazarus, 1966). Out of 78 categories, she indicated that the following four continue to cause her a great deal of fear:

Dead people
Prospect of a surgical operation
Darkness
Doctors

This was a considerable reduction from the list compiled one and a half years earlier when her phobias were first being assessed.

Interestingly enough, one month after completing this form, Ann became ill from the heat on the subway, an ambulance was called, and she was taken to the emergency room of a nearby hospital by herself. In spite of her stated fear of doctors, her reported level of anxiety was well within normal limits. She correctly interpreted that she was not seriously ill, that no one would try to hospitalize her for psychiatric reasons, and that she would be helped. This experience was a very positive one for her as it represented to her that what she stated as a current fear was not as strong as she actually believed.

On the Assertion Training Questionnaire (see p. 49), Ann reported having no problems. During her last year in treatment, Ann had successfully attended a city work training program where she had been given an award for outstanding achievement. Her evaluations by her employers were excellent. Ann had made numerous friends. She related well to peers and authority figures with warmth and directness. As she gained confidence, her rich sense of humor and sensitivity to others emerged, qualities which made her extremely popular.

As her life experiences broadened, Ann began to discuss a number of normal, age-appropriate topics in therapy, including how to get along with peers and authority figures at work, as well as dating. She had suddenly become quite popular and was beginning to be asked out on dates with increasing frequency. At this point, it became evident that the earlier hypothesis made about her lack of problems in assertion and social skills was indeed accurate. Once Ann moved out into the world, it became apparent that she related to people very well and simply needed an opportunity to discuss her experiences with a supportive adult.

In spite of improvements in other areas, Ann's level of anxiety remained high. On the Anxiety Checklist (Beck, 1978), she reported experiencing the following symptoms during the past week at a (2) moderate to (3) severe level:

Level*	Symptom	Frequency†
3	Like I'm smothering (especially on subways)	1
2	Dizzy, lightheaded or faint	1
2	Frightened	2
2	Heart pounding or racing	1
2	Strange feelings of unreality	2
2	Difficulty breathing	1 (only on trains)
2	Shaking	3
2	Alarmed	1 (on street or in her bedroom only)

* 1 = mild; 2 = moderate; 3 = severe.
† 1 = sometimes; 2 = most of the time; 3 = all or almost all of the time

She reported feeling the following symptoms which she labeled as mildly unpleasant (1):

Level	Symptom	Frequency
1	Nervous	1
1	Jittery	1
1	Sweating (not due to heat)	2
1	Nausea or vomiting	1
1	Anxious (hyperactive)	3 (at home only)
1	Numbness or tingling hands	1
1	Jumpy	2

Although Ann's anxiety level remained relatively high, it did not interfere with her vocational and social growth. In her therapy sessions, we reviewed the relaxation techniques, went over hierarchies, anticipated possible problems, and discussed in detail new ways that she could develop to adapt socially. Referring back to the behavioral formulation posited earlier in this paper, by directly working to reduce her fear of loss of control, we were able to work on helping her to stop the phobic avoidance of anxiety-producing situations which she felt would make her become angry or "crazy." Once Ann learned to tolerate anxiety, she could begin to develop new social skills as a result of her expanded contacts and experiences. Ultimately, she became able to discuss in detail her experiences of becoming psychotic and to learn that speaking about these experiences and the feelings which this produced did not have a catastrophic result but, rather, led to mastery.

As Ann's social contacts and range of experiences increased, her extreme anger responses diminished. This was due, in great part, to her being away from home much of the time. We discovered that Ann became most angry with family members. She was more detached and objective in her dealings with others. In fact, her assertive skills with others were quite good.

Because she was extremely angry less often, and because she had learned to articulate what made her angry, an angry response no longer led to a fear of loss of control with the resultant phobic avoidance. When Ann became very angry at a family member, she was now able to leave her house and cool off, go to her room, or state what she felt. Having so many options made her feel less trapped and at the mercy of her aggressive impulses. She was still angry, but she could now act to prevent hurting herself or others. In addition, she began to plan an independent life when, in the near future, she would get a full-time job. This plan was accepted by her parents, who supported her efforts at independence.

During Ann's last year in the program, her teachers no longer continued the behavioral program, but instead focused on teaching her practical skills such as banking. She no longer needed the reinforcement, as her real-life experiences had become very reinforcing to her and motivated her to continuously broaden her range of experiences. This achievement was possible in part because her program over the years had been designed to insure a high probability of success. Both in her therapy sessions and in her classes, tasks were broken down into small steps which she could accomplish. She was placed in a highly reinforcing environment for seven hours a day, five days a week. As she became more capable, her program was gradually extended to include a broader work training program. The integration of therapy with her educational and vocational program was vital for the success which we saw because of the opportunity it provided for continuous reinforcement coupled with direct skill building. Without the opportunity to practice each day, she would not have steadily improved. In addition, the support given to Ann's family helped them to participate in the total therapeutic process and to evolve shared goals for Ann at home and in her center.

SUMMARY

The reformulation of Ann's core problem led to a different handling of her treatment. Although a schizophrenic process was acknowledged and appropriate medication prescribed, emphasis was given to working on the more neurotic aspects of her problems and to teaching her techniques to control and regulate her feelings and anxiety levels. This approach necessitated looking beyond her obvious diagnostic label of paranoid schizophrenia with all its implications to the more subtle but pervasive problems which were in reality limiting her growth.

As Ann became more aware of the differences between anxiety states and a psychotic process, she became able to respond differently under different conditions. She became able to seek medication changes to avoid a psychotic episode. This ability led to a sense of greater control over that area of her life that was of greatest concern to her—her stated fear of "going crazy" and being hospitalized.

Ann gradually learned to label when she felt anxious and to tolerate high levels of anxiety while she forced herself to try new experiences such as taking trips or staying outside of her house for increasingly longer periods of time. She no longer avoided anxiety-producing situations and so was no longer withdrawn. Her expanding circle of social contacts increased her self-esteem and sense of competence.

A second chain of behaviors stemming from her fear of loss of control was to become oversensitive to inner physical and mood changes, and to attempt to control herself only as an option to a fear of hospitalization. Once Ann could realistically imagine what it would mean to be hospitalized, the image lost its emotional charge and she began to deal with anxiety through more neutral cognitive or relaxation techniques (including breathing and imagery).

The range of Ann's anger responses became modified to include normal levels of appropriate anger. She learned to set up controls or to arrange charged situations so she would not totally lose her temper.

To refer back to the behavioral formulation, the focus on self-regulation and self-control appeared to be a good choice. As Ann gained control over herself and became better able to differentiate between emotional states, the amount of phobic avoidance, both of external situations and of internal states, diminished greatly. She became increasingly more involved in outside activities which absorbed more of her attention and energy.

If in the future Ann should experience another acute psychotic episode, she will be in a different position to cope with this possibility. She could seek help and rely on internal methods of control. Hopefully, as a result of her treatment, such a possibility will be averted by early intervention. It is clear, however, that Ann has developed skills which will continue to lead to further personal, social and vocational growth.

In working with patients who, like Ann, present a mixed diagnostic picture, it is essential for the therapist to realize that psychotic and neurotic processes can coexist and dynamically interact to produce a complex clinical picture. To focus on one aspect of this complex process limits the development of a comprehensive treatment plan. More important, it results in a disservice to the patient, who is viewed in a skewed, limited manner. In the case presented here, the patient also possessed a number of strengths which emerged in the course of treatment and which were considered in forming the ongoing treatment plan. By simultaneously considering the psychotic, neurotic, and developmentally normal aspects of her personality, a treatment plan could be designed to enhance growth as well as symptom reduction.

REFERENCES

Beck, A. *Anxiety Checklist.* Philadelphia: Center for Cognitive Therapy, 1978.
Fishman, S., and Lubetkin, B. Maintenance and generalization of individual behavior therapy programs: Clinical observations. In R. Karoly and J. Steffens (Eds.) *Improving the Long-Term Effect of Psychotherapy.* New York: Gardner Press, 1980.
Goldfried, M., and Davidson, G. *Clinical Behavior Therapy.* New York: Holt, Rinehart and Winston, 1976.
Wolpe, J., and Lazarus, A. A. *Behavior Therapy Techniques.* London: Pergamon, 1966.

7

A Case of Agoraphobia
with Complications

Helene Sands

The behavioral psychotherapist is often faced with complex and multiple problems during the course of treatment. Even when the patient presents with an apparently straightforward symptom, the complexities surrounding it may make direct treatment of that symptom impossible. During the course of treatment, further complications may emerge from the patient's life situation. These complications too may necessitate the diversion of treatment from the main target behaviors. Therefore, treatment strategies must be flexible, and the therapist may have to call upon a wide variety of therapeutic techniques.

The treatment of Mrs. C. illustrates just this point. Her chief presenting complaint was a longstanding agoraphobia, a condition for which there is a standard behavioral treatment. However, the complexities surrounding the symptom made it impossible to conduct this treatment. Further, the complications arising from the patient's life situation during the treatment required immediate and direct interventions. As a result, several approaches, including social casework management, counseling, and psychodynamic considerations, were carried out, all within a behavioral psychotherapy framework.

CHIEF COMPLAINT/PRESENTING PROBLEM

Mrs. C. was a 62-year-old divorced Caucasian woman. Her major complaint involved a 40-year history of phobias and panic attacks. She described the symptoms typical of agoraphobia: fear of large expanses, as well as the fear of confined situations from which she could not easily escape, and travel phobias manifested as a fear of riding in trains, buses, and elevators. Also present were social fears, including fear of conversing with somebody face to face or unexpectedly encountering an acquaintance on the street; the patient experienced such situations as confining and felt that she would be unable to escape if she became panicky.

The core fear was of the panic attacks. The main symptoms of these were "hot flushes, pounding heart and rubbery knees." She was terrified of "losing control and screaming and fainting." When seized with a panic, Mrs. C. would bend over and hold her stomach in order to "hold myself together" and keep from fainting. But these actions, in turn, led to the fear that people would think she was acting strangely. Thus, her main coping method was avoidance. She was constantly vigilant for escape routes in case she met anyone on the street. She avoided all situations where she might become trapped. Hence, she had been unable to work for over 10 years and had led a severely constricted social life.

HISTORY OF CHIEF COMPLAINT

The patient's memory of phobias went back to primary school. She recalled an incident where she had to recite a memorized piece in front of her class, her parents and the principal. She panicked, was unable to perform, and felt stupid and humiliated. Her classmates teased her about this incident and also poked fun at her clothes and her hair (which had been cut by her mother).

At age 15, in high school, the patient had a number of panic attacks associated with being called on in class. She recalled one particular incident when she actually screamed and fainted. She suffered a "nervous breakdown" at that time and stayed in bed for three weeks. She described feelings of depersonalization during that period.

Life History

Mrs. C. was born and raised in a middle-class family in a small eastern city. She characterized her mother as a strict, harsh, and depriving woman who denigrated her and everyone else in the family, including her father. The patient felt helpless, frightened, and victimized by her mother. Her sisters, she believed, were better able to deal with her mother than she was; her brothers were not subject to quite the same harshness and so did not have the problem.

Mrs. C. described her father as a kind man who was subject to outbursts of temper. Under pressure from her mother to discipline the children, he would beat the patient with a leather belt. She never knew what she had done wrong. Although she reported being able to get along better with her father than with her mother, she nonetheless feared him and was not able to discuss her problems with him.

One of Mrs. C.'s sisters, whom she referred to as the "darling of the family," was at one time hospitalized for anorexia nervosa. Another sister had an unspecified behavior problem of sufficient magnitude to require that she withdraw from high school.

Mrs. C.'s phobic history started in primary school when she was about 10 years old. She would feel "trapped" when she was called on in class. In her senior year in high school, she had increased numbers of panic attacks associated with being called on. Nonetheless, she completed a four-year program in art school. She excelled in it and believed that she thus "showed" her mother that she could be successful.

Shortly after graduation, when she was about 20 years old, the patient experienced her first panic attack in the subway. She was "sitting opposite a man who was staring at her and she became panicky and frightened that she would lose control, scream, and faint, and that people would see that she was not "acting right." Later she experienced the same feelings while riding in a bus. The panic subsequently generalized to all moving vehicles, confined spaces, large open spaces, and to any situation in which she felt physically or psychologically confined, including such experiences as unexpectedly meeting an acquaintance and having to interact while standing or walking.

After she graduated from art school, the patient had great difficulty in holding a job. She would respond to an employer's instructions with panic and disorganization. Attempting to avoid these problems, the patient turned to freelance art work. However, here too she found it difficult to function. The need to travel to work, to use elevators, and to talk to clients gave rise to severe anxiety reactions.

The patient married when she was 22 years old. She described her marriage as a very bad one; her husband was depriving and abusive both to her and to their daughter. The marriage ended in divorce, and the patient was left in sole charge of raising her daughter. The daughter eventually became a drug addict, which Mrs. C. attributed to problems in the home caused by Mrs. C.'s anorexic sister, who lived with her. Mrs. C. characterized her sister as fiercely religious, reclusive, and paranoid.

Because her daughter was a drug addict, Mrs. C. gained legal custody of her daughter's child when the child was three years old. At the time the patient sought therapy, the child was 13 and had had so many problems that for a time she had been placed in a residential treatment facility. It was the child's problems and their effect on her that caused Mrs. C. to seek further help at this time.

Mrs. C. was extremely anxious. She felt overwhelmed and helpless to cope with the mounting problems in managing her grandchild and in dealing with other reality problems. She felt trapped by her phobias; they made it impossible for her to work and be independent and forced her to accept public assistance, which she found humiliating.

During her early thirties the patient had sought treatment for her phobias and for a brief time had received psychoanalytically oriented therapy. Later she periodically sought help at times of crisis and was treated with crisis intervention counseling and pharmacotherapy (Librium, 10 mg., prn.). She was strongly opposed to any kind of medication and took it sparingly and only when she had to travel. She did believe the medication had helped her to use buses. She could now travel without medication, provided the bus was not crowded and she could be close to the door.

MENTAL STATUS

The patient was a trimly dressed woman, slight in stature, with a thin, drawn, sad-looking face. She spoke freely and articulately with no indication of any thought disorder. Her mood was anxious and somewhat depressed; affect was constricted but appropriate. The patient was tearful when she talked about her past and her current problems with her family. She had a self-deprecating, apologetic manner and spoke tentatively about herself. She denied any current suicidal ideation, although she had thought about suicide in the past.

DIAGNOSIS

The DSM III diagnosis was: Agoraphobia with Panic Attacks (300.21) and Social Phobia (300.23) on Axis I; Avoidant Personality Disorder (301.82) on Axis II.

It should be noted that because of her prior lack of response to varied treatments and because of her current state of disorganization, one of the diagnoses suggested in Mrs. C.'s case record was Borderline Personality.

The most obvious core of Mrs. C.'s problem was her agoraphobia. This led to avoidance behavior which influenced her entire life-style. Beyond this, the avoidance-escape pattern of coping would serve to maintain and to perpetuate the agoraphobia. However, the intial examination revealed that the condition was not quite that simple.

Two other features were thought to be of major importance: reality problems and a deficit of self-control behaviors. The reality problems, such as those centering around the patient's disturbed granddaughter, presented situations with which the patient was unable to cope. This raised her general level of disturbance, aggravated her agoraphobia, increased her feelings of helplessness, and diminished her self-control behaviors. The deficit in self-control behaviors appeared to be of long duration and was most evident in Mrs. C.'s inability to control her anxieties, her disturbing thoughts, and her avoidance behaviors even when her livelihood was at stake. Beyond these, problems in assertion (as shown by her inability to stand up for herself with her family) were also evident. These problems also fed into her feelings of helplessness, which in turn helped to fuel the entire disturbed organization. These features are presented schematically in Figure 1.

In view of this formulation, it was believed that the usual treatment plan for agoraphobia could not be used. This treatment utilizes *in vivo* desensitization; the patient must enter and stay in panic-evoking situations. However, it was formulated that Mrs. C.'s self-control abilities were far too low to allow her to do this and that failure during the early part of treatment would markedly increase her feelings of helplessness. Further, her ability even to attempt this procedure would wax and wane according to her general level of disturbance, as it fluctuated in response to her reality problems. This would further increase her sense of helplessness.

Increasing her self-control skills and assertive behaviors and teaching her to cope with reality problems were therefore selected as the initial targets of therapy. It was hoped that some success in these areas would lower the patient's helplessness and increase her self-confidence. The long-term target remained, of course, the agoraphobia.

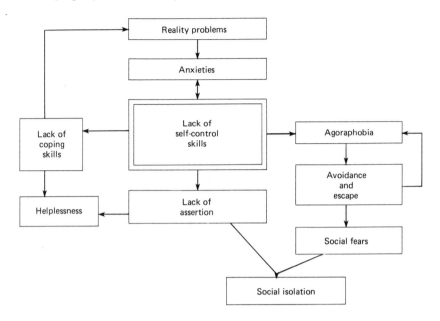

Figure 1. Initial behavioral formulation with lack of self-control skills as core and as maintaining other disturbances.

INITIAL TREATMENT

The first step in actual treatment was to teach Mrs. C. the progressive relaxation exercises. These were used as much for the purpose of training her in self-control skills as for reducing anxiety. It was hoped that through these exercises she would gain both the skill and the confidence necessary for eventual *in vivo* flooding for the treatment of the agoraphobia.

The first results of this approach were encouraging. The patient did achieve good tension reduction during the treatment session, and she agreed to practice the relaxation method at home and in life situations. However, a reality problem soon emerged to disrupt this program.

Mrs. C. reported that her grandchild was defiant, rebellious, and untruthful, and that she was unable to control or to cope with her. She feared that the child would repeat her own daughter's disturbed history, which had led to drug addiction. The patient was very frustrated and angry with the child for her disobedience. She also felt a helplessness that recalled trauma from her own childhood. The intensity of the disturbance was so high that the patient became agitated and disorganized. The deliberate practice of relaxation under these conditions was completely beyond her.

Such disruptions had been anticipated in the behavioral formulation, and the skills of coping with reality problems were among the initial target behaviors. Hence the treatment shifted away from relaxation training to the patient's problems with her granddaughter.

Although Mrs. C. was given ample opportunity to ventilate her distress about the situation, the main approach to the problem was the use of a counseling-educational model. Specific situations with the child were discussed, and the patient was instructed as to how she might have handled them. The therapist modeled things the patient might have said and done and what she could do when these behaviors recurred. The therapist also role-played the situations with the patient to give her rehearsal practice in the adaptive behaviors.

Mrs. C. was also given an assignment to initiate and record at least one positive interaction with the child each day. However, she was unable to perform this task; although she role-played the desired behaviors well during the office session, the intense disturbance in the actual life situation was too disruptive. Despite this lack of success, some therapeutic gains were made.

The major therapeutic gains from these procedures were a partial cognitive reorganization, which in turn had an impact on the patient's self-concept. She came to realize that there were ways of relating to her grandchild other than the ones she had been using, and that the reason she had not used those alternate ways was because of a skill deficit, not because she was a malicious, rejecting, or uncaring person. This new understanding gave her hope that she could learn to relate more positively to the child, and also made her more aware of her compassionate feelings towards the child.

There was a second gain that helped strengthen the therapeutic alliance. Mrs. C. had a new experience with an authority person (the therapist) who was quite different from her parents—an authority who was empathic, nondenigrating, nonjudgmental, and truly interested in teaching her to solve her problems. This experience probably helped make later stages of treatment easier.

Despite these gains, the patient's disturbances in life remained severe, and it became apparent that further training in tension reduction was needed. Clinical observation suggested a condition of habitual chronic hyperventilation (see Chapter 3). To test this, Mrs. C. was instructed to overbreathe for three minutes. However, her anxiety increased so much that the overbreathing had to be discontinued after only two minutes. With some slight difficulty the patient was taught the principles of dia-phragmatic breathing, and proper breathing indeed had a calming effect on her. With practice she would now have a new method to cope with disturbance.

REFORMULATION

At the fourth and fifth treatment sessions, a new and extremely im-portant reality problem emerged. Although Mrs. C.'s family lived out of town, her aged mother owned a building in the city in which the patient lived. The patient had lived in an apartment in that building for over 20 years, paying a very low rent. Now one of her sisters, apparently manipulating a somewhat senile mother, wanted to sell this house in a way that would deprive Mrs. C. not only of her residence but of her inheritance as well. The reality consequences, considering her limited financial resources, the constrictions imposed by her phobias, and her lack of recent work experience, were great. Further, she believed her needs would receive no attention within the family, and she felt be-trayed, abandoned, and humiliated by the injustice. Her disturbance, disorganization, and helplessness spiked to new highs.

At this time, enough additional information had been gained to re-formulate Mrs. C.'s behavioral dynamics (Figure 2). Her poor self-con-cept, characterized by feelings of helplessness, social incompetence, and weakness, were now placed at the core. She perceived herself as alone and unable to cope in a hostile world. This concept appeared to be maintained both by a series of fueling phobias relating to childhood memories and by severely stressful life situations. This self-concept kept Mrs. C. from acquiring coping skills, thus exacerbating her life problems and her assertive difficulties. These consequences, in turn, fed back into her poor self-concept, perpetuating the entire organization. Her main coping methods, phobic avoidance and escape, also served to reinforce and to maintain the poor self-concept.

This reformulation helped us devise a systematic therapeutic plan centering around the reality problem of the house. We retained the need to teach coping skills set forth in the initial formulation but also made most important the challenging of the patient's perception of being alone in a hostile world. We also designated the fueling phobias as target behaviors for treatment but decided to concentrate on the coping skills and the "aloneness" at this point. Changes in these, it was predicted,

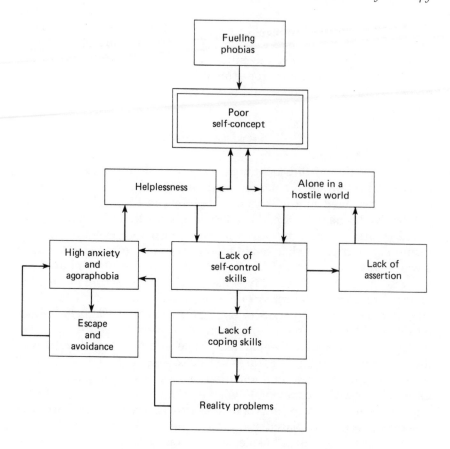

Figure 2. Second behavioral formulation with poor self-concept at core. Helplessness and aloneness flow directly from the poor self-concept and also maintain it.

would yield changes in the poor self-concept at the core of the organization.

Concrete social casework methods were introduced at this point. Mrs. C. was referred to Legal Aid in order to learn her rights in the housing situation and obtain legal representation. She was prepared for this step through assertion training and role-playing. Besides this, she was also given information concerning the availability of low rent and subsidized housing. These measures, in addition to increasing her coping skills, showed the patient that the world was not completely hostile—that there were helping people available to her. Her aloneness was further attacked by active listening on the part of the therapist, by empathic reflection of her pain and distress, and by encouraging the expression of her anger.

The therapist also supported Mrs. C.'s decision to visit her family to clarify her status in regard to the apartment. The therapist prepared her for the encounter with her mother and sister by crystallizing the purpose and goal of her pending visit and by rehearsing imagined scenarios. While Mrs. C. gained no satisfaction about the reality problem and was far from satisfied with her own coping skills when she did make the visit, she did see some improvement over prior visits and generally felt somewhat better about herself.

In order to make this family visit, she had to take a rather long bus ride. Here her agoraphobic problems played a role, but she managed to complete the trip, coping with the panic by pressing her feet into the floor and keeping her face buried in a newspaper. One consequence of the trip was that it shed some light on the possible fueling phobias, for during the trip she recalled many anxiety-provoking memories.

One of these memories appeared to be particularly relevant to her current social phobias. She recalled an incident in class when her name was called to recite. She panicked, ran out of the class screaming, and then actually fainted. The use of her name set off fears of being observed, judged, and being revealed as having done something wrong. It was believed that working with this memory would allow us to approach the fueling phobias, and a desensitization was attempted. However, the patient's self-control skills were not yet sufficiently strong to allow this. Even at the very lowest levels of a graded hierarchy she could not prevent the imagined scene from escalating to the very highest levels of anxiety. Due to the pressure of her reality problems, it was decided not to spend therapy time working through this difficulty, and the attempt at desensitization was discontinued.

ONGOING TREATMENT

At this point another social worker in the clinic took over some of the casework problems stemming from Mrs. C.'s pending housing problem. This allowed the therapist to concentrate more intensively on the target behaviors of helplessness, aloneness, and coping skills, mainly in the context of the patient's problems with her granddaughter. Although there were definite changes in Mrs. C.'s attitudes and perspectives—for example, she was becoming more aware that many things in her life could be modified through her own actions—she constantly suffered from high levels of disturbance.

Some of the work concerning the grandchild came to involve school personnel. The therapist maintained contact with the school psychologist and so was able to get the child into psychotherapeutic treatment. An anticipated meeting with the child's teacher brought about considerable anticipatory anxiety on Mrs. C.'s part, which was reduced by a systematic desensitization procedure with a graded hierarchy. The coming meeting was also discussed and critical behaviors were modeled by the therapist and rehearsed with the patient

The relative success of this meeting demonstrated to Mrs. C. that she was capable of learning and of exercising control.

Her high level of anxiety disturbed her, and for several sessions became the focus of treatment. Using a covert rehearsal model, Mrs. C. practiced during the session the act of relaxing herself. She reported some success with this procedure when she used it at home. She also reported further use of the diaphragmatic breathing exercises and their calming effect. The covert rehearsal method was also used for other tension-provoking situations. Although there was less success here, even the small gains she had made helped to support her in the face of her mounting life problems.

A program was now instituted to increase her awareness of these small positive gains and to increase her awareness of her own strengths. This program had several aims: It would weaken her poor self-concept and her helplessness, and it would serve to reinforce and to extend the gains she was making. To this end she was instructed to keep a record of something good that happened or something good she had done each day. She was also given assignments to do and was asked to record things that were either enjoyable or that would build her self-esteem. This program led her to reach out beyond the problems of her daily life, to go beyond the goal of minimizing the bad towards that of increasing the good in her life. One concrete action she took was to secure an art school catalogue with a view to taking a course, a big step for her.

In subsequent sessions Mrs. C. reported that she was going to visit her family again to discuss financial matters regarding the house. In connection with this visit, she was making a dress (an activity she enjoyed and felt confident about) as a gift for her mother. This was the first session in which the patient talked about her family without crying. She also did not experience the anticipatory anxiety occasioned by previous visits.

Mrs. C. reported that she handled herself more assertively with her family on this visit, despite an argument with her sister. She no longer expressed fears of "falling apart." The change in her mood was reflected in the new thought that she saw returning to work as her only prospect for gaining independence. Although her phobias made this impossible at this time, it was a positive goal and a motivator for eventually overcoming the phobias. These changes appeared to reflect changing cognitions about herself.

Up to this time we had done little direct treatment of the patient's phobias. Initially her self-control skills were too low for her to follow instructions, practice exercises, and keep records. The attempt to desensitize the fueling phobia concerning her name had failed. However, she had been successfully desensitized to her anticipatory fear regarding the meeting with her grandchild's teacher, and she had been able to take the bus trip to visit her family. She had gained greater ability to reduce her tension level and had acquired some understanding of how avoidance and escape behaviors maintained the phobias. Her new motivation eventually to seek work led us to make a more direct attack on the phobias themselves.

The target phobia chosen was that of being frightened of meeting people on the street. This was an often-encountered situation, and she herself described it as the most distressing of her fears. The core of the phobia, the fear of a panic attack and the consequent humiliation, fed into her poor self-concept and her helplessness. A result of the fear was the avoidance of such encounters, which maintained her social isolation and hence her feelings of being alone. This fear was treated with systematic desensitization and, after several sessions, some moderate success was achieved. Mrs. C. reported several incidents where she did not avoid the social encounters, where she did not escape from them, and where she did not double over in panic. This modest improvement served to reinforce her growing feelings of competence.

Then, once again, everything collapsed. The reality problems centering around the sale of the house and the problems with her grandchild had become worse. Mrs. C.'s newly acquired self-control behaviors could not be maintained under these mounting pressures, and she reverted to a state of fear and disorganization. She was constantly preoccupied with thoughts of imminent disaster and again described herself as "falling apart."

The problem with the grandchild appeared to be the more disruptive. The child had been acting out and had become involved in delinquent behavior. These difficulties raised Mrs. C.'s general disturbance to a very high level, and she was completely unable to cope. In consultation with the child's therapist, it was decided that separation was indicated as a therapeutic measure for both child and grandmother. With their mutual consent, the child was returned to the residential treatment school she had formerly attended. The removal of the child from her home relieved much of the pressure from Mrs. C.

The pending sale of the house, however, remained a major source of difficulty. With the patient's consent, the therapist contacted the family to learn of the actual plans regarding the patient's status in her apartment. It was found that the building was indeed being sold, and the patient would have to move. Despite this bad news, Mrs. C. was relieved and grateful to be so supported. She stated also that she was glad to have her family know that she was not alone, a statement that revealed a change in her own feelings of aloneness. She was also encouraged to resume the contacts she had earlier initiated for legal advice and representation, while at the same time making some specific emergency plans for housing. She was helped through structuring and rehearsing in each step along the way.

Thus, the therapeutic interventions in Mrs. C.'s reality problems had the therapist doing for the patient what she could not do for herself, while at the same time encouraging and assisting the patient to do those things that she was able to do. This approach did relieve much of the disruption, and we were once again able to approach the phobias directly.

ADJUNCTIVE GROUP THERAPY

With the relief of these reality stresses, Mrs. C. no longer presented as a disorganized and disintegrating person. Indeed, her personal strengths became so much more evident and her self-control skills so improved that the previously considered diagnosis of Borderline Personality could now be rejected with confidence. However, her general disturbance level remained high, and wherever possible she avoided phobic situations. To accelerate treatment in this area, she was now placed in a treatment group for agoraphobics. Individual treatment sessions continued as well.

Mrs. C. responded enthusiastically and hopefully to the suggestion of the group treatment. The group was newly formed, consisted of six members, and had co-therapists of which this therapist was one. The group program mainly centered around relaxation training methods and *in vivo* exposures to phobic situations. It was to meet for 10 sessions. Mrs. C. was the only group member who was also receiving individual treatment and the only one who had had a previous relationship with either therapist. This gave her the feeling of special status and served to further counter her feelings of being alone and victimized.

Entering the group had a catalytic effect in mobilizing all the patient's resources and determination to overcome her fears. In individual sessions too there was a marked increase in her motivation, accompanied by a dramatic increment in her progress. She was now able to use all the techniques and coping skills she had learned in individual therapy but had not practiced systematically.

To complement the group sessions, desensitization in imagination to phobias was conducted during individual sessions prior to the *in vivo* exposure in group or between treatment sessions. The behavioral literature reports that such a procedure has a facilitating effect on the patient's initiating exposure in real life situations. It appeared to have this effect here. Mrs. C. was desensitized to sitting in a center seat in an auditorium; following that, she actually did attend a lecture and stayed through to the end. She was desensitized to several other phobic situations, such as crowded buses and elevators. She was increasingly able to expose herself to these situations in life. She first rode elevators in an apartment building and then rode in a high speed elevator in an office building. In the high speed elevator she panicked and escaped the first time, but with the therapist's encouragement she was able to repeat this exposure successfully, on a more graduated (first-to-tenth floor) basis.

Her success in these few areas and the praise she was receiving from the group and her therapist encouraged Mrs. C. to keep trying in those situations where she continued to panic. For example, walking down the street between two other group members while conversing generated spiking anxiety. This scene was desensitized in imagination during individual sessions. The patient subsequently reported a chance encounter with a neighbor where she was able to stand and chat for five minutes. She felt a real sense of accomplishment at this achievement.

After this last experience, Mrs. C. reported that she was more active in traveling and in meeting people. On two occasions she conversed with another person while walking. She was able to cope with the momentary anxiety in those situations and to continue conversing without an anxiety buildup. The phobias appeared to be decreasing.

Thus at the termination of the group there was a definite diminution of her phobias. While the patient was still quite phobic, she had increased her ability to control her anxieties and no longer felt as helpless about them. She was optimistic about improving her ability to cope and to overcome her remaining fears. She also expressed a feeling of greater control of her life and to increase this, she was reading about assertive behavior.

LATER TREATMENT

With her newfound strengths, Mrs. C. turned once again to the still critical problem concerning the sale of the house. Now she tried a new approach: asking her brother for help and support. The therapist discussed the forthcoming conversations and rehearsed the patient in the desired behaviors. Mrs. C. was encouraged to use the assertive behaviors she was learning. She was also rehearsed in the process of reducing her anxieties during the conversations. When Mrs. C. spoke to her brother she learned, to her surprise, that she was not as alone as she had thought. He agreed to do all he could to help her retain her apartment.

Having made progress in traveling and in social interactions, Mrs. C. again turned to thoughts of achieving independence through work. But she was extremely anxious about the prospect, recalling her past difficulties with her supervisors and her panic in listening to instructions. She believed that she would not be able to do the same sort of work as in the past, so she needed to find out what kind of work she could do. The therapist referred the patient to the State Office of Vocational Rehabilitation (OVR) for help in evaluating her skills and aptitudes and for retraining and job placement. Mrs. C. made an appointment to be interviewed by OVR, and a session was spent in preparation for the interview. We reviewed such coping skills as diaphragmatic breathing and relaxation procedures.

In the interview itself, Mrs. C. was able to cope with her disturbances and was quite satisfied with her performance. She was accepted for a vocational retraining program and continued in therapy until it began. She and her rehabilitation counselor selected clerical work, which required a short training course, as an area compatible with Mrs. C.'s new coping skills, and one with good prospects for job placement. The patient felt confident of her ability to do this kind of work.

During this period Mrs. C. continued to accumulate positive experiences from her *in vivo* exposures. She was able to control her anxiety when she met an acquaintance on the bus, and she felt optimistic about continued progress in this area. She also reported that she had had a new experience while walking between her brother and the lawyer who was being consulted about the house. She had been able to attend to and participate in the conversation.

Mrs. C. had gained the active support of her brother and other members of the family. She felt better able to cope, more a part of her family, more instrumental in solving problems of living, and ready to try working again to become independent.

Treatment was discontinued by mutual agreement at the time Mrs. C.'s vocational retraining classes started. The treatment period had lasted one year, with 38 individual sessions and 10 group sessions, plus other professional consultations.

SUMMARY AND DISCUSSION

The case presented involves a woman with a more than 40-year history of agoraphobia with panic. A series of severe life problems complicated the picture and a rather complex treatment approach was necessary. Community resources were used, as were social work case management, rehabilitation counseling, legal advice, individual behavioral psychotherapy, and group behavior therapy. Good progress was made, although the treatment by no means could be considered complete at the time it was discontinued.

The crucial decision made took place at the very beginning of the treatment. At that time, even though the patient's chief complaint was her agoraphobia and this condition appeared to be the most disabling aspect of her life, it was decided not to choose that symptom as an initial target for treatment. In retrospect this was a sound decision. An initial attempt to treat the agoraphobia would most probably have failed, mainly due to the patient's lack of self-control skills. This failure, in turn, would have fed into her poor self-concept, increased her feelings of helplessness and aloneness, and made any future attempts at treatment more difficult.

The initial behavioral formulation led to the designation of the self-control skills as the first target for treatment. However, despite some signs that mastery of these skills would be helpful, the patient was unable even to practice them outside of the treatment sessions. In large part this was due to the high levels of disturbance elicited by her reality problems. In the course of treatment sufficient information was gained so that the self-control skill deficit could be placed within its own organizational context. As a result the second behavioral formulation placed at its core the patient's poor self-concept, which was allied with and maintained by her feelings of helplessness and of feeling alone in a hostile world. It was believed that until this organization was changed the patient would have neither the motivation nor the ability to do what was necessary to acquire self-control skills.

Because the patient's poor self-concept could not be approached directly, the helplessness and the aloneness became the primary targets of treatment. In this area, the alliance with the therapist became very important. In many ways the therapist demonstrated to the patient her concern and her willingness to help and to understand. The first changes in the feelings of aloneness thus came in relation to the therapist. Further, these target behaviors were the unifying thread in all the adjunctive consultations. More important than the specific help garnered through these consultations was the repeated demonstration to the patient that the world was not completely hostile, that there were people willing to help, and that there were things she could do that might improve the situation. The agoraphobic group, besides providing direct treatment for her fears, also contributed in a similar manner. The fact that the patient was able to perform tasks that others in the group could not do, the group support and approval, and her special relationship with one of the co-leaders of the group all served to attack her helplessness, her aloneness, and her poor self-concept. The ultimate effect came when, as a result of her own actions, the patient's brother sided with her. Even outside the therapeutic situation she was not completely alone.

As the target behaviors changed, the patient also acquired more self-control skills with self-esteem and confidence. Her newly emerged desire to gain independence through work motivated her to practice these skills and to use them in risk-taking situations. It is now probable that she will be able to get and to hold a job.

Despite her marked progress, the patient cannot be considered "cured," nor is her need for psychotherapy over. For one thing, we had formulated a series of fueling phobias feeding into her condition. An attempt to treat these phobias directly failed. It may well be that they will keep fueling some disturbance and that treatment cannot be fully completed until these phobias are reduced.

The patient's reality problems also remain essentially unresolved at present. She still has a problem about housing and severe problems with her granddaughter. These problems may escalate at any time and may bring about a relapse into disorganization and high disturbance. However, even should this happen, it is believed that the patient now has the resilience to weather the difficulties and to return to the new equilibrium we have established through behavioral psychotherapy.

8

A Case of Depression and Phobias: Report of a Supervised Psychiatric Resident

John Boronow and George Greenberg

This chapter recounts a brief behavioral psychotherapy case and its supervision. Since the therapy was a training case for a psychiatric resident, it exemplifies not only behavioral psychotherapy, but also the process of teaching behavioral psychotherapy to a trainee. Combining the delivery of service with ongoing training has probably become the norm in most academic settings, and it poses unique problems for the patient, trainee, and supervisor alike.

In this treatment, a great number of the diverse techniques used by behavioral psychotherapists were employed. The patient's treatment was not restricted to one or two simple regimens of repetitive exercises. Instead, she was relaxed with slow, regular breathing, muscle relaxation exercises, and hypnotic imagery; she learned new skills through role-playing, carrying out task assignments, and rehearsal in fantasy; she overcame fears with hierarchical desensitization, aversion relief desensitization, and suggestion; she recovered from her depression with the help of powerful rapport, medication, expanded social networks, physical exercise, and counterdepressive cognitions.

Such diversity demonstrates a basic principle of behavioral psychotherapy: responsiveness to careful observations of the patient's behavior as it manifests itself from moment to moment. Throughout the therapy, behavioral formulations are kept flexible and are revised as new data are presented. The therapy itself becomes conceptualized as a kind of test probe, the results of which produce further data with which to reformulate the case. There is a process of refining the understanding of the patient's behaviors with each session, and with every refinement there is a challenge to develop different therapeutic strategies. This on-going evaluation of a patient longitudinally over time gives much richer information about the patient and the illness. The patient's changing symptoms, far from being a "frustration" or a "disappointment," serve to aid the therapist in better understanding—and thus ultimately help-ing—his patient. Such an approach can only lead to a more rational therapy for the future.

THE SETTING

The patient came to an urban walk-in clinic where she was evaluated and referred to "brief behavioral therapy." The psychiatrists at the disposition conference settled on a "brief" therapy because they felt the patient was in crisis, had no premorbid psychiatric history, and demonstrated a previous satisfactory level of adjustment. They chose a behaviorally focused therapy because they believed that certain of the patient's symptoms, in particular her panic attacks and phobic symptoms, would best be addressed by behavioral means.

The resident assigned to the case was in his third year and had a strong background in psychopharmacology and dynamic psychotherapy. He knew very little about behavior therapy, however, and received a six-session course on behavior therapy only after he had already been treating the patient for some time. The resident had requested exposure to behavior therapy (which was optional) and was eager to learn about it.

The supervisor assigned to the resident had extensive experience in a wide variety of therapies. He was a clinical psychologist who had worked in psychoanalysis, gestalt, bioenergetics, and hypnosis, as well as behavioral psychotherapy. He had never supervised a resident before, and had not been told about the "brief" nature of the therapy. He did not accept the "brief therapy" paradigm as it related to behavioral psychotherapy, and felt that only the patient's behaviors and responses to therapeutic interventions would determine the length of the treatment. Despite this he was enthusiastic about treating the patient and teaching the resident, and he fostered an openminded attitude toward the patient.

PRESENTING HISTORY

The patient was a 58-year-old, widowed white European-born skilled craftswoman and mother of three who came to the clinic in January with the following chief complaint:

> I can't sleep since I came out of the hospital (two months prior). Several patients died there and the fear never left me. I lie there, ready to sleep, but then this dry constriction in my throat awakens me . . . scared, trembling. . . . I get diarrhea. The fear, such fear! I worry, I see the worst of events. I need encouragement but there is never anyone there.

The patient was well until a year and half before when her brother-in-law died of a heart attack. Two months later, the patient herself developed chest pains and was diagnosed as having mild angina pectoris. She was begun on low dose propranolol without much change in her symptoms. Propranolol is widely used in the treatment of angina, although it has been occasionally reported to cause depression as a side effect. The patient did well throughout the spring and that summer made a long-delayed return visit to her village and family in Europe. She had not been back since she emigrated at the age of 29. The family was apparently happy to see her and the trip was uneventful. However, the patient states that it was only after this journey home that she fully "realized" that not only her brother-in-law, but also her mother, were in fact dead. (The mother had died at the age of 89 two and a half years before, without ever having seen the patient since she emigrated.)

Upon returning home to the United States, the patient became depressed and cried every night. She blamed her feelings on the propranolol and her internist stopped it. Her chest pains worsened off the medication, however, and she was admitted for evaluation to the hospital to rule out a possible heart attack. The medical tests revealed no evidence of a heart attack, but during her stay in the hospital she witnessed two patients die of heart attacks. Upon being discharged from the hospital, she soon learned of the death of one of her friends by heart attack. The patient became increasingly anxious, was unable to concentrate or to sleep, developed mild phobic symptoms, and began to have trouble functioning at work.

The patient was initially treated for these problems by the same comprehensive medical clinic which had been following her for the angina.

They tried treating her with minor tranquilizers (flurazepam) for anxiety and insomnia but to no avail. They treated her subsequently with a tricyclic antidepressant (amitriptyline), but the patient refused to take the medication after the first night, saying it was "too strong."

Thus, when the patient came to the psychiatric clinic, she was suffering from symptoms that dated back as far as a year. They had become acutely worse following her medical hospitalization, and she was in crisis, unable to return to work and seriously impaired in the quality of her life.

Her mental status at this time revealed her to be a slightly heavy, large-framed woman with dyed hair and conservative clothes of good taste. She appeared unremittingly anxious and troubled, and her clothing and hair were somewhat untidy. She spoke fluently and her voice was whining. She was alert and oriented. There was neither psychomotor retardation nor agitation. Her affect was constricted but appropriate; her mood was anxious and depressed. She was often tearful. She did not demonstrate a formal thought disorder. Her thought content was notable for constant preoccupation about being alone, being sick, having a heart attack and dying. She denied any hallucinations, suicidal ideation, ideas of reference or first rank Schneiderian symptoms of schizophrenia. Although she doubted whether the doctors were being honest with her when they told her that she need not worry about her heart, when questioned further about this it was clear that she was in no way delusional. There was no impairment of her memory, abstraction, calculations, fund of knowledge, or judgment.

The patient described her anxiety as being consistently worse in the mornings. She denied early morning awakening. She reported difficulty both in falling asleep and staying asleep for several weeks prior to our first meeting. There was no significant weight loss but she did complain of diarrhea. She suffered from what sounded like panic attacks. She felt helpless but not hopeless. She denied guilty ruminations or feelings of worthlessness. She denied compulsive rituals but found that doing housework compulsively did decrease her anxiety somewhat. Lately she had developed an aversion to being alone in her house, and would dread going home after work unless she knew that her daughter would be there.

PAST HISTORY

The patient was the fourth of six children, and the eldest daughter, born to a Roman Catholic couple in a small, rural village in Europe. The patient recalled little of her childhood in the initial interviews except to say that she came from a warm, stable, and supportive family. She always was closest to her mother, whom she described as a rather strict and inflexible disciplinarian. She had little to say of her father except that he died of pernicious anemia at the age of 64 when the patient was 18. She was treated with special consideration because she was the eldest girl, and her brothers were protective of her. She completed high school and was trained as a skilled craftswoman. In her twenties she fell in love with a local man and planned to marry him. However, her mother apparently favored another man and the patient experienced her mother as forcing her to jilt her true love for the one her mother had chosen. The patient married this man and the couple moved to New York when the patient was 29. They settled in an apartment where she had lived ever since.

The patient had three daughters. When they started school, she went to work in a factory as a skilled craftswoman. Her marriage was difficult because her husband suffered from depression and was often in hospitals. He was emotionally distant. During the last three years of his life he essentially abandoned the family, moving in with his brother in upstate New York, leaving the patient to support the family on her own. In 1966, when the patient was 41, the husband was hospitalized at a psychiatric facility where he committed suicide.

The patient raised her daughters singlehandedly, feeling it would not be possible for her to remarry easily at her age. Her life consisted of a steady routine including work, housekeeping, preparing meals, chaperoning her daughters, and shopping. She left herself little time for friends or social activities. Her chief pleasures were her daughters and watching TV. She never made her daughters do any of the household chores, partly because she enjoyed the work too much and partly because it seemed to give her a hold over them, making them more dependent on her. She was vigilant about their dating and reluctant to let them leave home as they matured. She would often scream at them for being lazy good-for-nothings, but it is clear that she loved them very much.

Presently the patient lives with her youngest daughter, who is in her middle teens. Their relationship is amiable, but is often strained by frictions arising from the daughter's growing independence. Thus, for example, they quarrel when they go on vacation together, because the young woman stays up late flirting with men. The patient has had a particular dislike for the daughter's current boyfriend, feeling he is "not the right type" and objecting to the lateness at which he brings her home in the evening. The patient finds it increasingly difficult to be alone without the daughter at night. She fears the day when the daughter will leave the house and she will be left all alone.

The other two daughters are married and live close enough to visit on weekends. There is no history of any psychiatric illness in the patient's family. The patient has no past psychiatric history herself, and suffers from neither alcoholism nor drug abuse.

FIRST FORMULATION (JANUARY 14)

On the basis of the above information, the patient was diagnosed as having a Panic Disorder, DSM-III 300.01, with associated severe generalized anxiety. We were quite concerned about the level of her depression, and did not rule out the possibility that she might later become much more severely depressed. But the data did not support such a conclusion at this time, and we were prepared to conceptualize the depressive symptoms as secondary to the Panic Disorder. There was no clear-cut personality disorder (the so-called Axis II diagnosis of DSM-III) that could be made initially.

The observations led to the following formulation: The patient was acutely suffering from a Panic Disorder, the trigger for which was not yet apparent. She had developed generalized anxiety between attacks, as is common in this condition. Insomnia was a complication of this generalized anxiety. The patient's phobic avoidance of her work and home represented a response to situations in which she had had the panic attacks. This overall state of affairs led to marked constriction of her available supply of reinforcers, leaving her depressed.

In addition, it appeared that the patient was suffering from more chronically maladaptive behaviors. These included lack of an adequate repertoire of pleasurable activities, self-reinforcing social isolation (possibly due to subtle but pervasive social phobias), and deficiencies in assertiveness. These chronic behaviors were more difficult to assess in the beginning as they were so overshadowed by the acute crisis.

As a result of this formulation, the resident targeted the panic attacks as the principal symptom for treatment. He felt that by breaking the cycle of panic—anxiety—panic—more anxiety etc., he could bring the patient immediate relief. He chose to use low doses of the drug imipramine to accomplish this.* The resident felt that there would not be any

---

*Donald Klein and others have clearly demonstrated that tricyclic antidepressants are effective in preventing panic attacks in many patients, although not the anticipatory anxiety which precedes them. The latter symptom often responds to a minor tranquilizer and behavioral interventions.

incompatibility in combining psychopharmacologic and behavioral techniques, especially since there was good precedent for doing so (Liebowitz and Klein, 1979). He therefore started the patient on the very low dose of 10 milligrams of imipramine at bedtime, with the intention of slowly increasing it until the patient's panic attacks abated. In addition, he asked the patient to discontinue the flurazepam which the medical clinic had given her, as it was not helping her insomnia and might even be exacerbating it. An agreement was made with the patient to begin a time-limited behavioral psychotherapy, duration unspecified as yet, with a frequency of once a week.

SECOND FORMULATION (JANUARY 22)

The patient's symptoms failed to respond to the imipramine. Moreover, she complained of unusual side effects (e.g., feeling "drugged" and experiencing peculiar and vague bodily sensations) despite the very low dose. She phoned the therapist three times in one week and appeared in the emergency room in the midst of a panic attack.

After hearing the resident present the case, the supervisor laid greater emphasis on the patient's generalized anxiety. In his formulation, the patient's generalized anxiety became the principal target for the treatment, and the panic attacks, phobias, and insomnia were considered secondary to it. The depression remained conceptualized as a final complication of the overall absence of positive reinforcers due to the illness. In approaching the treatment of this generalized anxiety, the supervisor wished to forgo medication and rely solely on behavioral interventions. He hypothesized that the patient's panic attacks might be the outcome of acute hyperventilation, and her anxiety the result of a more chronic hyperventilation as described by Lum (1975). Both of these behaviors were directly amenable to behavioral psychotherapy. Obviously, they were prepared to use medication if it proved indispensable, but the present formulation led them logically to a behavioral strategy.

Using this model, the patient was reevaluated. Her baseline breathing was timed at 16 per minute, with an average of two sighs per minute. Characteristic of her breathing were shallow breaths taken by expanding the upper chest only. The patient was asked to hyperventilate. Her effort was suboptimal despite efforts to "coach" her with each breath. The hyperventilation produced only generalized discomfort and dizziness after two minutes, and the patient refused to continue.

Despite the failure of the hyperventilation to replicate the patient's symptoms, the therapist took her signs and shallow breathing as an indication that she might well benefit from breathing exercises. He taught her to breathe deeply using the lower part of her lungs, pushing her stomach out and thus pulling the diaphragm down. Once the patient learned this, he instructed her to say "calm" to herself with each exhalation. She was then told to practice this breathing technique for 15 minutes twice a day, in the morning and evening. He encouraged her to decrease her respiratory rate to four to six times a minute with practice.

During the rest of the session the patient was taught a muscle relaxation technique. She was asked to close her eyes and imagine the various joints of her body; the therapist would suggest to her that she try to feel the muscles connecting the hand and arm becoming so relaxed that they seemed to disappear. The patient would dwell on one set of joints for a few minutes, and then move on to another set, so that within 20 minutes the patient had relaxed all the major muscle groups in her body. The patient responded quite well to this procedure, with a noticeable decrease in her overall body tension. She reported a dramatic feeling of well-being which she called "beautiful." The therapist then instructed her to practice this relaxation technique at home for 20 minutes twice a day. He also encouraged her to use either the breathing or the muscle relaxation techniques whenever situations developed at home or at work in which she found herself especially nervous.

As for the patient's insomnia, the therapist told the patient to take an active role in combating this symptom. He recommended that instead of going to bed, she should resolve to stay up until she was exhausted, all night if necessary, and busy herself with her usual household tasks. She was to omit all coffee and napping, and continue this regimen for two weeks. The patient agreed to try. At this point the frequency of therapy sessions was increased temporarily to twice a week.

The patient did not benefit as much as we had hoped from these interventions. She continued to suffer from generalized anxiety as well as panic attacks, and it became clear that she had not mastered the breathing techniques correctly at home. Even in the office, with continuous coaching, it became difficult to get the patient to complete an entire breathing or relaxation exercise without her stopping to complain about how badly she felt. At home, the patient was still taking the flurazepam, despite being told to discontinue it, and thus was in no way complying with the prescribed treatment for insomnia. In short, the symptoms and degree of dysphoria were reaching a point which precluded the patient from even trying the therapy and cooperating with treatment recommendations, so distractible and anxious had she become.

THIRD FORMULATION (JANUARY 29)

The therapist reformulated the case when the patient came in reporting new passive suicidal fantasies and impulses to hurt her daughter. Although she had made no gesture, and the fantasies were egodystonic, the patient's depression was becoming clearer and the anxiety and panic attacks seemed more and more to be part of a depressive syndrome. She began to manifest diurnal variation of her mood in addition to her insomnia, anhedonia, poor concentration, and suicidal ideation.

In light of this further deterioration, the therapist focused on her depression as the principal problem, and assumed that the attendant symptoms of insomnia, panic attacks and anxiety were in most part consequences of this depression. The goal of therapy would be to treat the depression, with the expectation that the other symptoms would abate as the depression itself diminished. Behavioral techniques could continue to be applied to these secondary symptoms for the relief of distress, but would be considered palliative rather than curative. Curative treatment would have to address the depression itself, and this could be accomplished through a combination of pharmacological and behavioral means.

Obviously, the clinical situation had changed. The patient was worse, could not cooperate with a treatment regimen suited for less disturbed patients, and demonstrated some of the characteristic symptoms of endogenous depression. The extreme degree of the patient's suffering, corroborated by her family, along with the added potential of a suicide gesture, raised the level of urgency.

As a result of this reformulation, the patient was begun on an antidepressant, doxepin, 300 mg/day. However, the addition of medication for crisis management and rapid relief of the most severe symptoms did not blind us to the continuing need for other therapeutic interventions. Weissman, Prusoff, DiMascio et al.(1979) have shown how psychotherapy and medication complement, rather than duplicate, each other. We fully planned to implement new behavioral strategies once the patient was stabilized and more cooperative.

Specifically, the supervisor continued to see management of the patient's chronic anxiety and panic attacks as a task amenable to behavioral psychotherapy, and formulated the problem as one of overcoming the obstacles to learning which faced the patient. Thus, for example, repeated checking of the patient's deep breathing exercise revealed that she continued to have difficulty executing it properly, although she believed that she was doing it correctly. Strategies to surmount this seemingly tedious, but clinically very real, problem led to having the patient practice lying down, having her loosen her skirt and wear less tightly fitting clothes, and frankly discussing some of her fantasies about what it meant to stick out her belly. The latter revealed that the patient felt terribly embarrassed to be seen with a protruding abdomen, not because of any apparent pregnancy fantasies, but because it was "unattractive" and "humiliating." As the patient was able to relax somewhat about her appearance, her breathing technique improved, and after a few weeks she was a great devotee of the breathing exercises, doing them regularly and properly at home, and even at work as a means of warding off a pending panic attack.

In a similar way we continued to stress muscle relaxation exercises, and the patient was given a tape of the therapist's voice leading her through the 20-minute joint and muscle relaxation procedure.

For the depression, the supervisor formulated her difficulty as a cumulative result of a chronic deficit in both pleasure enhancing and self-esteem enhancing activities in the patient's daily life. To counteract this, new activities were introduced to the patient. The therapist asked her to begin making two tasks for herself daily: one was to think of something that she would do that day just for the fun of it, because she enjoyed it; the other was to think of something that she would do that day because it made her feel good about herself. We hoped with this method to help the patient explore the possible variety of things in her environment that could act as positive reinforcers, as well as demonstrate to her cognitively the extent to which she had control over such reinforcers. We wanted to create an opportunity for the patient to discover that she was free to choose many alternatives in her life. Recognition of such freedom in itself would reduce her depression.

The formulation of the patient's depression as the result of a constricted system of reinforcements, and in particular those of an interpersonal nature, led naturally to a better understanding of therapeutic leverage. The therapist, who had clearly become a very important person in the patient's life, would be able to exert a great deal of influence on the patient's behavior by controlling how often he saw the patient (source of pleasure) and how praising he was (source of self-esteem). By judiciously manipulating the therapist's impact as a positive reinforcer, we hoped to target certain behaviors for change, using his praise and time spent with the patient as a reward.

For example, the patient had trouble getting to work in the morning because she felt worst at the beginning of the day, so much so that she would take refuge with the therapist, either by phone or in person. The therapist handled this by keeping his contact with the patient very brief, insisting that the patient go to work instead. He would not spend time with the patient discussing her latest fears and obsessions, would not give her an extra session, and instead focused on the patient's strengths and ability to master her difficulties. The patient got little reinforcement for this avoidance of work. Conversely, when she came to a session and reported success at having gone to work 15 minutes earlier, the therapist enthusiastically congratulated her and asked for all the details of how she managed to do it, rewarding her with his praise, time and attention for her accomplishments. The patient was thus positively reinforced for behaviors that accentuated her active self-control.

As the patient gradually began to return to her previous level of functioning, she attempted a number of new activities with the therapist's active encouragement. She began taking walks, first around the block, then across town. Next she went shopping in department stores and became comfortable in negotiating with salespeople. She was able to go to the movies and, with urging, even asked a friend to accompany her. She managed to accept an invitation for tea with the neighbors and went to church for the first time in a long while. In addition to the choosing of such pleasure and self-esteem activities daily, the patient kept a log to monitor her progress. She recorded the frequency of her panic attacks, the percentage of the day that she felt well, the hour that she reported for work, as well as a list of the tasks she would set for herself. The results of all these assignments varied, and the patient was often only partially compliant. This was handled with both rephrasing the assignments and doing actual examples in the office, as well as by praising her and focusing attention on her when she did carry them out correctly. The therapist repeatedly emphasized to the patient that while she could not overcome her depression right away, she could perform these assignments, thereby stressing her active and effective participation in therapy.

Progress was not entirely smooth, to be sure. The patient came in frantic one day with the obsessional idea—very alien to her—that she should kill her daughter. She had even thrown a knife out the kitchen window as a magical gesture to ward off such impulses. On another occasion she came to a session with a bandaged thumb, explaining with rather striking indifference that she had run her thumb under a sewing machine. Despite these setbacks, the patient continued to make progress, and more importantly, was able to actively engage in the execution of her own therapy.

The patient's acute depressive episode was essentially over by the end of February. Her sleep was excellent, she was gaining weight, she was going to work earlier and earlier, and her panic attacks were diminished. She remained somewhat anxious, especially when her daughter would leave her alone on a weekend, but she was able to live with this. The patient, too, agreed she was better, and so together she and the therapist reevaluated the goals for therapy. It seemed appropriate at this point to examine the patient's everyday life more closely, now that she was less symptomatic, and to search for any maladaptive behaviors that could render her prone to such depressions. Sessions were decreased in frequency to once a week, and the patient consented to meet until the end of June, thus setting a definitive endpoint to the treatment for the first time.

First of all, the therapist gave the patient a habit schedule to fill out (Roberts and Fisher, 1976). This revealed that the patient's greatest pleasures in her daily life were eating, music, pets, watching sports, looking at beautiful scenery, working and shopping. It was of some interest that all of these activities could be done alone. This was in marked contradistinction to our earlier observation that the patient's principal reinforcers were significant others, i.e., activities of an interpersonal nature. We began to get a picture of a woman whose principal satisfactions in life revolved around caring interactions with people, but whose actual behaviors confined her to a lifestyle in which she isolated herself. Although she had developed a repertoire of activities to do by herself when her daughters were absent (clearly a second-best alternative, as far as the patient was concerned), these same activities actually prevented her from meeting new people who might eventually become significant people in her life.

Next, we administered to the patient a questionnaire covering various different noxious stimuli (Wolpe, 1973). The patient listed 58 out of 87 items as causing at least a "fair amount of fear or other unpleasant feelings." Of particular interest were the items she designated as causing the most fear. They were of three types: 1) open wounds, witnessing surgical operations, human blood, dentists, and the prospect of having an operation; 2) strangers, being alone, speaking in public; and 3) people who seem insane, losing control, and the sight of fighting. Without speculating as to the psychodynamic etiology, it is nevertheless easy to see that the patient was probably phobic to the idea of being ill, either physically or mentally, and that part of the acute depression had revolved around an obsession with the idea that she was in fact ill, thus eliciting a panic reaction from her. The panic reaction, in turn, led her to feel out of control and thus elicited further anxiety. In addition, it appeared that the patient suffered from at least some social phobias, perhaps fairly well disguised by her superficially developed social skills.

We were able to conceptualize these various behaviors as a coherent syndrome, and the patient was now given an Axis II diagnosis (i.e., personality disorder) of Avoidant Personality (DSM-III 301.82). Social phobias, a common complication of this disorder, were also added to her diagnosis (DSM-III 300.23). The patient's continuing and residual pessimism and anxiety could be accounted for most parsimoniously as associated features of her underlying personality disorder. It seemed reasonable, therefore, to attempt to alter such chronically maladaptive behaviors therapeutically in an effort to forestall further cycles of discouragement, withdrawal, and ultimately depression.

This formulation led to a two-pronged attack on her underlying behavioral style. We decided to address her phobic ideas head-on with a program of desensitization. For her social phobias, we chose to use a combination of assertiveness training and a schedule of activities. Meanwhile, the patient's antidepressant was tapered to a prophylactic dose (100 mg qhs), thus confirming to the patient that we indeed had entered a new phase of the therapy.

The supervisor's interest in new methods of desensitization led him to propose a program of aversion relief desensitization. This seemed particularly suitable to this setting because it was simple and lent itself readily to desensitizing ideas. The therapist initially tried a few sessions using breath-holding as the aversive stimulus, a modification of the technique of Orwin (1971). The supervisor felt this might work especially well in a patient for whom shortness of breath (as part of the panic attack syndrome) was already clearly defined as an aversive stimulus.

The patient was helped to relax with a muscle-relaxation routine that she had mastered. She was then told to gently exhale and lower her head. When it became uncomfortable for her not to breathe, she would raise her head and take a deep breath. At that moment, the therapist would introduce a noxious stimulus, such as, "Think about letting loose and getting really angry with your boss." The effect is to render the noxious stimulus ineffective by forcing it to compete with a stronger, more pleasurable stimulus, namely a much needed breath of fresh air.

As the body feels good and relieved from the built-up tension (air-hunger) being alleviated, it cannot simultaneously respond to the stimulus with the usual anxiety. For best effect, it seemed useful to keep the patient exposed to the noxious stimulus for about 10 seconds. After a two-minute period of nondirected conversation, the procedure was repeated.

As it turned out, the aversive stimulus of breath-holding was too anxiety-provoking for the patient, and she could not cooperate effectively with the procedure. This method also seemed to generate a host of depressive fantasies and memories in the patient which proved counterproductive. We therefore chose to modify the aversive stimulus, using a conventional shock generator (Mark II, Behavior Modifier by Farrall Corp.). The patient was allowed to hold the electrodes in her hand so that she could drop them herself if the stimulus proved too painful. This guaranteed that she remained in control of the procedure at all times and could choose when to terminate. The voltage was then raised from zero to a few volts rather gradually; the actual voltage was determined by the patient, who would indicate when the stimulus was uncomfortable but not very painful. At that point, the patient would nod her head and the therapist would immediately stop the stimulus. The patient would then take a deep breath and relax, while at the same time the therapist would introduce a noxious idea, such as "think about what you would be like if you went crazy." He would keep this image in the patient's mind for about 10 seconds, after which there would be a one-minute relaxation period of nondirected conversation. The whole procedure would then be repeated, up to 20 times in one session, with a variety of noxious ideas.

For the first trial the therapist chose to desensitize the patient to two phobic ideas: 1) being followed by a man who tries to break into her apartment; and 2) being alone. These were uppermost in the patient's mind during the unstructured opening of the session, and seemed to cause her a great deal of distress. She received a series of eight shock/image couplets centered around the first idea, and 14 around the second. The actual amount of time spent on any one phobic idea was determined by how rapidly the patient seemed to respond to the desensitization. Thus, when first trying to introduce an unpleasant idea, the patient would scowl, shake her head, and say, "No, no, I don't want to think about that!" After several repetitions, however, she became more used to the stimulus, and in fact was able to tolerate more and more vivid and disturbing depictions of the unpleasant idea. It was quite simple for the therapist to titrate the severity of the unpleasant idea, and gauge the degree of the patient's sensivity to it.

The upshot of this first treatment was that the patient was able to carry out our recommendation to join a health spa. Up to now she had complied only perfunctorily, going with her daughter to look over the facilities, but holding back for fear of the "naked women" and the "small, dark rooms" which made her feel trapped and alone. Our desensitization had the effect of diminishing these fears, and she returned the following week with the news that she no longer was afraid of the spa and had started to attend.

The notion of encouraging physical exercise also stemmed from a review of the patient's habit schedule. Further inquiry revealed that the patient did literally no exercise or physical activity, barely walking a few blocks each day. The supervisor believed that lack of vigorous physical activity predisposed people toward depression and suggested that the therapist inquire after the origins of the patient's inactivity. It turned out that the patient had a number of quietly held phobias which restricted her activity: "The park is too dangerous; I don't like people looking at me; I feel safer at home." As the latter were uncovered, they were systematically subjected to aversion relief desensitization as well. All sorts of physical activity were encouraged as the patient began to overcome her inhibitions.

The therapist continued to keep after the patient to make out daily pleasure and self-esteem goals for herself. He also instructed her to make notes on her reactions to every new person that she met each week, which were then discussed in session. In order to counter the patient's passive behaviors, she was assigned specific tasks of initiating new contacts with people. Such experiences were then examined by the patient and the therapist together in order to identify specific maladaptive behaviors that were creating difficulties.

Not all assignments produced the hoped-for results. The patient would often simply not attempt the assignment, despite her apparent agreement in the previous session. Her difficulty in saying no to the therapist became more evident in this way, and further care had to be paid to the way the assignments were chosen. Similarly, even when she would attempt an assignment, she would often return with reports of failure, due to lack of the necessary assertive skills to carry it out.

These difficulties—the patient's pseudo-compliance and her very real lack of assertive skills—led us to introduce another technique. Since there seemed to be a real discrepancy between what the patient said she

could do and what actually happened, we decided to role-play exten-
sively with her. The purpose of this was not merely to teach her a
"script"; after all, we wanted to free her behaviors, not simply exchange
one for another. Our aim was to impress upon her the wide range of
choices she had in responding to unpleasant situations, and then let her
choose what felt best to her. To do this, it was at first necessary for the
therapist to play the patient, because she could not imagine any alternative behavior other than the one she relied on. By letting her be the
voice of danger, we also hoped to help her become a little more desensitized to perceived hostility.

Thus, we would have the patient say, "Isn't it a shame your husband
died so young; wouldn't it be nice for you if he were still alive?"

The therapist then offered the following possible responses for the
patient to choose from:

"Yes, it would. I do miss him so."

"Yes, it would, but I've gotten over it, you know."

"Yes, it would, but I'd just as soon not talk about it."

"Yes, it would, but it hurts me too much to talk about him; so please
don't!"

"No, you know I've really learned to forget him."

"No, are you joking? I'm a much different person now!"

"No, he might have turned out like your husband!"

"Perhaps, but who can dwell on such things today? Aren't those
flowers lovely!"

The major practical difficulty in this technique (besides coming up
with such a wide variety of responses) lay in the patient's passivity. She
would quickly grasp the intent of the demonstration, but would not
really join in. Instead, she might say, "Oh, yes, yes, I see what you
mean. Sure I could say that." But the question was: Would she? Only
with repeated trials in which the patient gradually was given the responding role were we able to get her to try out new responses. The
patient never volunteered to do this, and the therapist felt that whenever
he began to role-play with the patient, he was more interested in the
outcome than she. This is not to say that as a technique it failed—only
that it required a good deal of enthusiasm and patience. Despite this,
the therapist used role-playing to address a number of problems in
assertion: how to say no to the boss; how to negotiate with a friend over
which movie to see; how to invite a friend shopping; how to cope with
a surly clerk. The patient would then try out her new skills and reported
a number of successes in obtaining a satisfactory outcome in her dealings
with people.

FIFTH FORMULATION (May 1)

In reviewing with the patient the progress obtained thus far, it seemed clear that she was eager to pursue further therapy. She acknowledged the difficulty she was having in expanding her social network and in changing her interpersonal behavior. Moreover, she clearly appeared to receive reinforcement in continuing to present herself as the troubled but helpless victim who received personal attention from a caring doctor. This supportive relationship threatened to perpetuate her dependent behaviors and thwart the very assertiveness we were trying to promote. The patient certainly had no investment in this being a "brief" therapy!

Our formulation at this point saw the patient as recovered from a major depression and in the midst of learning new behaviors that would eventually replace older, maladaptive behaviors which may have predisposed her to the depression. At this point, the patient's learning still required the active interventions of a therapist to serve both as a role model and a source of reinforcement. Although she could not be without some such external aid for the time being, it seemed that an assertiveness training group might be the next logical modality to employ; such a group would broach head-on the patient's fear of interpersonal relationships, offer multiple new role models, and diminish the patient's dependence on one special person.

As a result of these considerations, the therapist discussed frankly with the patient the prospect of coming to the end of their contract in June. She expressed sadness at this, and made clear her wishes to continue in therapy, even with another therapist. The therapist presented her with the option of joining an assertive training group in the fall. The patient found this to be an acceptable idea, even while admitting her instinctive dislike of groups.

With such a disposition in mind, the patient and therapist set about to make plans for the summer. Renewed emphasis was placed on developing an expanded repertoire of activities that would increase the patient's pleasure and sense of self-esteem. The prospect of being without the therapist was rehearsed in fantasy and in role-playing, focusing on how the patient would cope without the ever-present therapist to rely on. Further attention was paid to acquiring new friends with the intention of widening the patient's social network, increasing the number of alternative interpersonal reinforcements, and thereby decreasing her need for the therapist to supply them all.

During this termination phase, the patient presented additional symptoms. She often came to sessions furious with the boss, whom she

accused of making fun of her and calling her "crazy." She was particularly worried that she might "lose control" and more or less prove him
right! These thoughts plagued her and caused her enormous anxiety at
work. In addition, she complained of a persistent tickle in her throat
which made her cough at night. This symptom resisted all efforts of an
internist to treat it medically.

The therapist again resorted to aversion relief desensitization, and the
results were dramatic. The following week the patient had greatly diminished anxiety at work and the cough, which had troubled her for
weeks, was all but gone. When the patient began to obsess about how
awful it would be to be alone, without the therapist, the therapist responded by desensitizing her to the prospect of solitude. He then
checked her breathing exercise routine, found it wanting, and did a
refresher course with the patient on proper deep breathing. He ended
by praising her for her continued efforts at expanding her repertoire of
pleasurable activities, and thereby reinforced the tentative steps toward
independence which she was making. He gave no reinforcement at all
to the depressive cognition that she was "sick again" and back where
she had started.

The patient came to the final session feeling much better. She reported
decreased anxiety with the boss and was eager to try out her own wings
over the summer. To this end, the therapist reviewed with her the course
of the therapy, emphasizing all the areas in which she had taken active
control over her behavior and begun to shape her own life. He praised
her success and reassured her that she could now do on her own what
the therapist had helped with before. He reminded the patient that he
would be available in the event of problems for consultation over the
summer. In any event, he would see her at least once for a renewal of
her prescription. They then ended, as did the supervisor and the therapist after a final review of the case.

SIXTH FORMULATION (JULY 23)

The patient went for about one month before calling the therapist, but
when she did, it was for more than a prescription. She reported a new
symptom, brief "hot flashes" associated with sweating that lasted a few
minutes and which occurred as often as 10 times a day without precipitants. It seemed to the therapist that this symptom exhibited the same
sympathetic arousal as had the panic attacks previously, and was possibly a *forme fruste* of the latter. The therapist therefore reassured the
patient that she would be able to control this symptom as she had the

panic attacks. He again went over the breathing exercise routine with her, again found it wanting, and once more rehearsed it with her.

The attacks persisted nevertheless, and when the therapist met with the patient again in two weeks, she was able to link them to a specific ideational content to which she was phobic, namely "going crazy" and "losing control" of her anger. With this new information, the therapist proceeded to desensitize the patient to the idea of going crazy, this time using the more current imagery that the patient was reporting.

Despite this intervention, the patient reported only modest gains the following week. She was clearly depressed, although not sufficiently so as to warrant a renewed diagnosis of major depressive episode. In fact, the patient maintained that she had felt better for the two days prior to her therapy appointment, and the therapist began again to reconsider his role in the patient's symptomatology. His new formulation located the patient's principal problem in her continuing difficulty in separating from the powerfully reinforcing figure of the therapist. It appeared that the patient had been unable to establish adequate internal reinforcers in the time that they had worked together. With that in mind, the therapist gave the patient a new tape of his voice to take home with her. The tape contained a 20-minute relaxation exercise quite different from the muscle relaxation exercise she had tried earlier in the year. This exercise consisted of a series of vague and changing visual images which were presented to the patient every 10 seconds (Fensterheim and Baer, 1978). An example might be, "Can you imagine the distance between your ears? . . . Is it possible for you to become aware of how close your breath comes to the back of your eyes every time you inhale?" The tape produced a profound relaxation in session, and the therapist hoped that in giving it to the patient he would provide her with a tangible, audible reminder that he was still there.

At this point the therapist consulted with the supervisor, who agreed that the patient's difficulty was a failure to establish sufficient internal reinforcers to enable her to do without the therapist. He made it very clear, however, that he viewed this as a therapeutic problem, not the patient's fault. He felt that we had inadequately formulated the patient's dependent behaviors. In particular, we had allowed the therapist to become so powerfully reinforcing to the patient that she had never needed to learn self-reinforcing behaviors. With that in mind, he proposed a revised formulation, focusing on a strategy to develop the patient's sense of self-esteem and, more importantly, self-pleasure. The patient would again be admonished to engage in the various activities which had helped before: vigorous physical exercise, relaxation exercises, socialization, etc. This time, however, we would attempt to arrange for these behaviors to be self-reinforcing. To do this, we proposed helping the patient to develop a repertoire of joyful, pleasant images, taken from fantasy, childhood, or genuinely pleasurable sensations in her present-day life. If the patient was doing an activity which she liked, she would be instructed to tell herself how much she liked it, even as she was doing it, and literally remind herself that here, at least, there was pleasure in her life that she could give herself. She was also to rehearse this script, telling herself how much she enjoyed a particular activity, before as well as after she did it, so as to teach her to look forward to, as well as to savor, a pleasant experience. Similarly, this exercise could be applied to an activity which the patient did not honestly enjoy, but which she was willing to do because we recommended it as "good for you." In such cases, the patient could be instructed to think about a scene or memory which, though unrelated to the activity, nevertheless was pleasurable. In particular, scenes that reminded her of being loved by her mother, of making her mother proud of her, and of basking in such pride seemed to be the logical internal reinforcer for behaviors that would otherwise not seem self-motivated. In both instances, what was proposed was a systematic attempt to change the very way the patient thought about her own behavior, using thought itself as a potentially powerful reinforcer which the patient could learn to modify. To alter the pattern of reinforcing thoughts would lead naturally to a change in which behaviors were reinforced, and that would lead to behavioral change. This time, however, it would be the patient's own thoughts that served to maintain the progress, not some external reinforcer.

The results of these modifications in the formulation and their implementation resulted in improvement. The patient renewed her pursuit of new pleasurable activities with vigor, and would volunteer in session, "You know, I really do feel better after I exercise; I should do it more!" She began to go to museums spontaneously, walk in the park alone, and go to church. What remained was for the patient to include new people into these behaviors, which required additional assertive skills. She tolerated gaps as big as three weeks between sessions well. Her sweats diminished considerably and she even contemplated terminating therapy, this time because she felt the need to be more independent.

At this point the therapist discontinued the patient's medication, since the six months for continued prophylaxis was over. The patient rapidly developed renewed symptoms of insomnia, panic attacks and anxiety. At first, the therapist attributed this to a negative placebo effect, and worked with the patient to review her relaxation exercises, pleasure/self-esteem activities, and cognitions. However, the patient continued to deteriorate and became increasingly depressed, with weight loss, tearfulness, and diurnal variation in mood. The therapist therefore diagnosed the patient as again suffering from a major depressive episode and began the antidepressant medication again.

The patient's symptoms remitted after the usual two-week lag time. By the end of a month, she was again agreeing to focus on the business of furthering her assertive skills in a group setting. The therapist arranged for her to start a weekly therapy group. Simultaneously he began to decrease the frequency of contact with the patient. He used his remaining therapeutic leverage with the patient to overcome some of her specific phobias about group therapy, using a combination of role rehearsal and some dynamic interpretations. The patient is about to begin with a group as of this writing, and the therapist has terminated with her.

CONCLUSION: ON TEACHING AND SUPERVISION

From the supervisor's viewpoint, this case illustrates the feasibility of teaching a professional with virtually no knowledge of behavioral psychotherapy to reconceptualize the nature of his work and to utilize effectively procedures to which he has had no previous exposure. The resident's background in general psychiatry and psychodynamic psychotherapy were both an advantage and a disadvantage with respect to the treatment of this patient. We will consider each in turn.

The therapist was skilled in establishing a relationship that inspired confidence in the patient and was intrinsically reinforcing to her. He had experience in the assessment of symptom patterns and was competent to make use of medication for their treatment. Because of his psychodynamic background he was interested in the process of formulating an understanding of the patient that did not focus solely on symptom relief. His background in biopsychiatry kept him open to formulations of the patient's behavior that were not limited to psychoanalytic conceptions.

Nevertheless, these very strengths, as well as his limited exposure previously to behavioral work, also led to some limitations. The emphasis on the quality of the relationship as a therapeutic instrument led to some difficulty regarding termination. The availability of drugs that could affect symptoms may have led to some reluctance to rely solely on behavioral interventions to produce results. In such a way some expectations may have been induced in the patient that drugs and the therapeutic relationship were a critical factor in ameliorating her condition. This may have been compounded, at least initially, by the therapist's nonverbal cues and style of presentation, which perhaps conveyed to the patient the tacit implication that behavioral interventions were somehow limited, brief, and superficial.

As treatment proceeded, the power of behavioral procedures to affect the quality of the patient's experience became apparent both to the patient and to the trainee. A variety of relaxation procedures were used effectively. The patient learned, albeit with some difficulty, to reorganize her breathing in order to produce reliably significant calming whenever she felt anxious. Most dramatic possibly to both patient and therapist was the effect aversion relief desensitization had on areas of phobic distress and avoidance. Least effective, on the other hand, was the attempt to teach the patient assertive skills that would allow her to get a greater degree of satisfaction from social encounters. It is possible that more extensive preparation of the therapist could have been helpful in this area, but a group setting is probably better suited for modeling and practicing such skills.

As a teaching exercise the case allowed the trainee to be exposed to a very wide variety of procedures within a relatively short span of time, and thus demonstrated to the trainee the flexibility of behavioral psychotherapy in meeting the patient's clinical needs. The patient's remaining symptoms of social isolation and dependency on the therapist represented correctable error in formulation that in itself carried an educational value, as well as underscored the clinical reality that not all of the patient's behaviors could be changed within a brief therapy format.

From the therapist's viewpoint, the experience of learning and doing behavioral psychotherapy highlighted the conflict between many of the apparently contradictory but parallel explanatory systems current in contemporary psychiatry. It seemed hard to understand, for example, how recently "learned" behaviors could respond specifically to a drug; or why family therapy might not be the best treatment for a woman whose problem seemed coincident with the pending break-up of the last remaining vestiges of her nuclear family; or how relabeling transference as "rapport" accomplished anything except to simplify a necessarily complex phenomenon. Not that any of these explanatory systems —behavioral, biological, systems, or psychodynamic—has a legitimate claim to superiority. But the effective learning of a new system does require a "willing suspension of disbelief." The trainee must be flexible enough to work with his new supervisor, not against him. In this case, the therapist and supervisor more or less eschewed theoretical debate until the writing up of the case, in what amounted to an unspoken agreement to immerse themselves in the process of treatment. The supervisor's style of teaching the various techniques by actually demonstrating them on the therapist facilitated a kind of experiential learning. Such a process might be considered amost anti-intellectual, but it does serve to further the acquisition of a new gestalt, or what Jaspers (1963) calls understanding, as contrasted to explaining.

Nevertheless, the therapist could not free himself entirely of his former training, and this had an impact on the conduct of the therapy. For example, during the first sessions with the shock generator, the therapist discovered that each stimulus seemed to generate a new memory from the patient's childhood. He marveled at his ability to push a button and retrieve a piece of the patient's past. Far from seeing this as a mere epiphenomenon of the desensitization procedure, he was inclined to pursue each of these memories with the patient and explore their psychodynamic significance. This in turn led to a certain sense of guilt when he nevertheless continued steadfastly with the desensitization procedure, and certainly made for a curious blend of behavioral and psychodynamic therapy!

On other occasions, the patient would fill the session with a torrent of depressive reminiscences. The therapist would be inclined to allow the patient to speak and to listen attentively, but the supervisor would recommend active structuring of the session, maintaining that such repetitive and stereotyped behavior only served to reinforce the patient's already low sense of self-esteem and joylessness. The upshot of this divergence of opinions was an idiosyncratic compromise that often reflected the therapist's personal ambivalence more than any rational synthesis. Thus, he might let the patient talk on for 20 minutes, then cut her off abruptly without offering any interpretation, and yet have insufficient time remaining to implement his behavioral procedures effectively. Such solutions could maximize the worst in both systems.

Perhaps most disturbing of all to the therapist was his feeling of tacit complicity with the patient's denial of personal responsibility for her feelings and wishes. Little or no attempt was made to explore the patient's anger, for example, which so often appeared as the context for her panics and depression. To focus solely on these latter symptoms, of which the patient was a passive victim, seemed to beg the most important issue, namely that the patient was furious at the therapist, her children, her husband, her boss, and ultimately her parents. And such victimization was precisely what was "intended" by such symptoms: to belie the patient's responsibility for such angry feelings which she found unacceptable.

Of course, there are many dynamically informed supportive therapies which would equally have avoided the topic of anger in this patient, and the therapist himself felt that the assertiveness exercises were a most helpful device in enabling the patient to sublimate her aggression effectively. The therapist did come to accept the idea that learning new behaviors can promote dynamic change. His experience with behavioral psychotherapy was an essentially maturing one, and despite all the theoretical reservations raised above, he was able to mold himself to the form of a new model—to the ultimate benefit of the patient.

REFERENCES

Fensterheim, H., and Baer, J. *Stop Running Scared*. New York: Dell, 1978.
Jaspers, K. *General Psychopathology*. Chicago: University of Chicago Press, Part II, 1963, pp. 302ff.
Liebowitz, M.R., and Klein, D.F. Assessment and treatment of phobic anxiety. *The Journal of Clinical Psychiatry*, 1979, 40:480.
Lum, L.C., Hyperventilation: The tip of the iceberg. *Journal of Psychometric Research*, 1975, 19:375.
Orwin, J. Respiratory relief: A new and rapid method for the treatment of phobic states. *British Journal of Psychiatry*, 1971, 119:635.
Roberts, J., and Fisher, D. *How To Make and Break Habits*. New York: Dell, 1976.
Weissman, M.M., Prusoff, B.A., DiMascio, A. et al. The efficacy of drugs and psychotherapy in the treatment of acute depressive episodes. *American Journal of Psychiatry*, 1979, 136:555.
Wolpe, J. *The Practice of Behavior Therapy*, Second Edition. New York: Pergamon, 1973.

9

Indications for Central and Peripheral Approaches to Presenting Problems: A Case of Sexual Impotence

Stephen Wilder

The behavioral psychotherapist is often faced with the decision of whether to treat the presenting problem directly or to treat other aspects of the patient's behavior in order to solve that problem. With the use of the behavioral formulation the decision is based on whether the symptomatic behaviors appear to be functionally autonomous or whether they appear to be fueled, maintained, or reinforced by other aspects of the patient's psychological organization. This is illustrated in the treatment of a young man who presented with the complaint of sexual impotence.

INITIAL DATA

Simon was 26 years old, married, and a junior executive in a large and competitive advertising firm. He was tall, attractive, athletic, of medium build, but appeared less prepossessing than his objective characteristics indicated. This self-mitigation was achieved not by any deficiency in dress or grooming but rather by a subtle yet persistent avoidance of prolonged eye contact and a slouching posture which resulted in his appearing smaller and lacking in vitality. He also moved perceptibly backward when asked direct questions and excessively used conditional clauses, which diminished the impact of his speech.

Though Simon was overtly timid and unassertive in his demeanor, I rarely felt relaxed in his presence and was not surprised by sporadic unpleasantries which took the forms of carping, querulousness, and demandingness. These sallies were not directly aimed at me and were quickly denied or retracted and followed by apologies. Examples of these sallies included complaining about traffic en route to my office and repeated requests for a precise prediction of the length and outcome of treatment. Also issued were negative pronouncements about psychotherapy "as a science," and an almost whining refusal to recognize any of his behavioral assets. Incidentally, it was only in the more advanced and successful treatment phases that Simon was able to make positive statements about himself, about me, or about our mutual endeavors.

The client came to treatment because he was "impotent." This was stated flatly, frequently, and, in contrast to his customary self-effacing style, most demandingly. Also in contrast to his self-effacing style were his insistent demands for immediate systematic desensitization. Simon's demands for systematic desensitization were not merely the result of his reading about a procedure reputed to be highly efficacious, quick, and at that time very much in vogue. His demands were consonant with his presentation of his potency problem as "totally his fault," in no way related to his wife's actions, and as some culpable defect which caused his wife great pain. It was also consonant with a wish to minimize exploration of other life issues.

Inquiry during the initial session revealed the following chain of events. Simon was actually impotent, as defined by inability to erect and penetrate, about 50 percent of occasions intercourse was attempted. Premature ejaculation after penetration was not reported by Simon or by his wife. From a cognitive standpoint, it was critical that he never labeled himself "potent" during the other 50 percent of occasions when lovemaking was described as "good"; neither did he even internally challenge his wife when she blamed him. Simon was selectively unkind to himself in his self-evaluation.

Simon was most reluctant in early sessions to discuss his wife or to consent to her being interviewed with the possibility of her participating in treatment plans. He staunchly resisted the thesis that this could be a shared problem. Rather, he described Carol as a "fine woman, totally functional and totally free of anxiety," who was awaiting the restoration of his potency. He reported that she completely concurred with and reinforced this viewpoint. He was humorless and irritated when I mildly described him as a "knight seeking to purify himself and save a damsel in distress from his iniquities."

As I explored the antecedents and consequences of Simon's impotent behavior, the following became apparent. Simon could neither predict when he would be impotent nor identify even hypothetical events, affects, or cognitions preceding these occasions. Two phenomena were, in addition, extremely noteworthy. First, Simon had no concept of the right of the male to refuse or defer sex. His world view—shared by his wife—was that he must perform flawlessly regardless of the emotional context, his state of fatigue, his degree of desire, or his lack of interest. Second, his failures to perform were met by his wife with criticism, tears, and angry accusations of his lack of consideration. Simon would agree to all of the above, He and his wife would first argue, then cry, and when exhausted, fall asleep in each other's arms. Simon noted that they often felt closest to one another at the end of this chain of painful consequences. This interlocking choreography was so well ritualized as to be strongly suggestive of a sadomasochistic game with shared intimacy, otherwise unattainable, as the ultimate reinforcer.

When I asked about other areas of his life, Simon was grudgingly compliant in responding. In brief, the following information seemed most pertinent. Simon denied problems with his job functioning but did state he did not like aspects of his work and was considering a change. Upon listening carefully to the contradictory strains of his verbal report, I formulated the clinical hypotheses that Simon was anxious about competition in general and was anxious and angry mainly in connection with evaluative authority figures. He flatly denied or minimized these possibilities.

Simon maintained close ties with his parents. An elder brother lived in another city. Simon joked that his brother had "escaped" his mother but denied the accordingly plausible clinical hypothesis that either brother had any negative feelings about his mother. It is important to note that at the inception of treatment Simon denied both the nature of such events and/or that he responded to them with consequent angry or fearful feelings. That is, he denied both that his mother's constant scathing criticisms constituted attacks, and that he felt any consequent affect. As might be expected, therefore, this passive cognitive stance had generated no direct or assertive responses employed to deter or to counter his mother. Simon reported that his father was treated similarly by his mother and responded in a similar fashion.

Simon's descriptions of his early development were meager in detail but emphasized passivity, conformity, and a generally phobic life-style marked by ill-defined anxiety and strong avoidance of difficult interpersonal encounters. As is frequently the case with such individuals, copious obsessional thought was present and served to distract from more central anxieties.

It is important that neither Simon nor his wife reported other lovers or close involvements during dating or prior to marriage. More important were their independent reports that he was free of sexual dysfunction during their year of courtship and for the first three months of marriage. They had been married for ten months when Simon consulted me. Both had gone through academic and/or vocational pressure beginning after three months of marriage. The sketchy data indicated the following clinical hypotheses: 1) Each felt anxious, dependent and covertly blamed the other for being emotionally unsupportive; 2) Simon attempted to seek refuge in his customary passive demeanor and his wife reacted with a sharp increase in her critical behavior; 3) Simon became increasingly tense and angry but also sought to mollify her with increments in his habitual deference and submission. Simon was unable to manage the ever-growing discrepancy between his negative affect and his compliant behaviors. Eventually his sexuality, a respondent area of his life he could not voluntarily control, became the vehicle for and signal of disruption in the marriage.

BEHAVIORAL FORMULATION

The core of Simon's psychological organization in the problem area was formulated as being a long-term fear of angry and demanding women. This had generalized to a fear of any kind of confrontation. Early in life he had developed two modes of coping with this fear. One coping method was a passive-aggressive pattern of behavior and the second was a phobic avoidance. This latter, the phobic avoidance, concerned not only the interpersonal situations involved but even the very feelings these situations evoked; denial, repression and self-blame were major defenses. Hence Simon had only limited opportunities to learn appropriate assertive skills in this area and was inhibited from using even those skills he did possess. Nevertheless, it was formulated, anger did build up, an anger he was unable to express directly. He had learned a pattern for the indirect expression of these feelings, a pattern that I labeled "angry withholding." There were many instances of this, such as his withholding of generosity behaviors from Carol; he rarely did or said nice things to her. His sexual impotence was the most obvious expression of the angry withholding and he may even have perceived it as a punishment of Carol, although this was far from certain. Carol's reactions to his impotence, much as they appeared to upset him, actually served to reinforce it.

Simon's personal history tends to support this formulation. Simon's father passively accepted his wife's (Simon's mother's) attacks. His brother chose to escape from the situation rather than to adopt a more assertive stance. These models left Simon lacking a template for appropriate behaviors vis-à-vis a woman perceived as harsh and negative; indeed, his avoidant cognitive set left him with no basis for even the relevant perceptions of these qualities. These deficits, augmented by his social skill deficits, resulted in a lack of male or female friends sufficiently close and communicative to apprise him of alternatives in life. Rendering the likelihood of corrective information still more remote was Simon's grudging close-mouthed acceptance of Carol's family as the people with whom most recreational time was spent. In this setting, Simon was again exposed, in the form of Carol's mother, to a woman who criticized with abandon and vitriol her husband's and other intimates who threatened to refuse her various biddings. When directly addressed in this style by his mother-in-law, Simon's response was analogous to the ways in which he responded to his wife and mother. He avoided, if possible, submitted when necessary, and then minimized both the behavioral event and the presumptive consequent affect.

TARGET BEHAVIORS

The core difficulty, according to the above formulation, was his inability to deal with the anger emanating from such harsh, critical women as his wife, his mother and his mother-in-law. He also could not deal with his own anger toward significant others in an assertive and constructive way. Rather, he would tend to deny it, become overtly self-critical and covertly express it in disguised forms. Treatment centering around this area would be expected not only to bring about the widest change in his psychological functioning but also to bring about the most permanent change in his sexual impotence, the presenting problem.

Direct treatment of the sexual impotence as a consequence of anxiety alone was ruled out by this formulation. Because this symptom was formulated as being strongly fueled by his problems with anger, it was deemed that successful and permanent change was not likely. Even if this could be achieved, some other substitute behavior pattern aimed at achieving the same reinforcers would probably develop. A similar argument applies to working with the reinforcing impact of Carol's reproaches when sexual failure did occur. Through the use of cognitive and/or desensitization procedures it may have been possible to reduce Simon's sensitivity to these reproaches and accordingly reduce their reinforcing influence. However, at best this change would have been limited and the danger of the development of a substitute vindictive behavioral pattern remained.

One difficulty remained about selecting the anger constellation as the target for treatment. The behavioral formulation was basically a method for organizing my own thinking about the patient and his problems. Although based on data gained through record keeping and discussion with the patient, there was need for further verification. As previously noted, Simon was not an unbiased reporter and some external confirmation was desirable. Therefore, his wife was asked to come in to see me. Beyond the exploratory value of this visit there was also the possibility of her active participation in a treatment program.

Carol grudgingly agreed to come for one session. Though, as previously mentioned, Simon described her as a totally functional and anxiety-free woman, such was not my impression. In an individual session, Carol was insecure and defensive about her autonomous functioning and particularly about her marital relationship. Spontaneously and without provocation, she stated that I probably thought that she contributed to Simon's sexual problems "but they were strictly his own." The anger and rigidity of Carol's interview behavior served several purposes. First, it supported my own clinical inferences in contrast to Simon's descriptions of his wife and of their interactions. Second, it illustrated the inadvisability of persisting in attempts to gain her cooperation; it appeared highly likely that such attempts would frighten her further and risk Simon's leaving treatment to side with her. Also supported was the formulation that their joint anger and lack of perspective on their relationship were maintainers of his impotence. Thus, there was some confirmation of the behavioral formulation plus the knowledge that the treatment could not include Carol at that juncture. Also required was informing Simon that without Carol's cooperation we were dealing unilaterally with assertion training in a context of coercive marital control. It was stated and restated as therapy unfolded that Simon would of necessity find himself dealing with Carol in sometimes adversary interactions and the results of such dealings were not totally predictable in terms of consequences to the relationship.

THE INITIAL CONTRACT

As a first step, I presented to Simon my clinical opinion about his sexual impotence and about what would constitute proper treatment for it. I told him that I did not believe that he would receive full and lasting benefits from the systematic desensitization he desired. I explained to him that the complexities of his painful interactions with his wife strongly mitigated against the unrealistic flawless performance demanded of him by his wife and himself. I vigorously informed him that anger, criticism, and self-blame were neither aphrodisiacs nor contributory to a happy life; rather, it was necessary that he develop an effective repertoire of assertive behaviors. I suggested that his periodic impotence was not an intrapsychically determined symptom, nor was it a functionally autonomous or freestanding habit with a life of its own. Perhaps it was a signal of marital conflict, as well as an expression of some of his feelings in their own right.

Given Simon's initial set toward treatment, he was understandably reluctant to go into "such deep and esoteric matters." I told Simon that his difficulties in recognizing and appropriately expressing his feelings were neither deep nor esoteric but potentially observable events which were part of the repeating fabric of his ongoing life. I then proposed an initial procedure designed to verify or refute the validity of my proposed treatment model. Simon tentatively and cautiously agreed to "my approach."

RECORD KEEPING

Simon was requested to record, on a daily basis and in some detail, his perception of positive, neutral, and negative interpersonal events with significant others. He was asked to note concomitant and consequent affects when he could label them. He was further requested to record the occurrence, nonoccurrence, and nature of lovemaking, along with any antecedent, accompanying or consequent choreographies.

This monitoring task had to be presented to Simon with great care. His passive-aggressive behavior pattern and his need to avoid recognizing phobic situations suggested that he would have difficulty in following the instructions. Hence I emphasized that his task was being performed for its own values of being intrinsically interesting and of providing more information about his life. No immediate change was required. Further, his observations were discussed in detail during our therapeutic sessions. These discussions served to both reinforce the record keeping and to enhance the collaborative aspects of our relationship.

Perhaps partially because of this mode of presentation, Simon was unexpectedly diligent and reliable with respect to record keeping. This is not to say that Simon immediately would monitor and record all he had been avoiding or ignoring. Rather, my close attention and concern to the details of his life proved to be highly reinforcing to him, as long as the clinical inquiry did not touch on particularly sensitive areas. Simon was usually willing to reveal himself rapidly as long as we obeyed an unverbalized contract of not demanding change as an immediate consequence. In any event, extensive information was recorded which was elaborated by clinical inquiry.

Simon's early diaries revealed consistent patterns of criticism, pressure, and hostility from significant others, along with a general absence of effective assertion on his part. Furthermore, the mystery of Simon's intermittent impotence and intermittent potence was highly consistent with the data. Unanswered negative communications from his wife, his mother-in-law, his supervisor, and his peers were, in that order, associated with Simon's being dysfunctional later that same day. When he avoided or escaped negative communications or, more rarely, attempted rejoinders, he was usually functional.

Simon, upon inspecting the data, acknowledged the apparent correlations between being put down by others, particularly the women in his life, and subsequent sexual dysfunction. However, he blandly attempted to explain these as "perhaps accidental." Specifically limiting, in terms of the need for assertion training, was the absence of felt anger or any other labeled dysphoria as consequences. In short, despite viewing self-reported data to the contrary, Simon continued to minimize both upsetting antecedent event and consequent affect. This was formulated to be a repressive defense based on his pattern of phobic avoidance and also serving to maintain his passive orientation. Whereas he viewed systematic desensitization as based on an external locus of change which would allow him to remain passive, assertion training required from him the assumption of responsibility for effort and an active orientation. As long as he repressed dysphoric feelings, he was able to minimize the importance of the patterns that had emerged from his record keeping and so deny the need for active change on his part. The obvious next step in treatment was to help him become more aware of his own angers.

One method I used to increase his affective awareness I call "systematic sensitization." This method is based on the hypothesis that the phobic avoidance, the repression, is maintained by a series of physical or psychological avoidances and escapes from stimuli that elicit disturbed feelings. If we have the patient minimize these avoidances/escapes by focusing attention on these stimuli for some period of time, the disturbed feelings should emerge. With Simon this procedure was first carried out in imagery. Relaxation training was performed in an attempt to facilitate and intensify the imagery. He was then instructed to imagine as vividly as possible various events. These events were drawn either from his own reports or from my clinically based guesses about related but unreported happenings. The events were presented nonhierarchically in terms of my expectations of the level of distress they would elicit. Nor were they presented predictably in terms of content. Each scene was held long enough to allow the therapist, if necessary, to elaborate the description of the scene until affective responses could appear. When emotion was elicited, he continued to imagine the scene long enough to provide him with the full emotional experience but not long enough to bring about extinction. Every attempt was made to avoid suggesting specific affective responses but also to ensure that he persisted in focusing on the stimuli in question. When I doubted the vividness of Simon's focus, I asked him to repeat in detail his own experience of the situation. Persistence in redirecting Simon's attention to the component parts of these events began to bring observable tension to his forehead, faint perspiration to his face, angry scowls and, increasingly, reports of feeling hurt and angry. Scenes were repeated over several sessions to prevent attenuation of awareness of these seemingly new and upsetting feelings.

A second method I used to increase his affective awareness was a form of structured role-playing. Simon was instructed to play intentionally varied roles in events that had recently occurred with significant others. Through shaping and modeling, he was helped to practice a wide range of behaviors of all types, not merely appropriate or adaptive behaviors. For example, a series of scripts based on Carol's critical attacks was developed. Simon practiced a number of different kinds of responses to these attacks. Some of these responses were deliberately inappropriate in content or intensity, for the aim, at that point, was not to increase his assertive behavior but rather to increase his affective awareness. This was accomplished, probably helped along by the previous work with systematic sensitization. He did become more aware of his feelings, principally resentment and anger. He spontaneously began to question why he "put up with all this." These feelings generalized to everyday life situations, although he still did not know how to express them.

ASSERTIVE TRAINING

At this point in treatment Simon had become able to recognize interpersonal attacks on him and to experience his consequent resentment and anger. He also saw, through viewing his own record keeping, that such interpersonal and intrapsychic interactions were frequently related to his sexual dysfunction. The next step was to translate these new awarenesses into effective action.

A resistance to this step developed. Rather than seeking to acquire new behaviors, Simon became interested in "understanding." By this he meant a passive, more protracted and historical examination of how he came to this impasse. My clinical formulation of this attitude was primarily in terms of his dominant pattern of phobic avoidance, in this instance an avoidance of the confrontations his assertive acts might evoke. Reduction of phobic anxiety in this area would clearly be required before assertive training could proceed.

However, there was still the problem of having Simon accept this approach rather than the passive historical one he favored. I first disputed the need for such an approach. Using his own record keeping, I demonstrated to him that, although his behaviors did have histories, these histories were still active in the present. I read to him samples from his own reports of how he constantly but unwittingly elicited and reinforced Carol's attacking behavior; of how he frequently elicited and reinforced similar behaviors from mother and mother-in-law; of how his brother had recently "escaped" his mother but of how Simon remained and only now was conscious of the hurt and anger engendered within him; of the numerous instances of anxiety and avoidance in response to other threatening figures.

Rather than focusing on historical exploration, I proposed that we engage in certain experiments in living. The experiments consisted of three specific steps to be applied to various situations. The first was active scanning his intrapsychic and interpersonal environments to learn to correctly anticipate and identify prospective attacks on him. The second was the further use of imagery and systematic sensitization procedures to become even more aware of his own feelings about these attacks. The final step was to employ behavior rehearsal during our sessions, coupled with covert rehearsal on his own, to learn to act in such a way as to prevent these attacks or to respond effectively when they did occur. These, it was hypothesized, would lead to a more active and less blaming cognitive posture on the one hand and to an increase in his sexual potency on the other. The combination of my own persuasiveness and of Simon's burgeoning awareness of his own feelings induced him to accept assertive training as part of the working contract. Increasing trust in our therapeutic relationship was also invaluable.

The first behavior chosen as a target concerned his ability to say "no" to lovemaking. This was an important area and, although it had been explicitly targeted earlier in treatment, he had been unable to assert himself in this manner. Desensitization and cognitive procedures were used to reduce his anxiety and reluctance to practice the acts involved. In the desensitization scenes he would imagine feeling angry or feeling no desire or affection and then telling Carol that he did not want to have sex, that he preferred simple embracing or being alone. Other scenes included images of Carol's attacks or of her repeated questioning of him. During cognitive approaches we explored the wisdom and reasons for his attempting to make love while angry. We also explored the possible continuing damage to the relationship that was the consequence of the anger and self-flagellation following the impotence that would come about under those conditions. Simon was also advised to express to Carol, when he could honestly do so, the affection he actually felt. Simon was pleased to discover that Carol was generally accepting of his clear and direct expression of his desires or nondesires. Again note that early in therapy Simon had been advised to do these things but at that time he reported that he was too anxious or unwilling to do so. Now he was able to make such statements with reinforcing consequences.

Whereas 15 to 20 sessions were required before Simon was willing to attempt a more assertive life-style, once he began progress was swift. Essentially, Simon continued the same forms of record keeping described above. In addition, however, he recorded the increasing frequency of his attempts at assertive communication. He also recorded the affects experienced before, during, and consequent to attempts at assertion. Data were also collected in the context of teaching Simon to perceive the impact of his new behaviors on significant others. Of course, he continued to record the occurrence or nonoccurrence of lovemaking, along with 1) whether he was functional, and 2) his subjective enjoyment of lovemaking on given occasions. I stressed that his becoming a perfectly functional android was far less desirable than appreciating and acting in terms of his feelings about himself and others. I suggested that this improved sense of self would also affect both his relationship with Carol and his sexuality.

Treatment results were dramatic and notably free of sabotage by what had been thought to be an angry and resistant wife. There were two important reasons for this. First, Carol did like sex with Simon; it was never her aim to use her anger to destroy such a direct form of contact and pleasure. Rather, the impairment of their sexuality was an unwanted consequence of their unwitting interplay. Second—and crucial to the strategy of Simon's new assertiveness—the plan was to reduce Carol's inadvertent sabotage by reducing the mutual provocations in which Simon participated and which rendered him both submissive and symptomatic. However, I felt keenly aware of an unfortunate limitation in treatment goals achieved. Given Carol's resistance to participation in a treatment process, which could foster greater reciprocity and mutual nourishing, there remained for Simon one choice. He had to become relatively more dominant in day-to-day events on a unilateral basis.

TREATMENT CONSEQUENCES

The frequency of sexual dysfunction did not appreciably vary during early stages of treatment but this changed abruptly once assertive training began.

As Simon reported more frequent assertion, both with Carol and with significant others, reports of impotence decreased rapidly. Simon became quickly adept at noting and savoring his interpersonal gains, but had difficulty in noticing the effects of this increased assertion on his symptoms. Similarly, he had to be prompted to notice the reverse pattern—that on days of low assertion he was prey to dysfunction. Record keeping further indicated that the assertive balance he maintained with Carol was most important to the corresponding maintenance of his potency. His relationship with her generated both the most intense positive affect and the most intense negative affect. Other relationships mattered, particularly mother and mother-in-law, but not as much.

Within six sessions after the formal beginning of assertion training, Simon had demonstrated the following changes. He was consistently and increasingly being more assertive with Carol and with significant others. He reported feeling better about himself during and consequent to assertive encounters, as well as in terms of general self-confidence. The occurrence of impotence could nearly always be temporally correlated with failures of assertion or his allowing himself to feel compelled to engage in sex when such was not his desire. Simon, however, no longer berated himself for these failures; nor did he permit Carol to do so. Of particular importance were Simon's descriptions of his feelings about and during lovemaking; he now focused more on affectional, sensual, and sexual sensations and focused less on his adequacy as a lover. Sex was increasingly perceived as part of an expression of his feelings rather than as a vehicle for the measurement of success or failure or primarily pleasing another person.

Positive changes in the marital balance were notable. Carol was not only more satisfied sexually but also sharply decreased her attacking behaviors. She willingly engaged in some joint follow-up sessions and spontaneously reported perceiving and enjoying a different form of marital balance. Both Carol and Simon expressed satisfaction with the status quo and he expressed the wish to terminate his therapy.

However, many problems still required treatment. As an option to immediate termination, I offered Simon and Carol an additional treatment contract. I observed that his presenting sexual dysfunction had been associated with generalized interpersonal deficits in assertion and coercive marital control, clearly unfavorable to him. I commended him on his remediation of these difficulties but observed the following. Softer signs of a power struggle central to the marriage remained, though now more favorably balanced in his apparent interest. I also remarked on the persistence of deficits in giving or generosity behaviors—complaints that each echoed about the other. Accordingly, I broached another experiment in living. In this proposed treatment contract the targeted behaviors would be generosity behaviors, and we would monitor possible covariations with a finer appreciation of marital nuances as behaviorally defined. Simon understood the rationale for such a contract, recognized the strong remnants of the power struggle central to his marriage, and further acknowledged that he was still withholding everyday pleasures. He even could sometimes sense the spite which accompanied his withholding. He nonetheless restated that he felt "satisfied" with the status quo and would prefer the option of continuing only after a therapeutic vacation, despite my recommendation to the contrary.

Towards the end of treatment Carol did participate somewhat. She was seen several times both individually and in joint sessions with Simon for discussions of the changing marital relationship. She was particularly pleased with the improvement in sex, was neither unaware of nor overtly displeased with Simon's newfound assertiveness, and indeed expressed a preference for the new balance in their relations. She was interested in the proposal for increasing generosity behaviors but she too did not want to initiate a therapeutic program at that time.

Both Simon and Carol were alerted to possible signals of difficulty so that they could contact me. They agreed to monthly telephone calls as checkups. Treatment was terminated with good feelings all around.

FOLLOW-UP

The monthly telephone calls consisted of chats with Simon and/or Carol. During the first year they both felt that the relationship was "going well" although it could "use improvement" because there was a mutual feeling of frustration. There were no reported lapses in Simon's assertiveness or in his sexual functioning. At the end of this time Carol completed school and entered the job market. This was followed by Carol's having panic attacks in a series of job situations and eventually entering into a state of agitated depression so severe that a brief hospitalization was necessary. At the time of this writing Simon has been seeing me periodically for emotional support and Carol is under the care of another therapist. The marriage is tenuous as each has mixed feelings about the other. It is interesting to note that during this period Simon's sexual and assertive gains remained intact. Indeed, in other areas, particularly in his professional endeavors, he has shown increasing confidence and strength.

The final word is not yet in on this case. Carol's depression appears to have been directly precipitated by the new demands the job situation placed on her. It is most difficult to assess the role, if any, in this that was played by the changed relation with Simon. What happens in Carol's treatment will probably have a great influence on what finally becomes of the relationship with Simon. Nevertheless, as has been noted, Simon's therapeutic gains are holding and he is continuing to improve in other, nonstressful areas.

SUMMARY

Simon presented with the problem of sexual impotence and a desire for treatment through systematic desensitization. However, it was formulated that such a treatment approach would not be effective because the symptom was not functionally autonomous. Rather, it was part of a more general pattern which I labeled as "angry withholding." The core of the organization from which this pattern emerged was a phobic reaction to angry, demanding women. This in turn fueled a passive-aggressive mode of coping in interpersonal situations and a generalized pattern of phobic avoidance. These, in their turn, led to decreased opportunities for the learning of assertive skills and to inhibition in the use of those skills he did possess. The defenses of repression and denial allowed him to avoid the very recognition of his main problems.

Treatment first centered around circumventing his defenses so that he could recognize his angers, resentments and discomforts and the cues that set them off. Then, through desensitization and assertive training, his phobic reaction to angry, demanding women was reduced. Teaching Simon to exercise his right to refuse sex when he did not want it was one of the behaviors which received considerable attention. However, change in this behavior proved not to be crucial; although he did feel more comfortable following change in this area, it did not eliminate his sexual dysfunction. General assertive behaviors in social situations led to an amelioration of the symptom. His own records show that when he acted assertively he usually was sexually potent; when he lapsed into unassertive behaviors there were recurrences of impotence. Thus, modifying Simon's phobic life-style and changing his hypo-assertive response pattern led to the successful removal of the presenting symptom. The sexual impotence was never treated directly.

With the removal of his sexual impotence Simon terminated treatment against advice. During the first posttherapy year the gains he had made continued. At that time his wife developed a severe agitated depression precipitated by her unsuccessful entry into the job market. Even during this stressful period Simon's gains in the areas of sexual potency and assertiveness were maintained and he continued to make progress in such relatively nonstressful areas as his professional functioning. Probably much of the ultimate outcome of his marriage will depend on what happens in his wife's treatment. However, there appears to be a reasonable chance that Simon's own personal growth will continue.

10

A Case with Vomiting, Depression, and Sexual Problems

Daphne Burdman

The patient, Mrs. V., was a 31-year-old Middle Eastern woman who had emigrated with her husband and two children to the United States four years prior to the onset of her emotional disorder. She was first seen by a member of the psychiatric consultation-liaison staff in the hospital Emergency Room following a fainting espisode in the Gynecological Clinic. She was tearful, depressed, and anxious. The medical staff gave a history of frequent visits by the patient to the Emergency Room over a period of three months, with complaints of anorexia, nausea, constant vomiting, fainting attacks, "stomachaches," and weight loss of more than 20 pounds. Full medical workup including G.I. series was negative and failed to reveal any organic etiology for her symptoms.

Psychiatric referral had been refused by the patient on several occasions; on this occasion she agreed to visit the psychiatric outpatient department. Initial interview with the triage social worker indicated that the symptoms had started at the time when her husband became involved in a new business four months previously, in which all of their savings were invested. She had stopped cooking, cleaning and doing her household chores, and was sleeping constantly. She was reproachful, felt that she wasn't a good wife and mother, "hated" sex, whereas her husband had a "healthy sexual appetite," and felt that she was neglecting her children. She was having nightmares and had recently developed suicidal ideation with thoughts of jumping from the terrace, although expressing doubts that she could truly follow through with such an action.

She was seen shortly thereafter by the therapist. She appeared as a very pale woman, excessively overwrought, nervous and pressured, wearing no makeup. Although she was clean and neat, her harried appearance was striking. As the interview proceeded, she settled down and was able to talk and answer questions coherently and logically; although circumstantial, offering much detail, she began to reveal herself as a good self observer, highly intelligent and cooperative, and with a pleasing personality.

Further information began to emerge regarding the initiating circumstances of her illness. Her vomiting had commenced dramatically on the day the contract for the new business had been signed, at which time she had had to give up her job as a teacher in a parochial school. The business was a fast-food restaurant which was bought by her husband and herself, in conjunction with another couple. Although the family members all migrated at the same time, she was the only member of the group who spoke good English. Therefore, she was given the role of being the family spokesman and intermediary in dealing with all legal matters. She was designated as president of the company, signing and being responsible for all the contracts. At the same time she deeply resented the nature of the business and had tried to talk her husband out of becoming involved. She had always been considered as intellectually gifted, had been a journalist in her native country, and had hoped for some kind of academic career. The new business represented a source of lowered self-esteem, and the idea of working there as a waitress made her feel that she had no future—"I feel trapped."

Another serious area of concern was financial. In order to meet their share of the purchase price she had had to borrow sums of money from her sisters and mother. Although the sisters were well able to afford the loan, she was still burdened with fears of not being able to repay them. Realistically, the business had a good record and could be expected to do well, but her fears were those of bankruptcy and the shame of not being able to repay the money. Hostility had grown against her husband for initiating the purchase of the business, and their sexual activity became progressively less frequent. As their sexual situation worsened, they both began to focus more on this as a power struggle—he desiring sex more frequently, she resisting it. This led him to sulk for several days, during which time he would not talk to her. Her anger and sense of isolation would increase, as would her symptoms. This aspect of her problem was discussed at length in our first interview, and although she believed that she still loved her husband, she was beginning to have serious concern about wanting to break up the marriage. She began to see more serious faults in her husband and to see him as "stupid" and unable to cope with business matters. She later related that her husband, to whom she had been married at age 18, had been an automobile mechanic, and that her family had been against the marriage because they did not consider him "good enough" for her. Although she had loved him when they married, she had also been influenced by fears that she would have few other offers of marriage, as she was considered the brainy but plain daughter of the family. She had never criticized him or seen him in the way her family did, as a stupid person, until this present episode of depression. The couple have a daughter aged 10 and a son aged eight, both of whom she loves deeply and who attend a private parochial school.

The patient's father had died 10 years previously at age 75; the mother was aged 52, alive and well after having recovered from a myocardial infarction three months before the onset of the patient's illness. The father had been considerably older (33 years) than the mother, who had become his second wife after a long period of what amounted to being a concubine, while he remained married to his first wife. The patient recalled her feelings of shame when she first heard the truth about her mother's true situation (told to her by her first boyfriend), and the feelings of humiliation that she did not legally belong to the family of this man who was wealthy and prominent in the community. His life-style consisted of going up and back between the families of his two "wives," this not being unusual in the Middle Eastern country in which she grew up. Interestingly, the patient was unable to recall having had any feelings of anger at her "illegitimacy," but instead was angry at her mother for taking her father away from his first wife (an interesting dynamic displacement).

Mrs. V. was the third of four daughters. She believed the oldest daughter had been her father's favorite. The patient had felt very close to her father as she grew up. The mother had been the disciplinarian, had frequently shouted at her, and had sometimes hit her. Nonetheless, Mrs. V. described herself at the present time as feeling "close" to her mother. It was clear as she described various events from the past, however, that her mother had been emotionally unavailable to her, and her grandmother and aunt had given her the love and attention she needed.

Her sexual history was one of extreme sexual repression, typical of the society in which she was raised. The topic was unmentionable, and the act was unthinkable. Her first menstruation took her by surprise and grandmother was the one who took care of her. Her courtship with her husband did involve genital contact but no penetration so that she could preserve her virginity for the wedding night. The Middle Eastern custom of displaying the bloodstained bed sheets of the first marital night to prove the virginity was observed by her husband's family. She was so fearful that the required evidence might not be adequate and satisfy her mother-in-law that on her wedding night she fainted four times before the sexual act was finally consummated. She was only aware of fear of her mother-in-law and was unaware of any feelings of fear regarding the sexual act itself, if indeed these were present.

DIAGNOSTIC EVALUATION

Mental status examination revealed an emotionally labile, tearful woman, with no evidence of a thought disorder, no distortions of visual or auditory perception, no evidence of organicity, and no psychotic phenomenology. She appeared depressed, and when emotionally laden material was discussed, she would develop acute gastric pain, as evidenced by facial grimaces and holding her hands to her stomach. This was sometimes accompanied by the beginning of heaving motions indicating incipient vomiting. Mild suicidal ideation (such as thoughts of taking an overdose of pills or jumping from the balcony) was present but was counteracted by thoughts of her responsibility to her mother and children. There was no history of prior psychiatric intervention; at age 16, she had superficially scratched her wrists, but suture and medical care were not necessary, and she was not considered a serious suicide risk at this time.

The diagnosis (DSM-III) was:

Axis I. Conversion Disorder (or Hysterical Neurosis, Conversion Type) 300.11.
Major Depressive Episode, 296.23.
Inhibited Sexual Desire, 302.71.
Axis II. Histrionic Personality Trait.
Axis III. Severe vomiting.
Axis IV. Severity of Psychosocial Stressor, Moderate (level 5).
Axis V. Highest Level of Adaptive Functioning in Past Year, Very Good (level 2).

The provisional plan established at this first session consisted of: 1) frequent (two or three times weekly) sessions for at least two weeks as a crisis intervention measure; 2) inauguration of antidepressant medication, amitriptyline, with a starting dose of 25 mgm, three times daily. Although the 20-pound weight loss could be ascribed to a conversion symptom (vomiting), this together with other vegetative signs (hypersomnia and loss of normal functional activity) were of sufficient degree to be addressed immediately; 3) consideration of a plan for definitive therapy.

At the next session two days later, Mrs. V. reported that she had been sleeping a great deal (to be expected at inception of antidepressant medication): suicidal ideation had not recurred. Further exploration was undertaken to assemble the data necessary for a behavioral formulation.

BEHAVIORAL DATA

Recapitulation of Principal Problem

Vomiting and secondary depression following entry into the new business were obviously important. The patient was not aware of the thoughts, feelings, or events triggering the frequent episodes of vomiting, and for this careful observation and record keeping would be necessary. Already observed during the history-taking was the association of painful thoughts, such as references to signing the contracts for the new business, to the patient's increasing tension, epigastric pain, and incipient vomiting. Surprisingly, the patient was not in touch with this association; the therapist believed that this observation, if utilized well, might be a convenient and dramatic take-off point for therapy.

General Disturbance

Mrs. V.'s tension levels were high when she was first seen. Throughout the first two interviews her sud levels ranged from 50 to 80, peaking when her somatic discomfort appeared. However, at this point the interpretation of these observations was not obvious. It could not be determined whether the somatic distress was brought on by some unidentified mechanism and led to the anxiety or whether the somatic symptoms were secondary to the high anxiety levels. Further, it could not be determined whether the high tension was primary or whether it was really a lower tension level that was exacerbated by some mechanism such as passivity or a phobic response to the anxiety. Finally, and most important, it could not be determined if this was truly anxiety or rather the clinical signs of an agitated depression. Further investigation of these differentials was important in planning treatment but was postponed until the effect of the antidepressant medication could be evaluated.

Automatic Emotional Responses

Mrs. V. denied any obvious phobic responses and no Fear Survey Schedule was administered. However, her history suggests several possible phobic areas. Most obvious among these is the speculative fear of rejection. For example, she reported fainting several times on her wedding night, which she attributed to her fear of her mother-in-law and possible rejection by her. Earlier, at age nine, she fainted at a party when she thought of how pretty her sisters were and how plain she was—again very speculatively concerned with rejection. What does seem obvious is that somatic or conversion symptoms were conditioned responses to phobic stimuli.

Assertion

Again Mrs. V. denied problems in this area, but evidence of severe assertion problems was obvious. This was dramatically revealed at the end of the second session. The clear-cut relationship between her ruminative thoughts and vomiting had been demonstrated and use of thought stoppage had been recommended. She had doubts about her ability to use this method because her mother and sisters constantly talked about her problems during their frequent visits. When she was advised to ask them not to do this, her emphatic response was: "I could never tell my mother not to do something!"

Systematic examination showed the patient to be almost totally unassertive in her interactions with her mother. She did not state her opinions, was unable to request even small favors, and was totally unable to refuse the numerous requests and demands her mother made. She was comfortable with her mother only when she acted in a subservient manner. It was not clear whether this was an assertive difficulty based on the lack of skill and/or the lack of recognition of her own rights or a phobic avoidance of the mother's anger. The mother had been the disciplinarian and had frequently hit and criticized the patient. Despite the fact that the patient denied such fears (and also denied any consequent anger towards her mother), this remained a possibility.

Further examination showed Mrs. V. to have similar assertive deficits with all her intimate associates, such as her husband and her sisters, and to have them as well with strangers. The major difficulties were in making and in refusing requests. A major assertive strength noted was her ability to initiate, maintain, and end conversations of a purely social nature.

Obsessions

Many of Mrs. V.'s thoughts were of a low grade ruminative obsessive type regarding failure of the business, loss of self-esteem, self-reproachfulness for "allowing" her husband to enter the business, criticism of him, and self-pity. As described by her, these engendered and prolonged her feelings of apathy and passivity, and when acute led to vomiting and agitated behavior. While these thoughts were enhanced by her acute depressive illness, nevertheless they were a part of her ongoing personality style. She described herself as always having been a "worrier," as always feeling that she had responsibility for everything that happened in the family and consequently blaming herself for everything that went wrong.

Unwanted Habits

Inquiry in this area elicited the fact that she "yelled" at her children, and had feelings of shame about this. Also noted was her avoidance of her mother's anger. When this avoidance response was clarified to Mrs. V. by the therapist, Mrs. V. responded with the emphatic realization that her entire life had been characterized by avoidance responses; it was requested that she keep careful records during the following weeks of any response which she recognized as being avoidant. Over the following sessions Mrs. V. was seen to be perfectionistic, fearful of criticism and anger, and willing to take the blame for everything that went wrong around her.

It is important to note that many of Mrs. V.'s initial observations regarding herself were quite distorted or misunderstood by her, predominantly because of her use of the mechanism of denial. For example, the patient described herself as being "close" to her mother, and only later recognized her anger at her mother, and finally her fear of her mother, which prevented her from asserting herself properly.

BEHAVIORAL FORMULATION

After the first two sessions, sufficient data were available to set up an initial tentative behavioral formulation. There was some problem regarding the tension levels and their relationship to the vomiting in the presence of what might have been an agitated depression or an atypical depression. Nevertheless, the fact that several times during the interview there appeared a progression of painful thoughts leading to increasing tension leading to incipient vomiting suggested that this was a valid sequence. The painful thoughts expressed to me were angry hostile ruminations regarding her husband's involving them in the new business. These ruminations led to increasing tension which (even in my office) almost culminated in vomiting. The ruminative thoughts also appeared to have a direct effect in producing a depressive state. Similarly, the continuous vomiting with its implication of lack of control also fed into this depression. This organization is shown in Figure 1. Although anger has been placed at the core, its relationship with the remainder of the organization was not clear at this phase.

For this formulation the most practical point of intervention appeared

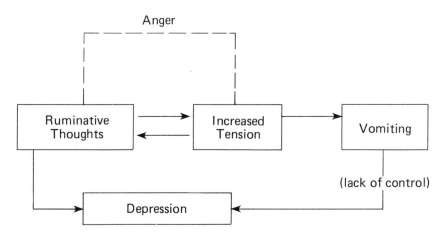

Figure 1. First behavioral formulation indicating organization of major symptoms. That the relation between anger and the remainder of the organization is not clear is indicated by the use of broken lines.

to be the interaction between the ruminative thoughts and the tension level. The increased tension level would increase these thoughts, which in turn would increase tension still further. In the formulation it was hypothesized that it was the tension level that led to the vomiting. Thought stoppage, which included both pushing the thought away and briefly relaxing, appeared to be a good method for breaking this thought-tension spiral. When this method was actually tried out during an office session, the patient reported that the feeling of nausea quickly subsided and the therapist could directly observe the diminution of tension. To accentuate the fact that it was her own actions that brought the relief from the nausea, some of the physiological effects of tension were explained to her. Mrs. V. was impressed that through the use of thought stoppage she could gain some measure of control of the symptom.

The explanation of the physiological aspects of tension and of the relation between her tension and her ruminative thoughts was used as an introduction for the Jacobson-type relaxation training procedures. These were demonstrated in the office and given to her on tape for use at home. Her instructions were to perform them once a day and a second time if she found her symptoms to be escalating. Along with this she was to use thought stoppage whenever the anxiety-provoking thoughts occurred.

EXPANDED FORMULATION

At this point her assertive difficulties with her mother and her sisters had to be addressed, for these were interfering with the successful use of thought stoppage. As previously noted, her family would constantly discuss her problems. They would lament over her illness and emphasize her husband's foolishness for having become involved in his business. These talks would exacerbate her angry ruminations about her husband. Further, their attention and solicitousness appeared to be reinforcing the somatic symptoms. In these ways the apparent concern of her relatives was serving to perpetuate the pathology and needed to be stopped. However, Mrs. V. was unable to bring herself to ask them not to talk about these things. It was this problem in assertiveness that needed to be formulated.

In the expansion of the behavioral formulation to evaluate the assertive problems, the fear of her mother's anger was placed at the core of the organization. This had generalized to a fear of anyone's anger and, in an attempt to avoid this phobic area, there was a general inhibition of her own assertive behaviors. The lack of assertion in turn had two effects.

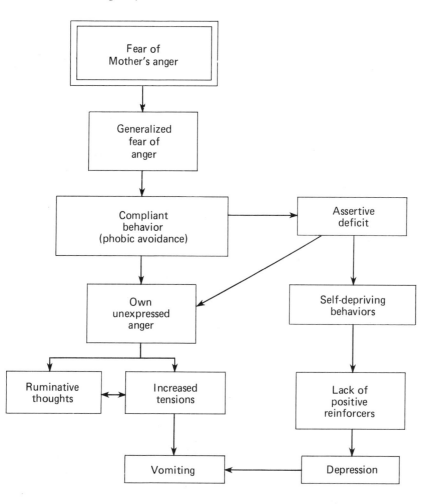

Figure 2. Expanded behavioral formulation.

The first was to increase her own feelings of anger which, although denied, fed into the tension-ruminative thought spiral (Figure 1) and eventually to the depression. The second effect was to produce self-depriving behaviors and low self-esteem. These too fed into the depression. The depression itself, of course, would further diminish assertive behaviors.

Based on this expanded formulation, the obvious main target for treatment was her fear of other people's anger. However, it was believed that the patient had not yet been properly prepared to cooperate in the desensitization techniques that would be used because she still did not have proper control over her tensions and thoughts. As some intervention was immediately necessary to limit the destructive effects of her relatives, assertive training was introduced. Through modeling and rehearsal she was taught to ask them not to talk about her sickness or about her husband. She was able to do this *in vivo*, resulting in some change on their part. However, based on our formulation, it was not believed that she could maintain this assertive behavior.

ONGOING TREATMENT (SESSIONS 3 THROUGH 7)

Treatment had developed momentum and some changes were coming about. She conscientiously practiced her relaxation exercises and these, combined with thought stoppage, reduced her daily tension levels to an average of 30 to 40 suds (from an initial level of 85), according to the records she had been instructed to keep. Her vomiting had decreased and she became increasingly able to work in the business. Because she developed "racing thoughts" and some pressured hypomanic behavior, the antidepressant medication was discontinued. Instead she was given diazepam (Valium) 5 mg. to be taken once or twice a day, as necessary. The side effects did disappear with the removal of the amitriptyline but no special deleterious effect was noted on her mood and behavior.

Treatment at this point centered mainly around assertiveness training. This involved two areas: 1) standing up to her family, and 2) doing nice things for herself to counteract the self-depriving behaviors. In terms of her family, she insisted on being treated with greater respect. When her mother and sisters attacked her husband, she would defend him; they stopped the attacks when they saw that she would not tolerate them. She did not offer to serve and to wash dishes and to make herself "the servant" at her sister's party as she had done in the past. Much to her surprise, after their initial shock at these changes in her, her sisters began to cheer her on: "Listen to this, she is speaking up for herself. What happened?" This encouragement reinforced Mrs. V.'s assertive behaviors but at the same time it must be noted that the sisters periodically would fall back into their old habits of criticizing her and her husband.

The patient had a long history of depriving herself of things, of not doing things for herself. This tended to lead to a lack of reinforcers in her life and may well have contributed to her depression. Hence, she was prescribed the task of doing something pleasurable for herself each day. She quickly developed a momentum in this area. She spent a day in town and bought lunch for herself, previously impossible and forbidden. She bought a dress and skirt for herself after years of hand-me-downs from her sisters. She bought for herself Swiss cheese and chocolate almond candy for the first time since coming to this country. She cooked her own favorite dish for dinner.

Many changes were taking place. She had not vomited for over two weeks. For the first time in months she was able to fulfill all her required work assignments in the business. She reported increasing assertion with her mother, her sisters, and her own children. She was able to reach complete relaxation through her exercises and her daily tension levels ranged from 20 to 40 suds. She came to her sessions transformed, smiling, with full make-up and bright lipstick. It obviously was time to move on to a desensitization of her fear of anger, the core target in our formulation. We started to form a hierarchy in this area.

Of course, as we had predicted, these changes did not hold. She came in for the sixth session in a state of obvious distress. Her vomiting had returned, she had ceased performing her assignments, and she was no longer working her full schedule in the business. Her sisters had again begun to criticize her husband. This time, however, she could neither ask them to stop nor express her anger at them for doing so. This, following her usual pattern, led to increased tension levels, to ruminative thoughts concerning anger with her husband, and to vomiting. This time, however, certain characteristics of her cognitive style became most evident. Therefore, besides reviewing assertion with her, the main thrust became one of changing these cognitions.

The style that had become obvious was her tendency to take one small aspect of a situation, to magnify that aspect, and to ignore all other facets of that situation. This would lead to a biased, distorted comprehension of the situation, feelings of helplessness to do anything about it and anger which she was unable to express. These would then lead to the chain of increased tension, ruminations and vomiting. This style of thinking was pointed out to her, as were its consequences. It was discussed concretely in three areas:

1) She focused on her husband's lack of academic ability and his difficulties in learning the language. She tended to ignore facts she had mentioned in passing, such as that he had a great deal of common sense and shrewd insights into matters of everyday life, and was an intelligent, albeit nonacademic, person. As this was discussed, she

became aware of the extent to which she had been influenced by her mother's (and sisters') values and the distortions to which they led.

2) In considering the business venture, she would magnify the difficulties and possible disasters. She would dismiss any of the positive reasons for going into the business, the opportunities that might come as a result. She also ignored the fact that she was helping her husband try to do something that was very important to him. This concentration solely on the negative aspects led to the feelings that she had been derelict in her duty ("to keep him from doing it"), lowered her self-esteem, and fed into her depression. With discussion, she was able to change the thought: "I shouldn't have let him do it," into the alternate thought: "I was able to go along with it for positive reasons, despite some misgivings."

3) The third problem came about when she was offered part-time work in journalism. She could see only that she was committed to working in the business, that she would never be free to do what she really wanted to do. With discussion she was able to see that her commitment to the business was such that, with some inconvenience and discomfort, she could still pursue journalism. She was also able to see that once the business was on its feet, she would have greater freedom and could branch out into other kinds of work.

This cognitive approach led to a better recognition of reality, helping to bolster her self-esteem and to diminish much of the self-blame. Along with the assertive training and with readings on assertion (bibliotherapy), her tension level again started to go down and her vomiting to decrease. She was back on the track and treatment was ready to progress.

ONGOING TREATMENT (SESSIONS 8 THROUGH 22)

During the next period, treatment centered around three themes. The major theme was an attempt to reduce her phobic reactions to other people's anger, the core target behavior in our formulation. Next in importance was the continued attempt to increase her assertive behavior. Finally, because they were a source of great distress to her, her marital and sexual problems needed to be addressed.

Fear of Anger

Attempts to reduce her reactions to anger used systematic desensitization with relaxation. In the first hierarchy used she would imagine various people expressing anger towards her because she had kept them waiting. Good anxiety reduction was achieved in the office and this did generalize to the life situation. She went four days without vomiting. At that time there occurred an extremely vehement argument with her husband's partner's wife (S.). The patient was unable to speak up or to defend herself against S.'s attacks on her and thereafter nausea and vomiting recurred. We now had several specific and recent examples of S.'s arguments and displays of anger setting off such episodes of vomiting. These incidents, combined with similar reactions to her mother and sisters, indicated a special sensitivity to women's anger. Still further examination indicated that the most sensitive area of all was her mother's anger. This last appeared to be the core of the phobia, as we had originally formulated.

Desensitization now centered around different images of her mother's anger. As her disturbed responses to these images decreased, a series of spontaneous realizations and cognitive corrections emerged. At times during the desensitization her facial expression would change and she would be questioned about her thoughts; at other times she would just volunteer this information. One such major change involved not her mother, but S., the partner's wife. In what seemed to be a cognitive-affective insight she said: "Why does she have to scream at me? I did nothing wrong. I don't deserve it." Following this realization of undeserved blame, her thoughts went to her vomiting and fainting at her own wedding. She now recognized her feelings of anger and indignation at not being trusted by her mother-in-law and at being made to undergo the ritual testing. She was now attaining her own awareness of the unexpressed anger—increased tension and rumination—vomiting chain.

As the desensitization proceeded, her assertive skills in life situations continued to improve. Yet the vomiting kept recurring. However, even here, changes were occurring. Following the tenth session there was another argument with S. and again the patient had the urge to vomit. This time, differently, she used the insightful thought that had emerged during the prior desensitization session: "Why should I get sick to show her (S.) that I'm hurt?" This was combined with the thought: "She doesn't care if I'm sick. She doesn't care if I die." At this point she made herself eat something and did not vomit. The next day she actually reprimanded S. for what had happened. Again she felt nauseous and again she ate something ("a pizza pie loaded with mushrooms and sausage") and did not vomit.

At this point it was also becoming clear that the phobia had generalized to include any expression of disapproval. The desensitization was expanded to include such images and was supplemented by training her in assertive responses to be used when they did come about. She reported several incidents showing decreased disturbance in life situations and better control over her symptoms. However, vomiting still did occur on occasion.

The last severe vomiting episode happened just prior to the fourteenth session. It was triggered by what she interpreted to be her husband's loss of interest in her. It turned out that he was suffering from a mild pneumonia and that his attitude towards her had not changed. This incident was used to supplement the previous cognitive restructuring concerning her selecting one part of a situation and ignoring others. It was a sharp lesson to her and seemed to hit home. Thereafter the vomiting did not recur. She did report at the sixteenth session that when she was required to assert herself she experienced increased tension and feelings of nausea. She was able to control the nausea and the feeling rapidly dissipated. From that time through a nine-month follow-up there was no return of the feelings.

Assertiveness Training

Assertiveness training was used throughout the treatment. She had been trained to ask her mother and sisters not to disparage her husband. She had been trained to respond assertively when others expressed disapproval. One incident occurred when her husband was hospitalized (for pneumonia) and she realistically needed help in taking care of her children. She became very angry because her mother did not offer such help and treatment centered around training Mrs. V. to request it of her mother instead of just passively waiting for it. For this and other situations, the training consisted of the selection of the appropriate response, modeling of the response by the therapist and rehearsal of the response by the patient. It did turn out that she had many assertive skills and that the major difficulty was an inhibition in their use. With practice and with the lowering of her fear of other people's anger, she became increasingly able to use these skills in a wide variety of life situations.

Sexual Difficulties

Mrs. V.'s sexual problem led to marital tensions, was of great concern to her, and was among her presenting problems. The difficulty was mainly expressed through the periodic avoidance of sexual contact. For example, when her husband came home at midnight (the end of his working day) she would be in bed sleeping or feigning sleep in order to discourage his sexual advances. Should he attempt to arouse her, she would become angry but would often give in to his sexual demands. She would also become anxious when he requested sexual acts (anal intercourse) distasteful to her. These requests brought about vomiting. Her husband had become quite angry, not just about the sexual avoidance but also about the general lack of contact. He would often sulk for several days which, in turn, made her more fearful and more symptomatic.

It was quite clear that the patient did enjoy sex when she was in the mood for it. However, after intercourse where she did have pleasure and did achieve orgasm, she would feel guilty and dirty. She would compulsively wash or shower and would change her panties. It turned out that she always had to sleep in panties because of her disgust with female odors. Preliminary discussion suggested that such attitudes towards sex were held by her family and that she had probably learned them there.

From the available data a behavioral formulation of the sexual problem was drawn up (Figure 3). The behavior to be understood was her periodic need to avoid sex. There appeared to be two roots to this avoidance. One root stemmed from attitudes that sex was dirty and wrong, attitudes she had learned within her family. The second root concerned her husband's pressures, her inability to meet them in an assertive manner, and the anger these pressures precipitated and the consequent stress this avoidance brought about in the marital relation in general. This marital stress also fed into the sexual avoidance behaviors through increasing her own unexpressed angers. It was recognized that this formulation left many questions unanswered, but it did furnish a basis for a beginning therapeutic intervention. It was assumed that in the course of this work further information would become available and a more adequate formulation could be derived.

One root of the avoidance behavior was already being treated, although not in a specifically sexual context. Her husband's pressures and sulkiness, her lack of assertion, and her unexpressed angers were being addressed through the phobic reduction and assertiveness training procedures already being used. Hence the area of her sexual attitudes was now chosen as the target for change.

In the behavioral formulation there were two components to her sexual attitudes. One was her feelings of guilt and dirtiness. This, at least in part, was being maintained by her compulsive acts. To help extinguish

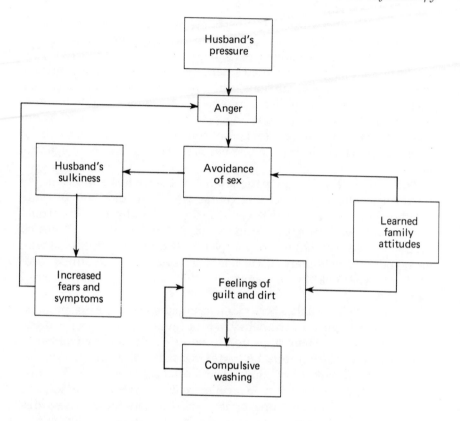

Figure 3. Behavioral formulation of sexual
and marital problem.

these feelings a program of response prevention was assigned. She was instructed never to wash following intercourse, no matter how great the urge to do so, and to wear the same panties throughout the night. The general family attitudes toward sex were discussed, misconceptions pointed out, and the healthful aspects of sex emphasized.

In the course of these discussions, as had been expected, important new material emerged. Most important among these were two memories. One, long buried and charged with shameful feelings, was an incident at age 10. She recalled her inadvertently observing her parents having intercourse and her terror of being discovered observing this.

The second memory concerned an experience with an elderly man at an earlier age. This man, a neighbor and the father of her girlfriend, molested her by putting his hand down her skirt. In the present, the memory set off strong feelings of guilt. Desensitization was conducted to both memories and did reduce the intensity of the disturbed feelings they elicited.

At this point changes in sexual behavior had started to take place. There was some decrease in the avoidance behavior and an increase in satisfactory sexual experiences. She reported a general increase in her relaxed attitude towards sex in general. Unfortunately, treatment had to be discontinued because the therapist was transferring to another hospital.

TERMINATION

The behavioral psychotherapy had brought about a marked improvement in the patient. The depression was gone and there had been no vomiting at all for about two months. There were a number of changes in her life situation. The most important of these was that not only was she able to handle business problems more effectively and without undue tension, but she was able to relinquish her need for complete control of the business. She was able to undertake several part-time projects in journalism. Besides some improvement in the sexual area, she now had greater trust in her husband and more respect for his good qualities. There did still remain problems in the sexual area and there remained a major problem in assertive dealings with authority figures.

When the patient was informed of the pending change of therapists for her, she expressed disappointment. She then failed to attend the next two sessions. At the last session she was tearful and expressed great sadness at the separation. However, with the replacement therapist who was not behaviorally oriented, she was able to express much anger. She also showed clear awareness about the areas that still needed work. Nevertheless, she decided to discontinue treatment after the third session with the new therapist.

FOLLOW-UP

Six months after termination the patient was contacted by telephone. She was delighted to hear from the therapist and reported that the changes were holding up and increasing. The business venture had been sold and her husband was back at his previous job. She had increased confidence in him and a "new respect." There had been no return of the vomiting or of the depression. She worked at journalism as the opportunities presented themselves. She recently had been able to assert herself with her children's school principal, something that in the past had appeared to be impossible. She frequently reviewed her notes from therapy and performed some of the exercises she had been taught.When problems arose she would run a dialogue in her head imagining how we would deal with it in a therapy session. All in all, as she put it, she had been "managing."

The sexual area was not really discussed during this conversation. In the area of assertion with authority figures, it appeared that although some further progress had taken place, there were still problems. One of these appeared to concern the therapist. The patient said that she had wished to call the therapist for an appointment but that she did not know the private fees and "it's not right to bargain with a doctor." Her right to do so was pointed out to her and her difficulty was presented to her as part of her assertive problems with authorities. She was complimented on how well she had been doing and told how valuable it was for her to continue to learn to handle her own life.

Three months later she did come for a session in a state of great distress. This had been precipitated by a television program regarding child molesters. The program had revived memories of when she was seven or eight years old and an upstairs neighbor, a man of her father's age, had molested her. She had allowed him to stimulate her genitals both orally and digitally. She also recalled feelings of shame and fear concerning her genitals which she strongly felt at that age. She had been taught by her mother that the genital area had to be especially clean and tended to or "worms would get in there." With difficulty she admitted that the experience was a pleasurable one; the guilt came only after it was over. In fact, she allowed this molestation to happen on three further occasions. She was unable to tell her mother about this and was fearful of her finding out. The revival of the memory following the television program elicited disturbing feelings of guilt and apprehension lest her husband find out about these incidents.

The current intense disturbance was treated during this consultation session through cognitive restructuring and relabeling. It was pointed out to her that her assertive deficit made it difficult for her to say "no" to an adult. It was also pointed out to her that her natural and healthy curiosity, so important for childhood growth, also led her to repeat the experience. In view of these, it did indeed take strength to stop them when she did; many children allow this to go on for years. Whether it was this cognitive approach or whether it was some other aspect of the discussion (such as the therapist's noncondemning attitude), there was a great relief of her disturbance.

Although her anxiety was greatly lessened, relief from this disturbance was far from complete and Mrs. V. remained concerned about it. It was indicated to her that desensitization to the memories might help but that she should think over our discussion. She did make an appointment for further work on this, but two days later she called to cancel it. She felt that she could deal with the problem herself and she sounded confident and cheerful.

During this consultation there was opportunity for a more detailed follow-up than had been obtained over the telephone. Until the television program she had been doing quite well. She regularly worked an average of two days a week at free-lance journalism. Her husband was starting a new business again, one she would have previously considered to be of low status. This time she did not interfere. Her insecurities and concern with status were minimal and she was able to respect his judgment and autonomy. Their sexual activity was markedly improved; it was much more frequent and more frequently enjoyable. When she became aware of inhibitions due to guilt, she would reason with herself that there was no reason to feel that way, that it was normal and natural. She was able to sleep without wearing panties. She was standing up to her mother and her sisters and was better able to make requests of them. Her birthday was coming up and her mother always bought her as a gift a long flannel nightgown. Now she was preparing to ask her mother to let her choose her own nightgown: a sexy lace one. There had been no return of the vomiting or of the depression.

SUMMARY

This individual presented with symptoms of vomiting, depression, and marital and sexual problems. Initial data gathering was made difficult by her massive use of the defense of denial. By the end of treatment there was a greatly lessened use of this defense, as illustrated by her reaction to the television program on child molesters. Despite early indications for the use of antidepressant drugs, she was treated essentially without the use of medication. Amitriptyline (Elavil) was discontinued after a one-week trial and diazepam (Valium) 5-10 mg per day was used for only six weeks. Complete symptom relief was obtained exclusively through psychological interventions.

The core of the disturbance was first formulated as a phobic reaction to her mother's anger and the further data obtained in the course of treatment support this formulation. This core fear led to compliant behaviors as an attempt to avoid the phobic area. These then led to unexpressed anger which fed into a ruminative-increased tension-vomiting spiral which also fed into her depression. Assertive deficits and lack of positive reinforcers were also formulated as fueling the depression. This general organization was modified through the use of desensitization, assertive training, behavioral assignments and cognitive restructuring. Dramatic changes in her symptomatology followed these interventions.

Her marital and sexual problems stemmed in part from this general pattern as illustrated by anger at "pressure" from the husband and her fears of his sulkiness. It also stemmed from sexual attitudes learned within her family. At the end of the treatment there was the suggestion that phobic reactions to childhood memories may also have been contributing to her sexual problems. The desensitization to anger and the assertive training that had been conducted are believed to have relieved part of this problem. The cognitive approach of challenging and disputing her (and the family's) beliefs about sex is believed to have played an even more direct role. At the end of treatment there had been a definite decrease in her avoidance of sex, an increase in both the pleasure she experienced and the frequency of the pleasure, and a marked change in her attitude towards sex.

The satisfactory outcome of this treatment owes much to the patient's intelligence and to the fact that she viewed therapy as a cooperative endeavor throughout. However, part of the satisfactory result may have been due to the nature of her phobias. There are some indications that her fear of authorities may have been active in her relation with the therapist and have elicited compliant (phobic avoidance) behaviors in treatment. This may have made her more accessible, particularly to the cognitive approaches used. This problem had only been partially worked through at the end of treatment. For example, she was unable to express her anger at termination directly to the therapist but she did not deny it and was able to express it to the replacement therapist.

Despite several not completely resolved problems, the results were satisfactory. Not only were the most distressing symptoms completely relieved but there was a general change in many areas of functioning. She was now free to follow her own career and to seek her own satisfactions. She had become more autonomous from her mother and sisters and in general was in more assertive command of her life. Her relationship with her husband had improved considerably with a great increase in mutual respect. Overall she had been transformed into a far more adaptive human being.

11

Managing Psychosomatic Symptoms: The Case of George

Jonathan H. Weiss

The challenge to the behavioral psychotherapist of managing patients with physical symptoms is, in principle, the same as that presented by patients with emotional or behavioral symptoms. The therapist must first assess the symptoms within the context of the cognitive, affective, and behavioral variables that can affect the course of the particular illness. He must then formulate how these variables interact. Finally, his formulation will suggest a treatment plan. In some cases, the therapist may regard the symptom as a (functionally autonomous) habit and undertake to control it directly through biofeedback training, aversive stimulation, negative practice, relaxation training, and the like. In most cases, however, the therapist will find the symptom to be functionally linked to a complex of antecedent, concomitant, and consequent events that will need to be altered if a satisfactory and lasting result is to be achieved (i.e., the symptom is to be prevented as well as merely controlled). Sometimes, a symptom will be life-threatening or cause a great deal of suffering. In such instances a direct approach to control will be taken initially and then followed at a later time by the comprehensive treatment of related variables.

For example, a teenaged patient who had been repeatedly hospitalized because of chronic, severe coughing (that was not medically controlled) was treated initially with a pain avoidance paradigm that led rapidly to suppression of the cough. The anxieties, family problems, etc., that were believed to be triggering and maintaining the symptom were then addressed. In another case, multiple somatic complaints that were interfering with the patient's job performance were quickly controlled by training in abdominal breathing. The assertiveness difficulties that triggered the patient's tension and, in turn, the hyperventilation that brought on her symptoms were then treated.

There is at this time no catalogue that the therapist can consult of the cognitive, affective, and behavioral variables that are relevant to specific physical illnesses. (Creer, 1979 has compiled such a catalogue for chronic obstructive pulmonary diseases that can serve as a model.) The therapist, the patient, the family, and the physician will, therefore, need to do some investigating to determine what is relevant in each case. Together, they can assess the basic paradigms that Fensterheim has described in Chapter 3. The therapist will then formulate how the relevant paradigmatic events are involved and plan treatment accordingly. I will illustrate this process in detail in the case that follows. First, however, I will describe how contexts affect physical illnesses. Because of certain considerations that will become clear, I have divided the context of illness into cognitive, affective, behavioral, physiological, and environmental-reactive components.

CONTEXT OF ILLNESS

Cognitive

There is a variety of ways in which cognitive variables can bear upon the course of an illness and its management. For example, how much a patient understands about the rationale for his treatment will influence the degree to which he complies with that treatment. Or how aware he is of the early warning signs of symptom onset and how to detect them will affect how soon treatment can be started. Or how well he is able to avoid excessive attention to his symptoms will determine how much unnecessary suffering and/or illness behavior will occur. Similarly, accurate expectations about the course of his illness will influence how much unnecessary medicating, doctor shopping, and secondary anxiety take place. In adolescents, faulty or incomplete knowledge about the etiology or course of an illness can lead to all sorts of complications based upon fear, shame, or guilt. Such complications also happen when parents of sick youngsters blame themselves (inappropriately) for the child's illness. For example, the mother of a nine-year-old girl whom I worked with blamed herself for having "made" her child asthmatic. Because of the guilt that this faulty understanding about asthma engendered, the mother was unable to deny her daughter anything, including the pets, chocolate, and nuts that triggered her child's symptoms!

The basic paradigm that most closely corresponds to the cognitive variables that affect physical illness is "obsessional thoughts." And in physical illness obsessional thoughts, as such, do occur. For example, unshakeable thoughts about dying, excessive thinking or worrying about symptoms, regretful ruminations about past actions that presumably led to the illness, etc., are not uncommon. I am suggesting, however, a broader role for cognitive variables in physical illnesses. Naive optimism, for example, is not an obsessional symptom, but can underlie neglect of important therapeutic or rehabilitative procedures. What might be of little or no consequence for somebody who is not sick can be very important in the case of illness.

How the behavioral psychotherapist deals with cognitive variables that are determined to be relevant will depend upon how they fit into the behavioral formulation. For example, lack of information may be a simple deficit that can be remedied by explanations or the assignment to read certain materials. In other cases, assertiveness training may be required to facilitate the patient's requesting relevant information from the physician. Or systematic desensitization may be necessary if phobic avoidance of knowledge about the illness is to be remedied.

Affective

Emotions obviously influence physical symptoms. The bulk of the literature on "psychosomatics" has been devoted to describing and explaining how emotions do their work. In terms of the basic paradigms of behavioral psychotherapy, "phobias" and "tensions" can be observed to affect the symptoms of almost any illness. Once again, however, a somewhat broader role for emotions must be defined. Thus, emotional states that would not ordinarily be considered to be phobias or even tensions can affect symptoms adversely. Eager anticipation of going to the circus, for example, was described by one youngster to have triggered his asthma. What *is* a phobia or an excessive level of tension will be, at least in part, defined by its effects on the patient's symptoms.

Another consideration has to be borne in mind in assessing the role of emotions in physical illness. In many instances, emotions trigger or aggravate symptoms only via non-emotional mediators that constitute the more appropriate jumping-off points for selecting intervention targets. Also, emotions are themselves reactive to symptoms and can, therefore, become part of a feedback loop. I would like to illustrate these points by describing four patterns in which I have observed emotions to operate in physical illness.

I. Emotions ----------------> Symptoms

In this pattern a direct connection exists between the emotion and the symptom (with, perhaps, some time lag between the emotional stimulus and the symptom response). No other stimulus *subsequent* to the emotion appears necessary for the effect on the symptom to occur. Examples are asthma attacks that start when the patient gets angry or arthritic pain that flares up when the patient feels tense. In such instances, the goal of treatment is to alter the emotional state. How this is done will depend upon the behavioral formulation. For example, the tension that sets off the arthritis pain may be a phobia that requires desensitization. Or, it may be occasioned by faulty understanding about the illness and require cognitive restructuring. Or, it may result from the patient having acted unassertively, in which case the appropriate treatment would be assertiveness training. The goal in each instance remains the same, viz., to reduce the noxious (and in a sense unnecessary or inappropriate) emotion. The means vary, depending upon the behavioral formulation.

II. Emotions-----------> Behavior------------> Symptoms

In many cases, emotions that correlate with symptom onset or exacerbation operate via behavioral mediators. In such cases, the emotion without its behavioral consequent would be of no significance for the illness. For example, in some asthmatics anger precipitates symptoms only if it leads to shouting or fighting. Tension leads to pain in some arthritics only if they also clench their fists. The appropriate treatment goal in such cases is to alter the expression of the emotion rather than the emotion itself.

Patients, parents and physicians frequently confuse patterns I and II because, perhaps, of a tendency to stop looking further once a "psychological" event has been found that correlates with symptom variability. Many patients have been advised to control their feelings when controlling the expressions of those feelings would have been more to the point, as well as more feasible or more appropriate. Thus the asthmatics referred to would be better advised to express their anger in more controlled ways rather than to suppress it. And the arthritics (who may be tense about a very real problem) would be better advised to learn to relax the muscles of their hands than to "remain calm." The tendency to confuse pattern II with pattern I is probably a legacy of the years when "psychosomatic" meant "psychogenic" and symptoms were assumed to be symbolic expressions of underlying anxieties, conflicts, attitudes, and the like. The behavioral psychotherapist must examine closely what takes place during the time between the onset of the suspected emotional precipitant and the ensuing change in the symptom. Such an examination will not infrequently reveal a behavioral mediator. For example, a patient of mine reported on one occasion that fright had triggered an attack of asthma. He had been babysitting at home when a strange noise in the attic had frightened him. Some minutes later he noticed that he was wheezing. When I asked him what he had been doing during the time between the fright and the wheezing, he recalled that he had climbed several flights of stairs to investigate the sound in the attic and the effort had left him breathless. Thus, it was the behavior rather than the emotion that was at work. Pattern II sometimes involves the emotion triggering a behavioral deficit. Pain, for example, will cause some patients to avoid prescribed rehabilitation exercises.

III. Emotions---> Behavior---> Physiological Stimuli---> Symptoms

In pattern III, neither the initiating emotion nor the behavioral link is responsible for the change in symptom status. Rather, the patient's behavior brings him in contact with a noxious stimulus or causes him to avoid a beneficial one. Thus, the asthmatic child who reports that excitement brings on his symptoms may be referring to the time he played excitedly with the neighbor's new puppy, when neither the excitement nor the exertion was the problem, but the danders he inhaled. Or the arthritic whose symptoms seem exacerbated when he is tense may also be forgetting to take his medicine. Note that in the case of the asthmatic child, since neither excitement about a puppy nor the urge to play with it is "inappropriate," the goal of treatment would be to redirect playing rather than somehow to suppress it. How that is done will, once again, depend upon the formulation. For example, it may be that the child is simply unaware that playing with the puppy is not good for him, in which case some instruction and explanation may be all that are required. Or the child may be embarrassed to admit that he has asthma and some combination of desensitization and assertiveness training may be needed. In the instance of the arthritic some sort of prompt, e.g., a chart, may be needed to enhance the likelihood that medication is noticed and taken. Or an explanation of the medical regimen may facilitate compliance. Or tension may be used as a cue to remind the patient about his medication.

The therapist should bear in mind when assessing these patterns that, in many illnesses, triggering and exacerbating stimuli may operate additively. It may take a combination of precipitants to push the patient over the threshold of clinical symptoms when any one alone would be insufficient to do so. In epilepsy, for example, it has been hypothesized that the nervous system acts like a reservoir, accumulating tensions of various sorts that eventually "spill over" and bring on a seizure. In asthma, running around in the winter may bring on an attack whereas the same level of exertion in warm weather would have no harmful effect. Such combinatory phenomena should be considered when there is a regular but less than perfect correlation between suspected precipitants or aggravants and symptoms.

IV. Symptoms----------> Reactions----------> Symptoms

In this pattern, the chain of events is initiated by the occurrence or exacerbation, for whatever reason, of the symptom. This motivates a reaction, e.g., panic, which in turn exacerbates the symptom or lays the groundwork for its recurrence under similar conditions. Miller's "autonomic conditioning" hypothesis incorporates this pattern. The pattern also describes the conditions under which "illness behaviors" that are independent of symptom severity or frequency are learned. Attention to the symptom or indulgence in response to it can result in unnecessary invalidism.

Some examples of pattern IV are: ulcer pain that leads to drinking presumably to kill the pain, but actually causes more ulcer pain; asthma-----> panic-----> more severe asthma; iatrogenic problems, e.g., incorrect diagnosis, unnecessary medical procedures, mismanagement of medication, etc. that can exacerbate the problem; pain behaviors that are maintained by secondary gains. Note that the pattern does not specify the form of the reaction. It may be an increase, e.g., excessive attention to the symptom, or a decrease, e.g., avoiding treatment when symptoms begin.

Behavior

Unwanted habits and behavioral deficits can figure importantly in physical illness. Many physical symptoms are affected not so much by what the patient thinks or feels, but simply by what he does or fails to do. Habits like smoking, drinking or overexertion, and behavioral deficits like unskilled use of medical equipment or low levels of exercise are frequent symptom precipitants or aggravants. They may have little to do with cognitive or emotional antecedents of any significance, and can be treated with habit control procedures. Where there is a link to other variables, e.g., drinking with the boys because the patient is too unassertive to say "No," the formulation will indicate the appropriate targets for change.

Physiological

Managing physiological variables is, of course, central to treating physical illness and usually involves administering drugs, regulating diet and so on. The role of the behavioral psychotherapist may simply be to help the patient to comply with a prescribed treatment program. Sometimes, however, the therapist will use his knowledge of the interactions between behavior and physiology to identify otherwise unimportant behaviors as targets for treatment. For example, one patient presented with complaints of dizziness and nausea that usually occurred in mid-afternoon. These sensations triggered panic attacks because they reminded her of several "bad trips" she'd had from LSD some years ago. Knowing that the patient was mildly hypoglycemic allowed me to select as the target for change the fact that she was frequently too busy to eat lunch.

Many hypertensives ingest too much salt, and some people drink to kill the pain of their ulcers. By themselves, these behaviors may not have much "psychological" significance. It is their (physiological) consequences, in the course of the patient's illness, that lead the behavioral psychotherapist to target them for change.

Environmental-Reactive

This category resembles pattern IV described above in relation to emotional variables. It is broader, however, in that it is not necessarily linked to a particular episode or change in the patient's symptoms but refers to the reactions of the patient and significant others to the fact of illness. Any of the basic paradigms described by Fensterheim may occur as a consequence of illness. Teaching the patient and significant others how to act, and interact, appropriately is an important part of comprehensive illness management. Teaching patients and doctors how to communicate effectively is one important example.

In thinking about the role of the environment in physical illness one must think beyond the confines of the immediate, e.g., familial, environment. The subculture within which the patient and his family live must also be considered as a source of significant input since models for illness management often transcend the family. Support for appropriate interventions may, therefore, need to be recruited at that level. To cite one interesting example, there have been moves in recent years to integrate Indian tribal shamans into the treatment team since their rapport with the patient, as well as some of their traditional remedies, seems to have a beneficial effect and help to make more conventional treatment acceptable to the patient.

I have tried briefly to show how a number of variables that come under the purview of behavioral psychotherapy can influence the course of physical illness. These variables comprise the context within which the illness occurs and comprehensive management includes assessing and managing them. At different stages of an illness different variables may come into play. For example, early on in the course of an illness, adequate understanding and essential skills training may be most important. Should the illness prove prolonged or chronic, however, emotional variables may come more prominently into focus.

In any event, the contextual variables must always be seen within the framework of the behavioral formulation since, once the involvement of a particular variable has been discerned, it is the formulation that will specify the intervention that will bring it under control.

The following case presentation illustrates these issues.

CASE HISTORY*

George was a 15-year-old boy of Italian descent with a presenting problem of chronic, intractable asthma. The doctor believed that, in light of George's overall physical condition, including his allergic and infectious profiles, George's symptoms were excessively frequent and severe and probably "emotionally" precipitated. George experienced some respiratory distress almost daily and had attacks of wheezing, tightness, coughing, etc., severe enough to interrupt ongoing activities two to three times a week. He took medicine to ward off as well as to control attacks,

---

*I wish to acknowledge the collaboration of Drs. Martin Gittelman and Vincent Fontana in this case. Portions of the case were presented at the Annual Meeting of the American Medical Association in 1975 and the Annual Meeting of the American Lung Association in 1978.

the amount varying with how much asthma he thought he was having or might get. He worried constantly that his asthma would get out of control and interfere with his life. According to his doctor, George's medication could be significantly reduced if the "emotional" precipitants were eliminated. George had no complaints other than about his asthma. He admitted to being tense but blamed that on his asthma. His motivation for treatment was low.

Life History

George was an only child, born to middle-aged parents in New York City. His father held a blue collar job; his mother stayed at home to raise her son. Mother's health during pregnancy was good and the delivery was normal. The first six years of George's life were apparently uneventful. Despite his mother's tendency to overprotect him, George had friends, played the usual childhood games, attended nursery school, etc. Developmental milestones were reached at appropriate times and George was reported to have had no more than the usual childhood illnesses.

At age six George developed breathing difficulties that were soon diagnosed as bronchial asthma. From the start, George's asthma was severe and required frequent visits to the doctor but not hospitalization. George was tested for allergies and put on an elimination diet. He also received desensitization injections to increase his resistance to allergens. Environmental control measures were taken that decreased George's exposure to odors, dust, and mold. His parents were counseled to remain calm during George's attacks, but mother found it difficult to control her anxiety or to stop cautioning him to be careful, take his medicine, etc. George's father, on the other hand, seems to have stayed largely in the background.

Before he developed asthma, George was an athletic and outgoing youngster. Asthma slowed him down. What had previously been merely vigorous exercise was now overexertion and brought on breathing difficulties. Baseball, football, skating, etc. had to be curtailed. (This was before the development of Intal, a drug that, taken prior to exertion, can prevent many exercise-induced attacks.) George soon became the last kid chosen for team sports. He started to think of himself as an invalid. He withdrew from group activities and spent much of his free time alone, often in his room, watching TV or reading a book.

At age nine George's asthma remitted as suddenly as it had started. For no apparent reason, he was able to run, be outside in cold weather, eat what he wanted, with no ill effects. George couldn't believe his asthma was gone. He was cautious, but as the months went by with no asthma, he became bolder. With practice he recovered his athletic skills and re-emerged as an active member of his peer group. George was happier than he could ever remember being. Then, at age 11, his asthma returned. For a time, George was devastated. He dreaded the possibility of being rejected and spending time alone in his room, and promised himself he wouldn't let this happen. The joy of athletics, his friends' admiration, and his own self-esteem were at stake.

By the time George was referred for psychological evaluation he was a husky, muscular five-foot-ten-inch youngster and a star at nearly every varsity sport. He was proud of his success and determined not to give it up lightly. He was aware that athletics had gotten out of hand and that he could hardly relax without becoming preoccupied with thoughts of playing. If a game was called off, he would feel tense and ruminate about playing. Sometimes the tension would get so high that it would trigger symptoms. This pattern was exacerbated if George had to spend his free time alone in his room, probably because this was associated with being sick. He fully appreciated the irony of his athletic talents, which made it possible for him to gain the admiration he cherished, being responsible for keeping his symptoms in high gear. A less physically gifted youngster might have settled for excellence in more sedentary intellectual pursuits—a pattern often seen in asthmatic youngsters and that is probably responsible for the myth that asthmatics are "brighter" than other children. George's primary recourse was medicine, taken at the first sign of trouble or even when there was no trouble, as a precaution, if a big game was coming up. George was determined to keep his illness a secret. In the course of a game, if he felt breathless, he would pretend to be hurt so that he could sit for a while and rest.

George's achievements were not limited to the playing field. Perhaps by the process of response generalization, George became a performer in other ways, and a worrier as well. He was an achiever academically, but at the price of worrying about exams, grades, classroom performance, etc.

Behavioral Assessment

George's problem was assessed in a number of ways. First a general behavioral interview addressed the diagnostic questions described elsewhere in this book. George was also given an Asthma-Precipitants Interview (Purcell and Weiss, 1970,) to get a factual account of those events that he had noticed brought on or aggravated his asthma. The results of the assessment were, in terms of Fensterheim's paradigms, as follows:

1) *General Tensions:* Moderate to severe. George reported few times when he was able simply to enjoy being relaxed. On a tension scale of 0-100, his tension varied between 30 and 50 on typical days.
2) *Phobias:* George was made especially tense by situations described earlier: onset of asthma, anticipation of asthma, the thought of being seen having asthma, the memory of being rejected, thoughts about poor performances in school, being alone in his room. These all seemed to have a common core, viz., the fear of appearing sick or inadequate and being rejected by friends. Other than this focal fear and its various expressions, there were no noteworthy phobias.
3) *Obsessive-Compulsive Symptoms:* George's preoccupation with sports was obsessional in its pervasiveness, and his playing had a compulsive, ritualistic flavor. The attention he paid to his breathing was more a hypervigilance related to his anxiety about asthma than an obsessional thought. Medicine-taking also had a compulsive, anxiety-reducing quality. George's athletic and school performances were compulsive behaviors engaged in to avoid anxiety.
4) *Assertiveness Problems:* George was able to assert himself in the usual ways, e.g., eye contact, expressing feelings, making requests, saying "No," having a social network—except one. He could not say, "I don't want to play today." This, however, was an outgrowth of his rejection phobia rather than an assertiveness problem due to a lack of appropriate skills. George knew exactly what he would like to say, he was simply afraid to say it.
5) *Behavioral Deficits:* None noted.
6) *Habits or Behavioral Excesses:* None noted.
7) *Special Problems:* One interesting aspect of George's behavior may be described as a special problem because, although the phenomenon is quite normal (see Weiss, Lyness, Molk, and Riley, 1974), it could trigger George's asthma. When George saw somebody out of breath, e.g., an athlete on TV or in a real game, he would experience "sympathetic" distress and this would sometimes trigger symptoms. This sympathetic response is seen in normals but does not, of course, trigger asthma in them.

Precipitant Interview Results

The following precipitants were reported to trigger or aggravate symptoms:

overexertion (forcing self to play sports)
foods
smells
dust
anxieties about school performance
seeing somebody out of breath
spending time in room alone (and thinking about not being out playing)
nonspecific anxieties
worrying about getting asthma

In terms of the psychosomatic paradigms described above, all but paradigm three are represented.

Behavioral Formulation

I said in the introduction to this case history that in doing behavioral psychotherapy one must decide whether to attack a symptom *per se* or to see it as a component of an organization that should be interrupted at some other point. In the present case, the choice theoretically was between treating the organization of asthma precipitants or using a technique such as biofeedback or relaxation training to teach respiratory control. In fact, however, there was little choice. First of all, George's overall tension level and his performance anxieties were not likely to be benefited by his knowing that he would be able to control his asthma once it started. He already had a technique for that, viz., medicine. Furthermore, unless he avoided his precipitants, he would undoubtedly continue to have symptoms that were too severe for control by breathing training. Third, George's concerns about school, which had generalized from his fears of being inadequate, would be unchanged if he was only taught to breathe better. One would anticipate continued worries about inadequacy in other areas of his life if this problem were not dealt with in treatment. About the only argument in favor of treating George's symptoms *per se* was that George was less than enthusiastic about the proposed behavior therapy. He was not interested in seeing a "shrink" and certainly not interested in his friends finding out that he was in therapy. His attitude was, of course, predictable. In George's instance the treatment choices were not mutually exclusive. We could treat the "underlying" precipitant organization while teaching George to control symptoms as much as possible through relaxation and breathing exercises. The behavioral formulation we worked with is shown in Figure 1.

We conceptualized the core problem as a phobia about rejection. The hypervigilance to breathing was seen as a direct consequence of his anxiety, and the compulsive playing of sports, denial of symptoms, excessive use of medicine, etc., as avoidance and escape behaviors. George's tension when alone in his room was seen as a conditioned response based upon his earlier experiences when he had had to spend time alone while ill.

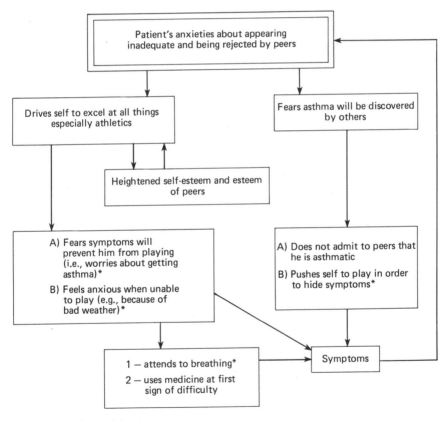

* = reported to be precipitants

Figure 1. Behavioral formulation

The formulation picks up the situation as we saw it when George presented himself to us. It does not explain why George was so devastated by his earlier experiences and why peer rejection was such a frightening experience. Why hadn't he found a way of being a group member in other ways, as many chronic asthmatic children do? We assumed that it had to do with his mother's overprotectiveness, a precondition that according to Salter (1949) is one of the primary childhood experiences that lead to excessive inhibition. In another child, the onset of asthma might well have motivated the adoption of other compensatory patterns that would have been nonprecipitating but age and peer group appropriate. Indeed, finding such patterns was one of the goals of George's treatment and is a standard part of the self-help training that we advocate for all asthmatic patients (Weiss, 1980).

Treatment Goals

Our goals were to help George to overcome his fears of rejection so that he could play when he genuinely wanted to, and to help him relax his demands on himself for performing in general. We believed that if we could accomplish these, the whole pattern of overexertion, anticipatory anxiety, preoccupation with achievement, etc., and the related asthma symptoms would break up. At the same time, we believed it was important to help George find substitutes that would enable him to function happily in his peer group and let him feel that we were not trying to deprive him of something highly reinforcing. Finally, we wanted George to learn to relax in the presence of symptoms, so that he would suffer less and perhaps rely less on medication. Note that in this formulation the symptom precipitants were regarded as the products of an "underlying" or antecedent condition, viz., his rejection phobia. It would have been possible, presumably, to target the individual precipitants e.g., overexertion, anxiety, etc., and to deal with them directly. This would have been inefficient. Also, George did not regard *playing* as a problem, but accepted that worrying about what others thought of him was something to be resolved. There were reasons for formulating the case in this way.

Treatment Course and Results

Our first step was to explain our formulation to George and outline our proposed treatment goals. As we expected, George was skeptical. First of all, he was proud of what he had accomplished and not inclined to view it as a problem. He was also concerned that word would somehow get out that he was seeing a "shrink." Second, he was suspicious that we would put restrictions on his playing and threaten his place in his group. Finally, George wasn't sure he wanted to be bothered with the appointments, daily measurements, and telephone contacts we explained would be necessary to follow his progress. However, using what Salter calls "past conditioning," we appealed to two things we knew George valued, viz., greater independence and the possibility that he might actually have less asthma (although we could not promise that). Greater independence meant that as he demonstrated more control and less tension, his mother might hover over him less. We offered to support this by instructing mother to stay out of the picture more. He would also, of course, be freer to be himself with friends. He might also be less at the mercy of asthma and less dependent on medication as he learned to control the precipitants and aggravants of his symptoms. This last we couldn't guarantee because asthma is multidetermined and we couldn't be sure that removing our targeted precipitants would significantly change his illness course. However, clinical experience made it a real possibility.

We assured George that his treatment would be kept totally confidential and that our contacts with him by phone and in the office would be scheduled at his convenience. We explained that he would be able to see his records as treatment progressed and that he would be the judge of whether continuing was worthwhile. George agreed to give treatment a try.

The next step was to gather baseline information about George's respiratory function, his subjective estimates of how much asthma he was having, his medication intake, and his exposure to symptom precipitants. George was taught to use a Wright-McKerrow Peak Flow Meter, a portable device (see Purcell and Weiss, 1970) that he took home and used three times daily at specified times. Frequent Peak Flow measurements are necessary, as has been shown (Purcell and Weiss, 1970), in order to have a meaningful picture of ongoing pulmonary function. Each day George was called at home and in about three to five minutes reported the following: 1) his three Peak Flow scores during the previous 24 hours; 2) the amount of asthma he thought he had had (estimated on a 10-point scale); 3) his medication intake (scored using a technique developed at the Children's Asthma Research Institute and Hospital); and 4) whether or not he had been exposed to any of 10 precipitants that were listed and read to him.

George found that using the Peak Flow Meter and being called were not as inconvenient as he had feared. Furthermore, in a way he had not anticipated, but quite consistent with his "past conditioning," George began to think of his treatment as a contest, with Peak Flow and medication scores that he could strive to better!

For three weeks we did nothing but collect the baseline data reproduced in Figure 2. Several things are noteworthy. First, Peak Flow moved through a range of about 350 points from 100 to 450. George's predicted normal score was about 400. Since a 10 or 15 percent drop from the predicted normal is considered clinically significant, George was having enormous fluctuations in airway function. Some daily fluctuation is expected because of normal circadian rhythms but George's pattern could only be described as extreme and erratic. Since it could be seen that as his Peak Flow fell his subjective estimate of asthma rose and his medication intake increased, it was unlikely that George was either using the Peak Flow incorrectly and thereby generating erratic results or merely making up scores.

With regard to the exposure to precipitants, we were especially interested in numbers 5, 9, and 10: "forcing self to play," "worrying about asthma," and "overexertion." These were reported on the average of two, three, and four times per week respectively. Table 1 gives the mean

Table 1

Pre-post Scores on Four Asthma Index Variables and Nine Precipitant Variables.

	Mean Baseline	Mean Therapy
Asthma Indices		
+ Peak Flow	303	330
Med. Score	0.57	0.52
Subj. Asthma	3.1	1.1
Clinical Rating	11.5	1.7
Precipitants (Occurrences/week)		
Foods	0.3	0.0
Smells	0.7	0.1
Dust	0.7	1.5
*Forced play	2.0	0.7
Seeing TV sports	0.7	0.7
+ Alone in room	1.7	3.3
Worries (nonspecific)	1.3	1.3
*Worry about asthma	3.0	0.6
*Overactivity	4.0	2.7

*Target precipitants
+ Desirable change is an *increase*

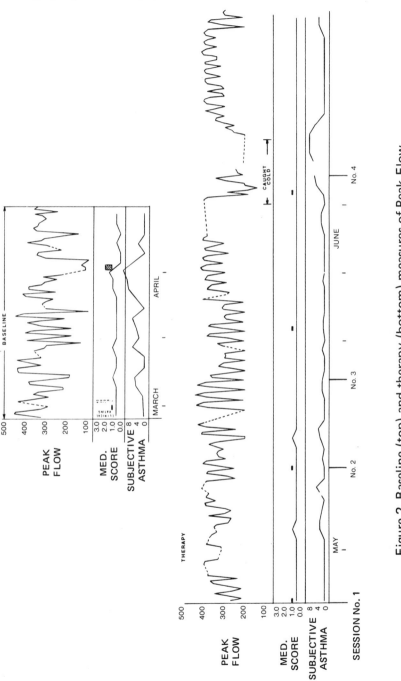

Figure 2. Baseline (top) and therapy (bottom) measures of Peak Flow, medication score, and subjective asthma.

Peak Flow, subjective asthma, medication and precipitant scores for the baseline and treatment periods. (One other score reported is a clinical rating assigned by a physician who examined George periodically. Since this was an infrequent measurement, its validity as an index of the patient's overall condition is low.)

After the three-week baseline period and a short break, treatment was begun. Measurements continued as before.

The first thing we decided to work on was relaxation. This was for several reasons. First, we wanted something that would benefit George quickly and we knew from work with other patients like George that relaxing results in a significant, if temporary, rise in Peak Flow.

George used a relaxing tape at home and in his somewhat compulsive way did it religiously. He soon noticed that when he relaxed his breathing was easier, even if he had been feeling well.

During the second session we began to discuss with George how he could use relaxation in a variety of ways, including overcoming his reluctance to speak up to his friends, staying calm when he needed to be at home, and staying calm when he felt tightness in his chest. He agreed that the rationale was sensible but we neither assigned him, nor did he volunteer, to do any of these things yet.

We had considered several ways of dealing with George's fears of rejection. Systematic desensitization in imagery would have been used if urging George to do *in vivo* risk-taking had not been possible. The *in vivo* approach, i.e., assigning George to refuse some activity, to relax his studies a little, etc., seemed more sensible because it attacked the problem most directly, would produce actual decreases in precipitant exposure, and appealed to George's action orientation. To prepare George for these assignments we did what amounted to assertiveness training, using role-playing, covert (imagined) practice, and much support from the therapist. We constructed a hierarchy of statements going from, at the low end, such statements as, "I want to rest a moment" (during a game) through, "I don't feel like playing today" to, at the upper extreme, "I don't feel up to playing now, my breathing's bothering me."

George's response was a growing enthusiasm. He thought of everything as a contest and was given to asking, "How did I do this week?" Even though George was taking his own PF's at home, he did not keep track of his scores and was genuinely surprised and very pleased whenever he saw his cumulative record.

While George was working on being less afraid of his friends' opinions, which, as it turned out, didn't seem at all affected by George's newly articulated attitude, we turned his attention to finding and suggesting alternative activities. George learned to bowl, play pool and chess. Not surprisingly, he was good at these and found them an adequate outlet for his competitive drive when more strenuous sports were out.

Results

The results of the nine-week treatment program will be discussed in relation to the following variables: 1) Peak Flow; 2) subjective asthma; 3) medication intake; 4) precipitant exposure; 5) clinical assessment.

1) Peak Flow

The Peak Flow record reveals several things. First, there continued to be a daily cyclical pattern but the amplitude of the cycle became progressively smaller—due to a progressive elevation of its trough (while the peak remained at about 400 liter predicted normal level). In other words, George was showing fewer, and less extreme, instances of bronchoconstriction (at least at the times he was using the PF meter). One might be tempted to assume that this represents a change in effort, or that George was simply giving us what he thought we wanted. This is gainsaid by several observations. For one, during the sixth week of treatment, George caught cold and his PF dropped sharply until he recovered. For another, he continued to report subjective asthma at levels consistent with the objective measurements. Third, as mentioned above, George seemed genuinely surprised and pleased whenever he saw his cumulative record. He wanted to know if other patients did as well as he did.

A statistical test of the mean PF during the baseline (303) versus the mean during therapy (330) showed a significant difference. This test is a most conservative estimate of change since it did not take into account the *pattern* of change we have described. George went from wide swings and erratic fluctuations to small (40-50 liters) swings in a much more regular cyclical pattern.

2) Subjective asthma

As George's PF was stabilizing, his subjective asthma scores still reflected the up and down movements, but the overall level of asthma he reported was lower. During his cold he reported a higher level of asthma, as one would expect if he was reporting accurately. Again, looking at averages, his baseline mean was 3.1 and his treatment mean was 1.1, a significant change but one that minimally reflects the pattern of change.

3) Medication

The medication score fell as Peak Flow increased and subjective asthma decreased. More than that, during the baseline and early treatment weeks medication usage was nearly perfectly correlated with subjective asthma. As treatment progressed, however, medication intake remained perfectly level even on days when George reported increases in subjective asthma and Peak Flow had fallen. This reflects the fact that his tolerance of distress had increased to the point where he no longer ran for medication at the smallest sign of asthma. George could be appropriately aware of changes in his breathing without running scared.

4) Clinical assessment

We did not place much stock in the clinical assessments done by George's physician because of their infrequent occurrence. Nevertheless, before treatment the clinical rating was 10, a significant amount of respiratory distress, and during treatment the ratings were normal. (An examination of the record shows that the clinical assessment reflects PF on the day of the assessment.) The ratings during treatment constituted the longest string of "normal" ratings in his physician's experience with George.

5) Precipitant exposure

Was George's improvement due entirely to "psychological" changes? Hardly. George was *behaving*, as the precipitant occurrences show, in less noxious ways vis-à-vis his asthma. He was not merely less anxious or more confident of his assertiveness, but was able to avoid precipitants and aggravants because of that confidence. George was engaging in less strenuous exertion as well as less worry. The precipitant occurrence scores for "overexertion," "forcing self to play," and "worrying about asthma" all dropped. Interestingly, "being alone in room" *increased* but with no ill effects. George had apparently extinguished his old associations of illness, rejection, anxiety, etc., to this stimulus environment and was able, appropriately, to spend more time there without the negative consequences he had previously experienced.

REFERENCES

Creer, T. *Asthma Therapy: A Behavioral Health Care System for Respiratory Disorders.* New York: Springer Publishing Co., 1979.

Purcell, K. and Weiss, J.H. Asthma. In C.G. Costello (Ed.), *Symptoms of Psychopathology.* New York: Wiley, 1970, pp. 597-623.

Salter, A. *Conditioned Reflex Therapy.* New York: Capricorn Books, 1949.

Weiss, J.H., Lyness, J., Molk, L. and Riley, J. Induced repiratory change in asthmatic children. *Journal of Psychosomatic Research,* 1974, *18*: 1-9.

Weiss, J.H. A practical approach to the emotions and asthma. *American Lung Association Bulletin,* 1980, 2-6.

PART III

Conclusions

12

Future Development of Behavioral Psychotherapy

Herbert Fensterheim

Behavioral psychotherapy is action-oriented. The behavioral formulation, which draws on biological, psychodynamic, behavioral and social concepts, serves as a basis for identifying target behaviors and for determining the order in which they will be modified. The behavioral paradigm, the process underlying specific behaviors, determines the change technology to be used. The general model of this approach was presented in Part I and illustrative applications of the model to specific, complex and difficult patients in Part II.

The formulation of the behavioral organization in the problem area is crucial. A man presenting with partial impotence was formulated as having fear of women's anger as a core problem. This led to assertive deficits, to self-incriminations, and to the impotency. Treatment centered mainly around reducing the core fear and establishing more assertion rather than around direct treatment of the impotence. A man with severe obsessive-compulsive behaviors was formulated as having a core fear of helplessness. The obsessive-compulsive pattern helped him to avoid feelings of helplessness and these patterns could not be relieved until the core fear was at least partially removed.

The point must be stressed that the behavioral formulation is not about the patient; it is a method for organizing the therapist's thoughts about the patient. It also must be stressed that the formulation is not a conclusion but rather an opinion based on admittedly incomplete information. Hence, as new information becomes available, it often must be revised. Nevertheless, it provides an important core around which to plan organized and systematic treatment. It can even be applied to discrete segments of treatment. Should a specific obstacle to treatment arise, for example, a behavioral formulation may be drawn up for that particular problem and this formulation may serve as a basis for making therapeutic decisions and for selecting target behaviors for change in order to remove that obstacle. All action decisions in behavioral psychotherapy are based on such formulation. If the actions to which they lead do not bring about the expected results, it is the therapist's responsibility to reformulate and to re-reformulate until it does lead to such results. If the therapist cannot achieve that, the patient must be referred on to another therapist or to a different type of treatment.

As we gain increased clinical experience with the behavioral psychotherapy perspective, we have found new ways of applying it. One area where we have progressed since the initiation of this book concerns the further use of psychodynamic concepts in the behavioral treatment of certain patients.

Fensterheim (1981), for example, has reported on a behavioral use of dreams. Although the behavior therapy literature does report the use of desensitization methods to remove anxiety elicited by a recurring dream, in this instance flooding to the dream content was used to reduce a claustrophobia. Because it has not been elsewhere published, the case will be reported in some detail.

The patient was a 40-year-old woman who had presented several years ago with a variety of problems. Among these was a moderately severe claustrophobia, a fear of being confined and unable to escape from the situation. This resulted in a high level of anticipatory anxiety, a fair (but not complete) amount of avoidance behavior, discomfort in confined situations occasionally rising to panic levels and escapes. Over the years this had been treated in a variety of ways: systematic desensitization and flooding in imagery, in vivo exposures and flooding, relaxation training, diaphragmatic breathing and thought stoppage methods. It had some, but far from complete, results. For over two years now there had been no avoidance behaviors and very few escapes. However, her anticipatory anxieties were still great and there had been little change in the amount of discomfort she experienced while in the actual situation. Recently she had been in an elevator, believed that the doors were opening too slowly, and began to scream and tear at them. This was a major reason for her returning to continue treatment at this time.

Two other problems are relevant to this presentation. She had had a difficulty in reading comprehension and had taken several courses to improve this. She now felt ready to take a college level course and had registered for one. The problem was that whenever she was in a class-room she would have a recurring thought about the door being locked and being unable to get out. This set off moderate levels of anxiety. A variety of treatment methods and four semesters of in vivo exposure failed to reduce this anxiety. Now that she was taking a college level course she was particularly concerned about her classroom discomfort.

The second problem, relatively trivial, concerned a brother ten years older than she. He was very authoritarian and hypercritical. She would respond to his sharp put-downs with a flash of anger. Through asser-tiveness training she learned to respond to these put-downs, but the phobic reaction of anger remained unchanged.

During the current course of treatment, we again tried a variety of phobic reduction methods and again achieved some slight but limited results. These approaches were not working any better than they had in the past.

At this point the question of a possible fueling phobia was raised with her. She could recall no childhood memory that appeared to be relevant, but she did tell of a dream that she thought might be important. This was a dream that had recurred many times over a period of years; she had even had it several times recently. The memory of the dream was very vague. In it two men came to the door of her house, were quite angry with her and were berating her. When they left they locked the door as punishment. The dream would end with her futilely and des-perately trying to get the door open, crying as she did so. She could not recall the actual feelings she experienced in the dream but just knew that she was very upset.

Recalling the dream for brief periods of time (I was investigating the possibility of using a desensitization procedure) elicited no feelings what-soever. However, when she held the dream in mind for a five-minute period, vague but disturbing feelings began to build up. It was therefore decided that we would use a satiation method with the dream and see what the results were.

The behavioral formulation considered the claustrophobia to be main-tained by a fueling phobia, a phobic reaction in the present to some set of childhood memories. However, because of resistance, the unaware avoidance of anxiety-eliciting information about herself, the fueling phobia could not be directly identified or approached. The dreams were formulated as being an indirect manifestation of the fueling phobia. By reducing the disturbed reaction to the dream, some of the phobic elements might be removed from the memories. Should this happen, should the fueling phobia be indirectly reduced, the defenses might not be as necessary, the memories themselves might be allowed into awareness, and then could be approached more directly. At the very least, should some reduction of the fueling phobia take place, the claustrophobia would no longer be as strongly fueled and might disappear of itself.

The patient was familiar with the satiation method, as we had previously used it with some limited results for her claustrophobia. She had demonstrated that she could minimize escapes and that she was able to maintain the disturbance-eliciting thoughts and images for long periods of time. She believed that she would be able to do so with the dream. But she did raise one point. She had had another recurring dream over the years, although not for many years now. This dream too was very vague. All she remembered of it was that there was a coffin and in it there was a chopped-up body. She had a very strong feeling, without any reason for it, that the two dreams were connected. She wanted to satiate herself to both dreams at the same time, which she was given permission to do. She was to do the first two exercises at home for 20 minutes. After that the time was raised to 40 minutes. Following the third satiation period, she began to keep notes on the thoughts and images she had while concentrating on the dream.

As she continued the satiation procedures with the dream at home, details gradually emerged and the feelings heightened. The two men accused her of killing someone, of chopping him up. She was handcuffed and was going to be locked up in jail. One of the men became her brother and he was accusing her of killing him and chopping him up and was putting the handcuffs on her. She was screaming over and over: "Don't lock me up. I can't get out." Then she hysterically insisted that she had to kill him, that he overpowered her and monopolized and didn't let her grow up. So she had to chop him up. This was accompanied by "really hysterical crying." In the middle of the fifth satiation session there was a sudden change. She imagined herself turning to her brother and saying: "But look, you're here. If you are here I couldn't have killed you, I couldn't have chopped you up. It was in my mind that I chopped you up. How could you know what was in my mind and punish me for that?" During the sixth and last satiation session she told her brother:

"I'm not afraid anymore. You can't lock me up for my thoughts. I didn't really kill you and you can't kill me." Although there was still hysterical crying, at the end she experienced "a wonderful feeling of peace."

Before reporting on the changes that immediately followed this procedure, I want to report some changes that did not occur. She has absolutely no memory of ever having fantasized killing her brother or of his dying. Although she recalls (and still experiences) some resentments towards him, she is unaware of any of the feelings of being confined, overpowered, or punished by him. Almost all the feelings she had experienced during satiation were new to her.

Three distinct changes were noted following her work with the dreams. 1) The very night of the last satiation, she had dinner with her brother, who made one of his usual disparaging remarks. This time, however, instead of her customary flash of anger, she experienced instead a strong feeling of being sorry for him. She thought: "How can he live if that's the way he talks to people?" She felt no need at all to make any of the assertive statements she had been trained to make in that situation. 2) On instruction she rode elevators. Although there was considerable anticipatory anxiety, she felt completely comfortable in that situation. 3) When she attended class, she did not think of the door being locked. She did briefly recall that she had had such thoughts in the past and she thought of how silly they were. For the first time she was completely comfortable in the classroom.

This case is indeed open to many differing interpretations and the results obtained did not necessarily come about for the reasons suggested by the formulation. However, the behavioral formulation did suggest the treatment action used and did allow for the use of behavioral techniques in what has been considered to be an exclusive area of psychodynamics.

Continuing clinical experience has provided other suggestions for the behavioral formulation of psychodynamic concepts. One such suggestion concerns possible similar fueling phobias connected to similar types of overt symptoms. We have treated three patients with the overt symptoms of agoraphobia with panic and severe separation anxiety. In these three patients there was also a Rankian-type conflict between merging and independence. In behavioral terms this was formulated as a double phobia centering around parents. One phobia consisted of automatic feelings of guilt and resentment when the parents appeared to be critical or displeased. The second phobia consisted of automatic feelings of humiliation and self-betrayal when the parents appeared to be pleased. Although it was possible to establish approach behaviors in these patients, habituation of the agoraphobic anxiety did not come about until both fueling phobias had been reduced. Other changes such as increased ability to form close personal relations and crystalization of career choice also took place at that time.

These are some examples of how continuing clinical experience with behavioral psychotherapy has led to increased therapeutic flexibility. It is also possible to cite similar examples from areas other than psychodynamics. From the biological perspective, for example, we are becoming increasingly aware of the clinical importance of chronic hyperventilation and the complex behavioral pattern it maintains. The behavioral formulation can take all such different variables, consider their possible interactions and their relationship to problem areas, and directly influence therapeutic targets and the choice of intervention procedures.

It is always important to remember that the approach is pragmatic and action oriented. Behavioral psychotherapy does not advance a theory about patients. Rather, it aims at helping the therapist to assume his responsibility for maintaining a systematic and pragmatic control of the treatment using whatever concepts he believes to be most applicable to that patient, at that time, for that problem. Its value as an organizing focus of treatment is shown in the complicated cases presented in this book. Most impressive in these cases is the willingness to quickly give up what doesn't work, to reformulate, and to try something new that may be successful. We are working therapists; our job is to help patients.

REFERENCE

Fensterheim, H. Phobic reactions to childhood memories can fuel current anxieties. Paper presented at the Third Annual Phobic Conference co-sponsored by the Phobia Society of America and the Mental Research Institute, San Francisco, 1981.

Index